Anarchy in Athens

Manchester University Press

CONTEMPORARY ANARCHIST STUDIES

A series edited by
Laurence Davis, *University College Cork, Ireland*
Uri Gordon, *Loughborough University, UK*
Nathan Jun, *Midwestern State University, USA*
Alex Prichard, *Exeter University, UK*

Contemporary Anarchist Studies promotes the study of anarchism as a framework for understanding and acting on the most pressing problems of our times. The series publishes cutting-edge, socially engaged scholarship from around the world – bridging theory and practice, academic rigor and the insights of contemporary activism. The topical scope of the series encompasses anarchist history and theory broadly construed; individual anarchist thinkers; anarchist-informed analysis of current issues and institutions; and anarchist or anarchist-inspired movements and practices. Contributions informed by anti-capitalist, feminist, ecological, indigenous and non-Western or Global South anarchist perspectives are particularly welcome. So, too, are manuscripts that promise to illuminate the relationships between the personal and the political aspects of transformative social change, local and global problems, and anarchism and other movements and ideologies. Above all, we wish to publish books that will help activist scholars and scholar activists think about how to challenge and build real alternatives to existing structures of oppression and injustice.

International Editorial Advisory Board:
Martha Ackelsberg, *Smith College*
John Clark, *Loyola University*
Jesse Cohn, *Purdue University*
Ronald Creagh, *Université Paul Valéry*
Marianne Enckell, *Centre International de Recherches sur l'Anarchisme*
Benjamin Franks, *University of Glasgow*
Judy Greenway, *Independent Scholar*
Ruth Kina, *Loughborough University*
Todd May, *Clemson University*
Salvo Vaccaro, *Università di Palermo*
Lucian van der Walt, *Rhodes University*
Charles Weigl, *AK Press*

Other titles in the series
(From Bloomsbury Academic):
Anarchism and Political Modernity
Angelic Troublemakers
The Concealment of the State
Daoism and Anarchism
The Impossible Community
Lifestyle Politics and Radical Activism
Making Another World Possible
Philosophical Anarchism and Political Obligation
(From Manchester University Press):
The Autonomous Life?

Anarchy in Athens

An ethnography of militancy, emotions and violence

Nicholas Apoifis

Manchester University Press

Copyright © Nicholas Apoifis 2017

The right of Nicholas Apoifis to be identified as the author of this work has been asserted by him in accordance with the Copyright, Designs and Patents Act 1988.

Published by Manchester University Press
Altrincham Street, Manchester M1 7JA
www.manchesteruniversitypress.co.uk

British Library Cataloguing-in-Publication Data
A catalogue record for this book is available from the British Library

Library of Congress Cataloging-in-Publication Data applied for

ISBN 978 1 5261 0059 7 hardback
ISBN 978 1 5261 0063 4 paperback

First published 2017

This work is licensed under the Creative Commons Attribution-NonCommercial-ShareAlike 2.0 UK: England & Wales licence. Permission for reproduction is granted by the editors and the publishers free of charge for voluntary, campaign and community groups. Reproduction of the text for commercial purposes, or by universities or other formal teaching institutions, is prohibited without the express permission of the publishers.

The publisher has no responsibility for the persistence or accuracy of URLs for any external or third-party internet websites referred to in this book, and does not guarantee that any content on such websites is, or will remain, accurate or appropriate.

Typeset by Out of House Publishing

For Jamie and Oli

CONTENTS

Acknowledgements ix

Introduction 1

1 Hellenic turmoil 6

2 Social movement theory and collective identity 18

3 Militant ethnography and taking notes in a furnace 45

4 The early years of Greek anarchism: 'it just doesn't mean anything to me' 65

5 A contemporary history: 'Fuck May 68, Fight Now!' 84

6 The anarchist and anti-authoritarian space: tensions and tendencies 108

7 Street-protests and emotions: a temporary unity 128

Conclusion: imagining and fighting for alternative realities 150

Glossary 156
Bibliography 158
Index 195

ACKNOWLEDGEMENTS

Writing this book was a collaborative process. This is not to shirk my responsibility for the final construct but to acknowledge the reality of knowledge production. There are some wonderfully passionate, hospitable, and inspiring anarchists and anti-authoritarians in Athens. My work is, absolutely, blank pages without their words and deeds. Any misrepresentation of these words and deeds is my fault and I sincerely apologise if that is the case.

Thank you to the following:

In Europe: Arianna, Bill, Acacia, Kyriako, Anna, Taki, Zizo, Electra, Mary, James, Deme, Aris, Sam, Pari, Dino, Georgia, Stavro, Panayiotta, Penelope, Aleko, Kosta, Vasili, Tina, Sofia, Emma, Yianni, Andreas, Helena, Christo, Tony, Julie Fraser, John Karamichas.

In Australia and New Zealand: Skye R, Amy P, Chris C, Adam W, Sarah DW, Andy C, Dudley W, Will P, Ben Proxy L, Rosie Sniper, Luke N, Steve Boff H, Claudia M, Craig L, Stevie V, Deme K, Dean K, Eddie F, Pops, JS, James Y, Tim G, Ewan M, Ra'cing FC, Jeremy K, Sid P, Tom E, Eddy T, Phil Benito R, Ally R, Jura Books, Karen K, SlackBastard, Ed N, Sarah S, Tim E, Weens B, Patty B, Emma P, Demelza M, Declan K, Emma W, Mark T, Caitlin Hamilton, Emilie Auton, Emma C, Chris W, Kev McF, Danny H, Andrew Bennie, Sue Wills, Diana Perche.

In North America: Jacqui P, Nick D, Paul G, Colleen S, Serge L, Stephanie C, Michele B, Dave W, Adrienne C, Jeremiah W, Chris M, Basel AK, MP S-L, Adele G, Andrej Grubacic, Michael Truscello, Jeffrey Juris.

Special thanks: Uri Gordon, Danae Bosler, Will Mailer, Aleko Moulis, Georgia Van Toorn, Sturnbull, The Gouns, The Vels, Sarah Maddison, James Arvanitakis, Manchester University Press, Macquarie University folks, University of New South Wales folks and my actual folks, Mum and Dad, who alongside my brother Alex provided unquantifiable support.

I am forever indebted to the inspirational Lloyd Cox. His endless anecdotes are a small price to pay for the privilege of his guidance. Without Annie Legendre and her unconditional love, this book would not have been possible.

Introduction

Modern Ελλάδα (Greece) finds itself navigating a treacherous confluence of economic, social and political headwaters. In the wake of the 2008–09 global financial crisis, the Greek Parliament, struggling to cope with ballooning debt and economic contraction, enforced austerity measures demanded by the European Central Bank, the European Commission and the International Monetary Fund. Structural adjustment has been the price paid for successive bailouts and continued financial assistance. This has resulted in sharply falling real wages for a majority of Greeks, a massive increase in unemployment, and significant declines in health, education and welfare services. The impoverishment of millions of working-class and middle-class Greeks has seen the chasm between rich and poor grow wider than ever, thereby exacerbating the economic crisis and giving it a political face. Here, mainstream political parties, such as the centre-left PASOK (Πανελλήνιο Σοσιαλιστικό Κίνημα or Panhellenic Socialist Movement) and the centre-right ND (Νέα Δημοκρατία or New Democracy), formed previously unthinkable coalitions in their struggle to maintain power in a context of dwindling voter support. Meanwhile, relative newcomers SYRIZA (Συνασπισμός Ριζοσπαστικής Αριστεράς or The Coalition of the Radical Left), a left-wing political party, have been the chief electoral beneficiaries of economic and political crisis, charging into government in 2015. The Communist Party of Greece (Κομμουνιστικό Κόμμα Ελλάδας (KKE)) has had its support base halved, while the explicitly fascist Golden Dawn (Χρυσή Αυγή; see Glossary) has grown alarmingly, often taking its reactionary, anti-immigrant politics onto the streets. In short, political polarisation in Greece has accompanied economic polarisation and dislocation.

Away from the parliamentary battles over votes and seats, graffiti heralding the resurgence of another actor in the drama of Greek politics similarly express political polarisation: 'Fuck May 68', the walls scream, 'Fight Now!' Discussed in detail in later chapters, this is a call to arms from the world's most militant anarchist and anti-authoritarian movement. This book is centrally concerned with this movement and its contemporary form, dynamics and internal constitution.

The Athenian anarchist and anti-authoritarian movement has been reinvigorated in recent years. Its public protests and battles against the Greek state, police and other capitalist institutions are prolific and highly visible, replete with rioting, barricades and Molotov cocktails. Away from the intensity of the street-protests and the glare of mainstream media, however, its militants implement an anarchist and anti-authoritarian praxis of which the outcomes are less visible. These militants are feeding the hungry and poor, protecting migrants from fascist beatings and trying to carve out an autonomous political, social and cultural space in the ancient city of Αθήνα (Athens). Activists within this milieu share an anarchist and anti-authoritarian politics broadly centred on hostility to the capitalist state and all forms of domination, hierarchy and discrimination. Yet, beneath the apparent unity of purpose are concealed tensions and fissures, which periodically reveal themselves in sharp political differences over a range of issues.

While these political ideas broadly involve a struggle against all forms of domination, questions about how best to apply them are a source of perennial conflict. Such conflicts can arise around general strategy and tactics, but also around specific questions on violence, anarchist practice with respect to the mainstream media, and female marginalisation within the movement itself. Nevertheless, the differences that give rise to these conflicts are transcended, albeit temporarily, in the moment of street mobilisation and action. When the Athenian anarchist and anti-authoritarian movement confronts neoliberalism, fascism, hierarchical rule and the state's police in public protests and demonstrations, difference and conflict within the movement gives way to group cohesion and solidarity. Militant protest action is here more than an expression of collective grievance. Rather, these actions are, as I argue later, key elements in the ongoing construction and reconstruction of Athenian anarchist and anti-authoritarian collective identity. Insurrectionist street-protests become as much an aspect of identity formation as they are a tactic.

In this context, this book is concerned not so much with anarchist theory, as with examining the forces that give the Athenian anarchist and anti-authoritarian movement its specific shape. What are the historical and contemporary factors that are influencing and helping to construct what it means to be part of this vibrant milieu? How do the activists themselves understand the terms 'anarchist' and 'anti-authoritarian'? What are the conversations that they are having and what do these reveal about the movement, its dynamics and boundaries? What role do emotions such as anger, humiliation, fear and loathing play within the movement? In answering these questions, I draw on Alberto Melucci's (1995a) work on collective identity, while offering a first-hand, ethnographic account of Athenian anarchists and anti-authoritarians in action, based on my time there in 2011 and 2013, living, squatting and protesting within this milieu.

Throughout this book I have tried to balance academic obligations to the form and presentation of my ideas, with a desire to keep the work accessible to those without experience of academic jargon. This is an important political point to which activist-engaged writing needs to be constantly attentive. Further, I have segmented the book into stand-alone chapters so they can be read somewhat independently of each other. Activists who offered feedback on early drafts suggested that I had fused too much social movement theory with the history chapters (4 and 5) and contemporary observations (6 and 7). The concern was that you had to wade through the theoretical mud to get to the 'good stuff'. As much as I personally enjoy a good theoretical wade, and this probably leaves me open to academic critique on the book's form, I want the book to be relevant and accessible to activists. As such, I disentangled a lot of the social movement theory so it now reads as its own chapter and, depending on your interests, can be skipped at will. The same goes for Chapter 4 (on the older Greek anarchist history). For some, this got in the way of the contemporary discussions of Athenian anarchists and anti-authoritarians.

The primary aim of this book is to illuminate the complexities of the Athenian anarchist and anti-authoritarian milieu. In the course of the following chapters, I argue that varying shades of anarchic tendencies, and ensuing ideological and practical disagreements, are overcome for the most part in (often violent) street-protests. In Chapter 1, I set the scene with a sketch of Greece's contemporary economic, political and social turmoil. Chapter 2 provides a discussion of social movement theory, and outlines my own position on some key debates. I begin with a discussion of the nominally North American tradition of social movement scholarship. Although there might have been the inclination merely to mention this tradition's existence before moving to the preferred viewpoint, I have taken the time to unravel this theoretical trajectory because it is particularly problematic for the study of anarchist collectives. I argue that the North American tradition of social movement theory often focuses on factors that create a false perception of an internally homogeneous political identity. I pay particular attention to this narrative because it can produce misleading conclusions, undermining the heterogeneous nature of anarchist and anti-authoritarian collectives. Having rejected these assumptions, I explore new social movement theory and ideas about collective identity, acknowledging the pioneering work of Alberto Melucci. His work rightly problematises contentious assumptions about internal homogeneity within collectives. It also provides a set of conceptual tools for understanding the dynamic, reflexive and negotiated process through which collective identities are constructed. Finally, it sensitises us to the 'field of opportunities and constraints offered to collective action' (Melucci, 1985: 793). This allows me to explore a number of important factors that give shape to the Athenian anarchist and authoritarian space. These include discussions on the way in which contemporary actors view their region's anarchist and anti-authoritarian history, the internal tensions and sources of unity within the movement, and the important role played by emotions within the space.

In pursuing these theoretical leads, I conducted intensive fieldwork in Athens from the beginning of January through to late March of 2011 and again in December 2013. Communicating directly in Greek, I participated in countless political protests, events and actions with Athenian anarchists and anti-authoritarians, while living in anarchist squats and shared housing. Furthermore, I had over 90 interviews and conversations with Greek anarchists and anti-authoritarians. These interactions are the foundations of this book. Throughout *Anarchy in Athens*, I refer to my Athenian collaborators by pseudonyms. They are as follows: Arianna, Bill, Acacia, Kyriako, Anna, Taki, Zizo, Electra, Mary, James, Deme, Aris, Sam, Pari, Dino, Georgia, Stavro, Panayiotta, Penelope, Aleko, Kosta, Vasili, Tina, Sofia, Emma, Yianni, Andreas, Helena, Christo, and Tony. Chapter 3 explores the methodological premises on which this fieldwork was based and the real-life issues that come with engaged fieldwork. My research methodology was guided by Jeffrey Juris's militant ethnographic approach (2007). This method is premised on intense, reflexive collaboration between ethnographers and activists, in which, as far as possible, researchers assume the role of active political practitioners. By focusing on the activists themselves, it brings to the fore their agency and voice. Consequently, the way in which actors in the anarchist movement interact, negotiate and share emotions, ideas and beliefs, is central. I detail some of the strengths, nuances and functional issues associated with my preferred qualitative research approach, ending the chapter with some of the fieldwork issues I encountered.

Chapters 4 and 5 move from method and theory to history, discussing Greek anarchist history and contemporary attitudes to that history. Chapter 4 gives some historical depth to contemporary attitudes on pre-World War II Greek anarchist history. I reveal that the Athenian anarchists and anti-authoritarians I spoke to had severed nearly all emotional, theoretical and practical links with the region's early anarchist history. Even when specifically asked, my interviewees were largely indifferent to the old anarcho-syndicalist history, instead clamouring to discuss the more recent insurrectionist history. I discuss the possible reasons for this towards the end of the chapter. Chapter 5 discusses the more recent Greek anarchist history. I provide a post-military-junta (1974) history that is celebrated and embraced by the collaborators of my militant ethnography. Here I show that although a plethora of political actions and events inform these contemporary historical reflections, militant and often-violent direct actions dominate the narrative presented in the chapter.

Moving beyond history and into the contemporary period, Chapter 6 details some of the more prominent tensions within the Athenian anarchist and anti-authoritarian space. I discuss tensions around gender and sexuality politics, tactics and media engagement, as well as violence and solidarity. I argue that negotiations and interactions around these issues contribute to the processes of collective identification within the space.

Whereas Chapter 6 focuses on tensions, Chapter 7 builds towards a conclusion regarding unity. Set against the backdrop of riots and street-protests, I make two claims: first, that there is nothing at all pacifist about the space; second, that a wide range of emotions are expressed, fermented and developed within acts of performative violence. Throughout the chapter, I show how experiences and elements of a street-protest contribute to the temporary unity of the often-fragmented milieu, and provide a focus for collective identity formation. I end with concluding remarks that summarise my findings regarding unity within the space, culminating with the observation that the movement's longevity stems from the unity produced within often-violent collective actions.

A final point: this book is the culmination of four years of research and throughout my study I was regularly asked by fellow scholars, family and friends why I had chosen Athens. Athenian anarchists and anti-authoritarians are a pertinent area of research because of both their politics and their geographical location. To begin with, there is the whole 'rise of anarchism throughout the activist world' phenomenon, visible from Seattle to Genoa, Quebec City to São Paulo. Anarchist and anti-authoritarian social movements are prominent actors in resistance to the current phase of capitalism in multiple, global locations (Gordon 2008; Graeber, 2009; Juris, 2007; Pallister-Wilkins 2009). Throughout Europe, North and Latin America, Asia and the Antipodes, radical resistance to neo-liberalism often has an anarchist and/or anti-authoritarian cast. If not openly waving the red and black flags of the anarchists, many of those challenging contemporary capitalism, consumerism and impending environmental catastrophe are anarchist inspired. They favour non-hierarchical decision-making processes such as those witnessed in the Occupy and *Indignados* movements, while advocating militant direct street action as an alternative means of political change to parliamentarianism. Their prominence in social movements over recent years makes understanding the anarchist and anti-authoritarian movement both a pressing political and scholarly task. As one of today's go-to destinations for anarchist-inspired activism and activist-inspired scholarship, Athens is the ideal place in which to undertake this task. That is why I chose it.

1
Hellenic turmoil

Greece is in the midst of a profound economic, social and political crisis. Hardly Greece's issue alone, it is a crisis shaped by a prevailing neo-liberal economic doctrine in Europe and elsewhere. Here, the 'logic' of markets and associated policies like austerity, privatisation and deregulation, are imposed on societies as life-saving cures for contemporary economic woes. Leaving aside for other scholars the problematic relationship between these 'cures' and the disease itself (see Amin, 2013; Shannon, 2014), it is nonetheless worth sketching the origins of this crisis as they specifically relate to Greece. This construct forms a backdrop to my discussion of the Athenian anarchist and anti-authoritarian movement.

In 2001, Greece entered the eurozone, but on the basis of economic modelling and data that were deliberately misleading (BBC News, 2004). Entry into one of the world's richest clubs opened up tremendous new economic possibilities for Greece, though ones that would in the longer term come at a high cost. In particular, membership of the European Union along with the new currency enabled the Greek state, Greek capitalists and Greek consumers to borrow at very low interest rates relative to rates prior to joining the European Union. For a time, this fuelled a credit-driven economic boom. Times were good as flourishing consumer spending augmented tourism and shipping – the traditional mainstays of the Greek economy. But the economic boom concealed the deeper reality that both public and private debts were soaring to levels that would be impossible to service should there be an economic downturn (Choupis, 2011). Unfortunately, for Greece, such a downturn began in 2006, accelerated in 2007 and reached a crescendo in 2008–09, as the international banking system teetered on the verge of total collapse. The consequences for Greece were swift and devastating. In the midst of a sharply contracting economy, tourism slowed to a trickle of its former self, shipping plummeted, consumer spending slowed dramatically and the proverbial debt chickens came home to roost (Behrakis and Maltezou, 2012). The crisis arrived in earnest in 2009, when the newly elected PASOK announced the government's fiscal balance was not in deficit by 4.1 per cent of gross domestic product (GDP) as proclaimed by the previous New Democracy government, but was instead a staggering 12.7 per cent of GDP and growing

(Smith, 2009). Equally concerning, Greece's public debt to GDP ratio was 114 per cent (Reuters, 2010).

As a result of the global economic crisis, international lending dried up, or at least became much more difficult to secure for a state with an indebted economy such as Greece. Where the Greek government was once able to pay back loans by 'rolling them over' (in effect, issuing new bonds to repay maturing ones), this became increasingly difficult in a context of soaring interest rates on bonds that were of a questionable quality. Neither able to use monetary policy to stimulate the economy (because interest rates are set at a European level), nor regain competitiveness through a depreciating currency, the Greek economy continued to contract while its debts mounted. Equally, the government was limited in its fiscal stimulus measures, having already reached an ultra-stimulus zone and now being unable to fund adequately such stimulus (Choupis, 2011). International bond markets froze Greece out, which required an injection of capital in order to avoid a sovereign default on debt repayments. This may have resulted in a Greek withdrawal from the eurozone and a return to the drachma, with very uncertain consequences for Greece, Europe and the World.

As austerity sucked demand out of the local economy, Greek economic statistics appeared weaker than originally anticipated by the International Monetary Fund (IMF) and the European Central Bank (International Monetary Fund, 2010). Hence, these institutions demanded even harsher austerity measures. In early May 2010, a troika consisting of the European Central Bank, the IMF and the European Commission granted the National Bank of Greece a three-year, €110 billion loan (Traynor, 2010). Attached to this loan were onerous obligations, including significant austerity measures aimed at cutting the government's expenditure, increasing revenues and restoring fiscal balance. Amongst other measures, these involved a 15 per cent cut to public-sector wages,[1] the closure of nearly 2,000 schools, the movement of the retirement age from 61 to 65 years and the privatisation of a host of government assets. Added to these were increased income tax and a hike in the regressive consumption tax known as the VAT (value added tax). In essence, this punished the average Greek for their government's ineptitudes, while rewarding gamblers (like banks and investment firms) for their morally hazardous investment in Greek bonds, an investment now protected by the troika's bailout. The effects were devastating for most working- and middle-class Greeks. At the beginning of 2011, around the time I was first in Athens, the national rate of unemployment was 15.8%, which included 43.1% unemployment for those aged from 15 to 24 years (Sedghi, 2011). By July 2013, 27.6% of the population was unemployed, while youth unemployment had risen to 55.1%. In early 2015, opportunities had only marginally improved with unemployment at 25.7%, with 50.1% unemployment for the 15–24 age cohort (ieconomics, 2015). In circumstances of rapidly dwindling welfare services, this often meant homelessness, malnourishment and destitution for those thrown out of employment, or else it meant relying on the generosity of family and friends.

Massive protests throughout Greece exploded in response to economic decline and fiscal austerity. Protesters demanding a more equitable loan arrangement frequently brought Athens to a standstill (Reuters, 2010). Others called for more radical solutions, bringing them head-to-head with Athens' police. This had been anticipated most vividly in December 2008 when riots and protests erupted throughout Greece after a policeman murdered a teenager in Exarcheia (I explore this in Chapter 5). The city was shut down as tens of thousands of disenfranchised people charged into the streets. The anger was palpable as protesters vented their emotions, with anarchists and anti-authoritarians out in force. Buildings were occupied, while others were torched, covered in graffiti or simply smashed up (Schwarz et al., 2010a). Amidst the repeated mass protests that followed, the government appealed for patience, insisting that the situation was soon to improve.

There was, however, no improvement. By the end of June 2011, daily protests swarmed the streets of Athens and other large Greek cities. A general election was finally held in May 2012, allowing the Greek electorate to participate in the political process and cast judgement on the policies of the day. All of my interviewees refused to participate in the election, as to do so would confer tacit legitimacy on the process of parliamentary democracy. For Greeks who did vote, the election was billed as a vote on the austerity measures (Malkoutzis, 2012). Pro-austerity parties only managed 30–35 per cent of the votes, which appeared to signal a resounding rejection of the austerity programme. None of the parties were able to form a coalition to govern, however, so another election was called for the following month (Smith, 2012a). This time the pro-austerity vote increased to around 45–47 per cent of votes (Owen, 2012). On 20 June 2012, pro-austerity parties and bitter political rivals New Democracy and PASOK (plus the smaller Democratic Left party) came together to form a coalition. With over half the population against the austerity measures, the streets again swelled with resistance and protest as the government extended the budget tightening.

All this bespoke a serious questioning of the current economic and political system by significant numbers of Greeks. As the fabled neo-liberal prosperity or even economic recovery failed to materialise there have been dramatic shifts in the political landscape.

From a parliamentary perspective, the January 2015 election of the left-wing SYRIZA marked a paradigm shift in Greek politics. In December 2014, after three failed attempts to elect a president, the Hellenic Parliament was dissolved and elections set for 25 January 2015. Built on the back of success in the 2014 European parliamentary elections, and a clear agenda to renegotiate the terms of the austerity programme, the 2015 election saw SYRIZA receive 36.3 per cent of the vote and 149 of the 300 seats in the Hellenic Parliament (the largest party gets an additional 50 seats to help them form a government). Falling two seats short of an outright majority, SYRIZA formed a coalition with right-wing nationalists Ανεξάρτητοι Έλληνες (ANEL or Independent Greeks), with SYRIZA's Αλέξης Τσίπρας (Alexis Tsipras) installed as prime minister of Greece. By forming a government, SYRIZA ended 41 years of alternating and uninterrupted ND and PASOK rule. In the snap election of 20 September 2015, SYRIZA consolidated their dominance, albeit with a slightly reduced margin of 35.5 per cent of the vote and 145 seats.

While SYRIZA's 2015 election result reflects a political shift, there is also more radical potential in the air – be it fascist, communist or anarchist – which is but the latest instalment in a long history of political upheaval in Greece. In the last 120 years, Greeks have been ruled by military juntas, monarchies, dictatorships and a Nazi occupation. In this context, the phase of parliamentary democracy since 1974 seems an exception rather than the rule, and a fragile one at that. It is little wonder then that for Athenian anarchists and anti-authoritarians revolution, or the creation of an autonomous neighbourhood, city or even region, is not beyond the realm of possibility. The imagining of radical political alternatives, however, is not the exclusive preserve of anarchists, anti-authoritarians and leftists more broadly. The Far Right has also energetically responded to, and been a key beneficiary of, the contemporary Greek crisis.

Golden Dawn

Forty years since the fall of the military junta, Greek fascism is on the rise again (Bistis, 2013). Its contemporary face is the cadres leading Golden Dawn and their black-shirted members out in the streets of mostly urban Greek centres. In 2009, Golden Dawn gained only 0.29 per cent of the vote in the national elections. This equated to roughly 20,000 votes. By 2012, this party of the Far Right had increased its vote to around 7 per cent, or 400,000 votes (Dalakoglou, 2013), and by 2013 Golden Dawn was Greece's third largest party with 18 seats in the 300-member parliament (Smith, 2013d). Led by a Holocaust denier, the party's symbolism is awash with Nazi imagery, vocalised in vehemently anti-migrant, anti-Semitic and anti-Muslim rhetoric (Dalakoglou, 2013; Margaronis, 2013; Occupied London, 2014). In 2013, during a 'Greeks only' food distribution to struggling Athenians, it was reported that party members blasted the Nazi-German anthem on loud speakers (Smith, 2013c). Despite the arrest of its leadership and many of its governing Members of Parliament under criminal-gang legislation in late 2013 (the constitution forbids the banning of a party for their political stance), the January 2015 election saw Golden Dawn maintaining the position of Greece's third largest party, with 17 seats in parliament. This result was marginally improved in the September 2015 election, with the gain of an extra seat. While its parliamentary presence is temporarily arrested, out in the streets and in the offices of the Greek police and military, its racist, homophobic and sectarian politics are thriving. It is here, away from parliament's doors, where anarchists and anti-authoritarians come into regular contact with proponents of this far-right ideology.

Before musician and anti-fascist Παύλος Φύσσας (Pavlos Fyssas or Killah P) was stabbed by a Golden Dawn member in 2013, which led to a public furore and ultimately the banning of the organisation, the party and its members took full advantage of the legitimacy that came from parliamentary representation. Racist attitudes and actions had credence now that they were represented so openly in the Hellenic Parliament. Coupling this newfound validity was a rabidly complicit police force. In the May 2012 elections, around half the police officers in the country voted for Golden Dawn (Το Βημα, 2013). Furthermore, it was reported that the chief of the Hellenic police, Νίκος Παπαγιαννόπουλος (Nikos Papagiannopoulos), told his officers to make the lives of immigrants 'unbearable' (Smith, 2013e). It is not surprising, then, that in this climate the radical Right felt they could run free. Their attacks on immigrants have been relentless. A daily stream of violence, stabbings and attempted murders were reported alongside the vandalism of migrant centres, synagogues and mosques (Dalakoglou, 2013). Members of the coastguard unit have been accused of beating and stripping migrants and dumping them at sea in Turkish territorial waters, or mock waterboarding them as a form of torture (Smith, 2013e). Communists were not immune either, with Golden Dawn members viciously beating KKE members who were leafleting in Athens (Smith, 2013c). Particular hostility is reserved for anarchists and anti-authoritarians, with regular, violent attacks on activists, social centres, protests, squats and outdoor assemblies (Occupied London, 2014).

During a number of these attacks against migrants, it has been claimed that police stood by idly, as was the case during the stabbing murder of the musician Fyssas (Smith, 2013a). My respondents told of countless incidences in which fascists and neo-Nazis were protected by the riot police. One incident had Golden Dawn members climbing into the back of a riot police van where they had stored their weapons. Others saw riot police watching as neo-Nazis violently attacked an anarchist squat. I too saw a police line protecting and supporting fascist antagonists. In this light, the words of former Greek President Κάρολος Παπούλιας (Karolos Papoulias) that it is the Greek population's duty 'not to allow any space whatsoever to fascism, not even an inch', appear rather hollow (Smith, 2013d). In the streets, where police complicity is consistently evident, it is left to anarchists and anti-authoritarians, as well as anti-fascists more generally, to challenge authoritarian and racist activity.

One of the more recent responses has anarchists, anti-authoritarians and anti-fascists riding on motorcycles in the search for fascist pogroms, who are themselves looking for migrants to assault (Occupied London, 2014). Often outnumbering fascist militants, the radical leftists engage in violent tactics to confront these forces. Other responses involve anarchists and anti-authoritarians setting fire to the offices of Golden Dawn, and more recently and drastically, the assassination of two Golden Dawn members outside the party's offices in the northern Athenian neighbourhood of Νέο Ηράκλειο (Neo Iraklio) (Legge, 2013; Occupied London, 2014). Inasmuch as it is still unclear who committed these murders, their timing so close to the murder of Fyssas suggests that it was in retaliation.

All these events may be a precursor to a more bloody confrontation. Activists within the Far Right are fostering conditions for a civil war. Before the mass arrests, Golden Dawn Member of Parliament Ηλίας Παναγιώταρος (Ilias Panagiotaros) said as much during an interview with the BBC (YouTube, 2012). With the support of a large percentage of the police, alongside the army's fascist historical tendencies, the possibility of fascism again seizing the reins of state power cannot be discounted. It is against this backdrop of rising fascism and economic and political crisis that the contemporary Athenian anarchist and anti-authoritarian milieu has grown – in both size and political significance.

The anarchist and anti-authoritarian space/movement/milieu

A favourite pastime of social scientists involves categorising phenomena. This book is no exception. A large component of my study explores a particular group of people: Athenian anarchists and anti-authoritarians. Before I got to Greece, my intention was to engage fully with anarchists and anti-authoritarians in two other locations, Θεσσαλονίκη (Thessaloniki) in the north and Πάτρα (Patras) in the west. However, because of the sheer scale of the movement in Athens, I limited my research to this explosive city.

Shortly, I will examine a number of ways to categorise and conceptualise the phenomena in question. In so doing, I will explain my interchangeable use of the phrases 'anarchist and anti-authoritarian *space*', 'anarchist and anti-authoritarian *movement*' and 'anarchist and anti-authoritarian *milieu*'. Before moving to this discussion, I will explain what I mean by the terms 'anarchist' and 'anti-authoritarian'. Ultimately, the many individuals and groups who identify with aspects of this body of political ideas inform my use of these terms.

As I reveal in Chapter 6, there is a plethora of differences within the Athenian anarchist and anti-authoritarian movement. Nonetheless, in the sense that I use these terms, anarchist and anti-authoritarian tendencies and currents share three critical characteristics. First, there is the struggle against all forms of domination in society, be they based on gender, ethnicity, capitalism, sexuality, the state or other hierarchical systems. Second, all anarchist and anti-authoritarian politics is committed to an ethos of prefigurative politics. This means that the way in which you conduct yourself on a daily basis should reflect an anarchist understanding of social relations. In practice, this can involve challenging hierarchical authority in all its forms within social interactions, and participating in direct actions that inject anarchist politics into society. Finally, anarchist and anti-authoritarian ideas do not constitute a closed system of thought. They are diverse and open-ended, in a state of perpetual development (Dixon, 2012; Gordon, 2008; Marshall, 2010). Peter Marshall usefully describes this anti-dogmatic aspect of anarchism as being like a river, 'with many currents and eddies, constantly changing and refreshed by new surges but always moving towards the wide ocean of freedom' (2010: 1). This means that despite shared commitments, there is no one approach to anarchist politics that necessarily dominates. Although anarcho-syndicalism once prevailed in Greece, for example, a more insurrectionist, anti-authoritarian anarchism is now popularly preferred.

Affinity networks link the individuals who embrace anarchist and anti-authoritarian ideas. These are voluntary and self-regulating political and social networks, steeped in non-hierarchical principles, a commitment to direct action, and consensus decision-making processes. Affinity groups in turn make up these networks (see Glossary). These are small, sometimes ephemeral collectives that are autonomous and based on high degrees of trust, camaraderie and emotional connections (Clough, 2012: 1673; Gordon, 2008: 15). Affinity groups are a core part of the Athenian space, conducting a multitude of direct actions that give life to the three components of anarchist politics I have just introduced.

Throughout this book, I refer to the groups and individuals embracing these ideas as both anarchists and anti-authoritarians. The subtleties between the beliefs of anarchists and anti-authoritarians are important as they reflect different currents and different outlooks on political ideals. Within the Athenian milieu, and this was certainly the case for my respondents, people variably describe themselves as anarchists, autonomists, insurrectionists, anti-authoritarians or a mishmash of all these identities (Schwarz et al., 2010c). When it came down to the specifics of the differences, conversations varied between the explicit and the opaque.

We Are an Image (Schwarz et al., 2010c), a collection of articles on the December 2008 Athenian revolt published by Greek anarchists and anti-authoritarians, contains a glossary with a helpful summary of the many descriptors at play within the Athenian milieu:

Many, but not all, Greek antiauthoritarians use these terms in the following way. Anarchists are those who identify themselves with the specific anarchist tradition, going back to (but by no means limited to) Bakunin, even though the major influences probably come from the events of May '68, as well as other more recent manifestations of new and old theories and struggles. The autonomists are not necessarily dissident Marxists as they are in other countries, but perhaps dissident anarchists who favour a materialist analysis ... All of these currents are grouped together as antiauthoritarians, although sometimes the term 'antiauthoritarian' is used in contrast to 'anarchist', to refer to those antiauthoritarians who do not specifically identify themselves as anarchists. These are all crass and clumsy generalisations. (2010c: 368)

I would add to these 'crass and clumsy generalisations' that some of my interviewees did not call themselves anarchists at all, because they perceive anarchism to be an ideal not yet attained. In other words, it is what you would call yourself if you were living within a society based on anarchist ideas (acknowledging that that too would be a constant work in progress). As a result, they refer to themselves as anti-authoritarians. Alternatively, I also had conversations with activists who describe themselves as anti-authoritarian for a specific political reason not mentioned by the editors of *We Are an Image* (Schwarz et al., 2010c), and separate to any sense of pursuing an anarchist ideal. One interviewee who I call Helena to preserve her anonymity, for example, explained to me that

'[a]lthough anarchism as a political doctrine fights against authority, by its very process of becoming an ideology in which to adhere to, it attains a position of authority. By calling ourselves anti-authoritarian, we are agreeing with elements of anarchism, without subscribing to the doctrine itself.'

In a way, Helena considers herself so vehemently 'against authority' that she is even sceptical of a body of ideas that explicitly articulates this position, lest it also become a governing dogma. That said, there were also many participants in my ethnography who were more than happy to embrace the term 'anarchist' as a description of their political commitments.

There can also be some confusion with respect to those who identify as anti-authoritarians but who are not fond of the Greek Αντιεξουσιαστικη Κινηση (Anti-Authoritarian Current or AK; see Glossary). I discuss this group in more detail in Chapter 5, but they are essentially a political network of anarchists and anti-authoritarians diffused throughout Greece, basing themselves on direct democracy and horizontal organisational principles. They tend to advocate permanent forms of resistance and anarchist praxis. In contrast, some anti-authoritarians are against this model of praxis, preferring ephemeral organisations that constantly and visibly attack capitalist and state institutions. An anti-authoritarian, therefore, can be supportive of or hostile to the Anti-Authoritarian Current.

Insurrectionist anarchists constitute yet another current within the broader milieu. Insurrectionists are more inclined to advocate ephemeral networks of organisations and small affinity-group structures, rather than the overt, permanent organisational frameworks, such as those involved with AK. They tend to be hostile to pathways of anarchist revolution that involve the building of a mass movement, which are actions more common with the anarcho-syndicalist current. Insurrectionists nearly always support constant attacks on capitalist, state and consumerist institutions and are synonymous with illegalism, propaganda by the deed and, often (although not exclusively), Black Bloc tactics (see Glossary, and Bonanno, 1977; The Invisible Committee, 2009). Despite the prevalence of insurrectionist tactics and politics in Athens, my interviewees mostly refrained from describing themselves as insurrectionist anarchists or insurrectionist anti-authoritarians in Greek. They referred to themselves as αντιεξουσιαστικοί (anti-authoritarians). Of course, to add to the confusion, some called themselves αναρχικοί (anarchists). To avoid further confusion, I refer to this current as insurrectionist throughout the book, because it accords with the English language description of this current.

Given these various nuances in the self-definitions of the actors themselves, it is inaccurate to describe what is going on in Athens today as merely anarchist-inspired. Rather, it is a fusion of anarchist-inspired – and anti-authoritarian-inspired –politics, with a strong penchant for the insurrectionist current.

In terms of demographics, the activists I engaged with were aged between 16 and 50, roughly half were female and nearly all were secondary-level educated, with some having completed tertiary education. In the absence of any statistical data assessing the demographics of the Athenian anarchist and anti-authoritarian space, I have relied on my own observations. For this reason, I have no concrete numbers on the size of the Athenian milieu.

Most people I met were originally from Athens, although some were from Πελοπόννησος (the Peloponnese, which is the big chunk of land south-west of Athens), northern Greece and the Greek islands, as well as from a few other parts of Europe. The other notable aspect of the space was that it was not strictly working class, in the sense of the activists all being blue-collar, manual workers or coming from such backgrounds. Although this was the case for some, a small number of my respondents came from reasonably prosperous middle-class backgrounds, where the main bread-winners were professionals or self-employed (although all claimed that they were financially alienated from their families). An overwhelming number of the people with whom I engaged were now unemployed or underemployed. In discussions, a significant number did not consider themselves as working class for this reason, despite some having recently been in work.

To be clear, these are admittedly impressionistic observations, which do not fully operationalise the rich notion of social class or make any claims to have measured it in the field. Such a task was beyond the scope of my fieldwork. Nevertheless, they do give some idea of the social composition of my interviewees and the broader anarchist and anti-authoritarian movement.

The heart of the Athenian anarchist and anti-authoritarian milieu is the neighbourhood of Εξάρχεια (Exarcheia). The lifeblood of Athenian radical leftist politics, it is a 10–15-minute walk from Πλατεία Συντάγματος (Syntagma Square) and the Βουλή των Ελλήνων (Greek Parliament). Since the fall of the military junta in 1974, leftists, radicals, artists, students, intellectuals, migrants, bohemians and hippies have gravitated to the neighbourhood. Known for its affordable rent, bookshops, squats and cheap food, over the course of a few decades it has cemented its position as a hub of radical leftist politics (Dalakoglou and Vradis, 2011b). Radical posters and graffiti adorn the walls of squats, social centres and migrant support centres. While Exarcheia can be seen as the heart of radical politics in Athens, as much as a physical space can ever give life to ideas and action, the anarchist and anti-authoritarian tentacles are spread throughout the city (in fact, one of the squats in which I stayed was some distance from the area).

With this in mind, I now discuss my interchangeable use of the phrases 'anarchist and anti-authoritarian *movement*', 'anarchist and anti-authoritarian *milieu*' and 'anarchist and anti-authoritarian *space*' as well as some of the ways in which the phenomena in question can be conceptualised. To be clear, I am fully aware that distinctions made in the categorisation and description of collective action can be problematic, political and rife for contestation (Opp, 2009). That said, I am not beholden to any one particular approach and I see all three of them as useful in creating a context for my research. While this may leave the book open to critiques of relativism, where equivocation offers little concrete substance to the discussion, I take as my lead the activists themselves. Like most of this book, I have been guided by conversations in the field, where, variously, my collaborators used *movement*, *milieu* and *space* to describe what was happening in Athens.

Beginning with the field of social movement theory, Nancy Whittier's definition of a social movement offers an appropriate definition for my research focus (2002). Whittier describes social movements as

> neither fixed nor narrowly bounded in space, time or membership. Instead, they are made up of shifting clusters of organizations, networks, communities, and activist individuals, connected by participation in challenges and collective identities through which participants define the boundaries and significance of their group. (2002: 289)

This could easily be describing the Athenian anarchist and anti-authoritarian movement. The 'shifting clusters of organisation' resemble Athenian affinity groups and networks. Moreover, Whittier's embrace of both the individual activist and the group reflects the idea of autonomy prevalent throughout the Athenian movement, whereby the individual is an aspect of the group, without being consumed by it. While not the most common description used by Athenian anarchists and anti-authoritarians, it did come up occasionally. For these reasons, I sometimes refer to the phenomena as a movement.

Another way of conceptualising the phenomena in question is to consider Hardt and Negri's use of the 'multitude' and the 'common'. In *Multitude*, the authors provide a template in which to examine the largely heterogeneous resistance to capitalism (Hardt and Negri, 2004). They essentially argue that as global capitalism expands, counter-forces develop in order to combat the ferocity of neo-liberal intrusions (Hardt and Negri, 2004: xiii). Hubs of resistance develop within and between the networks that perpetuate the changing forms of labour synonymous with the current phase of capitalism. Hardt and Negri call these hubs 'the multitude'. The multitude is 'an open network of singularities that links together on the basis of the common they share and the common they produce' (Hardt and Negri, 2004: 355). This common is unified in the struggle against capitalism and, importantly, against hierarchy. Regardless of whether or not Hardt and Negri's account of how resistance came to be is accurate, their work helps situate the Athenian space within a broader struggle. It also encouraged me to describe the movement and space as a 'milieu', in that it is one environment or one community amongst a sea of others fighting against capitalism and hierarchical domination. This also accords with some of the representations discussed during interviews.

Finally, I also refer to the collection of anarchists and anti-authoritarians in Athens as a 'space'. This reflects the language of many activists in Athens, who refer to the χώρος [space] (Boukalas, 2011: 281). As Drakonakis argues, space is far more than a 'linguistic choice' (2014: 2). Rather, it represents the contrasting views and identities within the space and conveys what he describes as a 'spirit of self-criticism' (2014: 2). Similarly, Schwarz et al. suggest that this is a preferred description in that it 'acknowledges that there is no single body or direction chosen by anarchists' (2010c: 368).

Consequently, the use of the term 'space' in the Athenian anarchist and anti-authoritarian context becomes politically charged. It encourages us, as David Harvey more broadly suggests, to use the concept of space as a way of examining relationships within urban societies under capitalism (2006: 120). We move beyond a physical description of space, and include the entire 'spatiality of human life' (Soja, 1996: 1). Encapsulated in Edward Soja's *Thirdspace*, space includes the following:

> subjectivity and objectivity, the abstract and the concrete, the real and the imagined, the knowable and the unimaginable, the repetitive and the differential, structure and agency, mind and body, consciousness and the unconscious, the disciplined and the transdisciplinary, everyday life and unending history. (1996: 56–57)

Anthony Ince sees this approach as moving beyond limited ideas of space and territory that are burdened by 'undertones of statism and authoritarian control' (2012: 1646). Instead, space and territory are re-cast 'as a tool of political praxis produced and contested chiefly through *relations*' (Ince, 2012: 1646, emphasis in original).

As a result, the term 'space' invites us to think of the physical aspects of anarchist and anti-authoritarian struggles alongside rhetoric and direct actions. I mentioned earlier, for example, the importance of the area of Exarcheia as a site of resistance. One such battle involved a successful struggle against the development of a car park in Exarcheia. After an extensive occupation, local residents as well as anarchists and anti-authoritarians converted the space into a communal park, at the corner of the streets Ναυαρίνου (Navarinou) and Τρικουρι (Trikouri). Here, space is as much a geographic tangible as it is a place of political experience (Pleyers, 2013: 118–119).

The politics of anarchism and anti-authoritarianism is as concerned with producing such autonomous spaces as it is about individual and group behaviour. This has given rise to theoretical discussions that give similar importance to different ideas around autonomous spaces. Contemporary elements of the post-anarchist literature that consider revolution as a 'multiplicity of insurrectional and autonomous spaces' (Newman, 2011: 353) have reinvigorated the importance of physical space. In addition to confrontations with the state over the control of space, anarchism is also about the rational planning of spaces 'based around the possibilities of cooperative and communal ways of life' (Newman, 2011: 346). Bringing the notion of space to the fore also acknowledges the significance of temporary autonomous zones like those espoused by Hakim Bey, alongside the importance of Richard Day's semi-permanent autonomous zones (Bey, 2003; Day, 2005). For these reasons, I also refer to the focus of my research as the anarchist and anti-authoritarian *space*.

The interchangeable use of *movement*, *milieu* and *space* throughout this work, gives some voice to the complexities and multiplicities that inform the Athenian anarchist and anti-authoritarian context. However, giving meaning to these voices is a perilous and contentious politicised process, as borne out in the next chapter on social movement theory.

Note

1 On average, Greeks work around 2,100 hours per year, placing them fourth amongst OECD member nations. As a point of comparison with a 'healthier' economy, Germans work around 1,400 hours per year (OECD, 2014).

2
Social movement theory and collective identity

Tiny flags attached to massive chunks of wood

On 15 January 2011, I was involved in a protest against the Greek government's plan to construct a 12-km, anti-immigration wall along the Turkish border. A group of leftists, anti-racists and migrants gathered to protest against the construction of a barrier that many saw as amplifying the dangers and miseries confronting already vulnerable migrants. By mid-morning around 3,000 protesters had convened outside the Athenian Metro stop at Πανεπιστήμιο (Panepistimio). The plan was to march two and a half kilometres to the park at Παντελεήμον (Panteleimon) for an afternoon of food, music and speeches celebrating cultural diversity and denouncing the erection of the wall. We never made it. Earlier, rumours had swirled that fascists were harassing activists setting up at the park, although being outnumbered they were forced to retreat. Undeterred, 50 fascists regrouped at the end of Αχαρνων (Acharnon) street, blocking the entrance to the park, obstructing the march's arrival. In front of them, a force of 150 armed riot police and four police buses were deployed, loaded and ready – as is the case in most Athenian protests – to bring us to tears.

As the march continued towards the police line, it was becoming too difficult to walk and take notes, so I snaked my way to a flank of the procession. Still walking at the pace of the march but with more space, I frenetically scribbled my observations. With a side view, the protest's structure became a little clearer. The KKE (Greek Communist Party) were scattered towards the rear, their party's acronym on flags and banners marking their procession. A strong contingent of a teacher's trade union occupied the middle, alongside a healthy gathering of Trotskyists and Stalinists. In front of them was a tight group of about 30 immigrants of Nigerian and Ghanaian descent, dancing and banging drums. At the front of the march anarchists and anti-authoritarians predominated, brandishing tiny flags attached to massive chunks of wood. These caught my attention and I began trying to decipher their symbolism.

Some of the flags were red, some black, and others half-red and half-black. Their symbolism was confusing; I could not work out what they represented. Most baffling of all, I saw a group of Black Bloc demonstrators carrying red and black flags synonymous with anarcho-syndicalism. It seemed strange that proponents of Black Bloc tactics, who tend to be more insurrectionist than syndicalist, would be flag-bearers for anarcho-syndicalism. Bewildered, I scurried back into the melee and found my insiders for the march, Sam and Helena, and asked about the flags. Sam replied first, only because Helena could not stop laughing at my question: 'You fool', he teased affectionately, 'what flags, mate? We use the poles for beating back cops.' It seemed that while activists chose anarchist colours generally, the specifics and permeations were not politically relevant. The flags were mere ornaments adorning weapons.

The point of this anecdote is that these flags nearly tripped me head first into a conceptual trap: I mistakenly assumed that they must represent clearly identifiable anarchist currents from which one could deduce relatively unified political identities. This conceptual trap stalks the field of social movement theory. In the North American tradition of social movement research, scholars broadly concentrate their research on the way in which groups, through collective action, engage with resources, political opportunities and threats (McAdam et al., 2001; Tarrow, 1994; Tilly, 1986). These studies have been richly rewarding, shedding light on a host of political factors that influence social movements. Indeed, I rely on some of this work later in the book. Nonetheless, research within this field tends to treat collective action as unified, creating a false impression of an internally homogeneous group identity. It was precisely such a false impression that I had had with respect to the flags.

Regularly, I saw that beneath the façade of collective unity lay complexity, heterogeneity and dissent. Even my 'flag-weapon' example is far more complex than a collective desire to 'beat back the cops'. Individual motivations with respect to violence and the police are nuanced and variable. Simply focusing on the visible actions of social movement collectives does not help us to appreciate fully these diverse motivations. We ignore the important elements of political identity construction that occur away from the public eye, where individual movement actors interact with each other. We miss the range of perspectives, meanings and relationships forged within social movements. Furthermore, we gloss over the influence of emotions, like explosions of love, rage and hate. We similarly may omit consideration of culture, symbols, affinities, rituals, bonds and interpretations of history – all of which inform and shape social movements and their collectives. The nominally European tradition of social movement theory – and in particular Alberto Melucci's (1985, 1989, 1995a) and other constructivists' new social movement theory – provides intellectual tools for avoiding these shortcomings.

Before exploring the intricacies of that tradition, it is helpful to consider some of the other paradigms against which it developed. In the following discussion, I have taken a rather longitudinal frame, introducing research agendas from as far back as the late 1900s. It is true that some of the theories presented below have been largely discredited. Nonetheless, there is still value in reminding readers of the various historical approaches to researching movements of change. These academic texts are more than historical relics: they helped produce stereotypes and perceptions that continue to permeate popular discourse. For example, early collective behaviour literature is dominated by characterisations of movement actors as crazed irrational beings (Burgess and Park 1969 [1921]; Le Bon 1969 [1895]). This is poignant when read alongside descriptions of anarchists in the same era as depraved desperadoes who prefer confusion and chaos to social order (Roosevelt, 1901). Tellingly, this politicised misrepresentation of anarchists and anarchism as inclined to chaos and mayhem continues to this day (see Williams, 2014).

The madness of collective behaviour

At the end of the nineteenth century, Gustave Le Bon called attention to the importance of *the crowd* as a social phenomenon (1969 [1895]). In a scathing account of the mental capacity of actors who came together in a political or social protest, Le Bon pioneered an approach to collective behaviour that would permeate the literature for the next 65 years; one that essentially viewed collective action as irrational behaviour (1969 [1895]: vi).

To Le Bon, *the crowd* appears as unruly and wild, full of individuals lacking in the rationality suitable for healthy social interactions. Participants are defined as 'impulsive savages', unable to respond to appeals of 'reason' and influenced by mystical powers compelling them to act like 'hypnotized subject[s]' (1969 [1895]: 11, 17, 19, 21, 23 and 33). Adding to their demonisation, Le Bon claims they are 'distinguished by feminine characteristics' (1969 [1895]: 20), a sexist stereotype aimed at perpetuating characterisations of irrationality, by dichotomising the rational-male and irrational-female ideal types (Addelson, 1991: 42). For Le Bon, all of these characteristics contribute to a palpable fear that the irrationality of the masses could ultimately 'utterly destroy society as it ... exists' (1969 [1895]: xvi).

Twenty-five years later, Robert Park viewed collective action in much the same way as Le Bon – primarily as irrational behaviour detrimental to society (1969 [1921]). Park explicitly extends Le Bon's characterisations of the crowd to include mass-political movements. These, he argues, 'tend to display, to a greater or less extent, the characteristics that Le Bon attributes to crowds' (Burgess and Park, 1969 [1921]: 871). The structural-functionalist logic within the work of Le Bon also influences Park's theory. It rests on a belief that there is a consensus within any given society on underlying morals, morays and norms, which provide a social glue ensuring order. When society suffers strains, including challenges to the established moral order, discontent spreads. Social unrest amongst aggrieved individuals increases, leading to displays of collective action (Burgess and Park, 1969 [1921]: 866; see also Buechler, 2004: 49; Rule, 1988: 83).

Like Le Bon, Park frames these collective actions within a rational-irrational dichotomy. For Park, collective behaviour is impulsive behaviour similar to 'religious fanaticism and fervor' (Burgess and Park, 1969 [1921]: 871), and is 'transmitted from one individual to another' in a way that is 'akin to the milling process in the herd' (1969 [1921]: 866). Park is clearly sceptical, then, that movements for social change are born out of reasoned reflection and discussion (1969 [1921]: 869). Underlying his approach is a persistent denial that participants of collective behaviour are acting rationally. Given that, it is hard to see how any meaningful change within any society could arise from the reasoned judgement of human agents. This is, of course, a broader problem of the structural-functionalist approach to societal order and disorder and is why it has been so widely discredited. Despite the naive and often superficial judgements within his work, however, Park played an instrumental role in the development of the collective behaviour tradition in North American sociology (Buechler, 2004).

Collective behaviour studies are further refined in the work of Herbert Blumer (1969a, 1969b, 1997 [1969]). He develops Park's work by including a specific focus on social movements (Blumer 1997 [1969]: 73–80). Even though he sees social movements as amorphous and poorly organised, he breaks from his predecessors, acknowledging their potential as purposeful agents of social change (1969b). As a result, Blumer 'definitively establish[es] collective behavior as a recognizable subfield in sociology' (Buechler, 2004: 49; see also della Porta and Diani, 1999: 5). In so doing, Blumer was an early pioneer of symbolic interactionism – that school of interpretive micro-sociology emphasising human agency and the symbolic construction of reality. He focuses on the way in which social movement actors challenge, contest and deconstruct social structures and norms. Blumer also rejects the notion underlying the structural functionalist approach, that collective action is a symptom of dysfunction in society and that challenging social norms can lead to the breakdown of society (1969a). Instead, Blumer argues that social movements are in fact participating in the development and interpretation of morals and values, rather than contributing to social decay (1997 [1969]: 80). Importantly, reason and rationality could inform collective action, a decisive difference in comparison with earlier approaches (Melucci, 1996: 17).

Although Blumer's analysis of social movements is more nuanced than that of his predecessors, it is still mired in a tradition troubled by collective action. This is evident with Blumer's idea of social contagion (with its resemblance to Park's *milling process of the herd*), whereby the intense emotions involved with collective action spread like a virus amongst participants, prompting 'vague apprehensions, alarms, fears, insecurity, eagerness, or aroused pugnacity' (1969b: 73). At best, social movements were semi-rational responses to changing social conditions.

Where Blumer waivered, Ralph Turner and Lewis Killian stepped forward, claiming in their work that collective behaviour could promote positive behavioural norms and moral codes (1957: 13). In so doing, they argue that there is a rational cognitive process within crowd settings (Turner and Killian, 1957: 331–453). Turner and Killian suggest that certain forms of social movements could be rational vehicles for social change, thereby dispensing with most of the irrational baggage that had previously defined analyses of collective behaviour (1957: 308). Nevertheless, despite the best efforts of Turner and Killian, and even Blumer, the characterisation of movement actors as essentially irrational continued to penetrate the literature. This was in no small part owing to the work of Neil Smelser (1962).

Smelser's structural-functionalist approach is a return to the assumptions that collective behaviour is irrational. It repeats many of the more questionable claims made by the earlier generation of literature (Smelser, 1962: 72–73). Smelser refers to collective behaviour as very much like magical beliefs, with actors guided by 'rumours, ideology and superstition' (1962: 80). Moreover, he views social movement participants as conspiracy theorists, irrationally fearing an imminent danger that did not exist (Smelser, 1962: 80; 1964: 118). To add further insult to activists pursuing social change, Smelser views their collective behaviour as forms of panic, crazes and fads (Smelser 1962: 72–73).

Smelser and many of the *irrational activist* brigade appear to be driven by what Seraphim Seferiades and Hank Johnston call a '*pluralist prejudice*': the idea that within Western parliamentary democracies there are 'sufficient expressive channels' for aggrieved protesters (2012b: 4, emphasis in original). Therefore, those who pursue change through non-establishment channels are irrational – which is particularly problematic for anarchists whose methods and desired outcomes exist outside the establishment. With Smelser, the political influence runs deeper. His ideas were formulated within a Cold War mindset, fearful of the 'dangerous' potential of collective action. This influence, arguably, underscores his focus on the irrationality of movement actors. Collective efforts resembling superstitious panics and crazes run contrary to normal societal behaviour that is rational, individual and conventional.

The constant description of movement actors as irrational played a significant role in the subsequent demise of collective behaviour approaches

(Mayer, 1995: 173). Collective behavioural theorists could not comprehend the actions of activists (Ferree, 1992: 42). For the new wave of theorists writing from the mid-1960s to late 1970s, some of whom were activists themselves, it was implausible that collective behaviour was indicative of irrational behaviour (Cox and Barker, 2002: 1–2). Collective behaviour approaches could not account for the wave of emerging social movements, such as the civil rights, anti-Vietnam War and women's movements in the 1960s.

Resource mobilisation and the clamour for rationality

In this changing political context, resource mobilisation theorists tried to 'bring in rationality'. Activists were rational beings using protest and civil disobedience as a political resource to achieve certain goals (Jenkins and Perrow, 1977; McCarthy and Zald, 1977; McAdam 1982). Studies began to emphasise the way in which social movements deployed tools and resources to compete with each other, mirroring the structure, rationality and logic of the economic market (McAdam, 1982). Movement actors would, it was assumed, rationally assess the costs and benefits of participating in action (Olson, 1965). The notion that collective action was 'impulsive, irresponsible outbursts of self-indulgence' was turned on its head (McAdam et al., 2001: 15).

It was Mancur Olsen (1965) who led the charge here. In *The Logic of Collective Action*, Olson uses micro-economic analysis and rational choice theory to conclude that, in the right circumstances, an individual's participation in collective action could be rational (1965: 21–25). Participation is rational when individuals receive adequate benefits for participating in collective action, therefore satisfying their own self-interest. In circumstances where participation in a movement would provide both material and non-material incentives to the movement actors beyond what non-participants would also receive, it was rational to participate (Olson, 1965: 51). For Olson, collective action was only irrational if individuals act against their own self-interest. He argues that it is illogical for humans to participate in time-consuming and potentially dangerous collective action, when those same benefits are also received by non-participants (1965: 21). Drawing on micro-economic theory, Olson concludes that it is perfectly rational behaviour to free ride on the efforts of others (Olson, 1965: 25, 51).

Olson's work was such an immense challenge to collective behaviour models that it shook the field of social movement theory (della Porta and Diani, 1999). Such an economically and mathematically anchored analysis of human behaviour, however, was ultimately found wanting. His core premise, that the satisfaction of individual self-interest is the ultimate gauge of rationality, is particularly questionable, and not subject to any empirical test. The anthropological and historical record of seemingly rational human beings subordinating their own interests to those of some collective or transcendent good, is testament to the variability of rational human motivations. Olson considered adding to his analysis a discussion of how emotional factors influence behaviour. Yet, because he believed it was 'not possible to get empirical proof of the motivation behind any person's action[s]', he removed them from his research agenda [1965: 61]. Consequently, Olson's work ignores emotions and identities, which are aspects of human behaviour that give us a much richer understanding of movements and participation, beyond mere self-interested action.

Extending Olson's application of rational choice theory, John McCarthy and Mayer Zald concentrated their attention on social movement organisations (1973, 1977). Challenging the structural-functionalist paradigm and its focus on system failures, McCarthy and Zald argue that grievances are constantly present in any given society. The challenge for social movement organisations is how best to take advantage of the resources available within this political reality (McCarthy and Zald, 1977). As a result, their work looks at the way in which organisations mobilise and compete for resources, and at the relative successes or failures of different strategies (McCarthy and Zald, 1977: 1212–1216). These resources include, but are not limited to, such things as strong leadership, funding and media access. A key finding was that successes and failures came down to a social movement organisation's access to resources and their ability to make the most of these resources. Resource mobilisation theories scrutinise the processes by which resources for collective action are mobilised, conceptualising these as an extension of conventional forms of political action (Tarrow, 1994: 16).

In order to challenge claims of irrationality, the resource mobilisation approach creates a 'rational being' – the standard activist. This standard is framed in the language of rational choice and cost–benefit ratios, creating a meticulously mathematical and calculated individual (McCarthy and Zald, 1977: 1216). But, of course, this is a completely fictitious character stripped of human agency: gone are any notions of 'values, norms, meanings and significations' (Buechler, 1993: 230) and, I would add, emotions. Indeed, Chapter 7 is loaded with stories of emotionally inspired acts of militancy – the sorts of insights deliberately excluded from resource mobilisation approaches. As William Carroll argues, in its valiant attempt to refute the irrationality claims of its predecessors, resource mobilisation 'falsely universalizes or reifies a certain form of rationality – the instrumental rationality of the isolated, profit-motivated individual – and misapplies this model to the sphere of movement politics' (1997: 15). Although it is a welcome challenge to previous analysis, the dichotomist response to the irrational actor – the creation of a perfectly rational actor – ultimately limits the insights of resource mobilisation theory.

Political process theory and predicting protest

By the early to mid-1980s, social movement theorists had significantly broadened their research focus. Underlying this shift was a heightened regard for movement groups in relation to their structural-political environment – and all that that entails. The rigidity and narrowness of the resource mobilisation approach expanded into detailed studies of a variety of social movements and collectives, and the political opportunities and threats with which they were confronted (Tarrow and McAdam, 2011: 4). This new research direction privileged protest cycles, the role of the state and state agencies, and the wider political environment (della Porta and Diani, 1999: 169; McAdam et al., 2001: 16; Noonan, 1997: 252). Political process theory, as it is known, revolves around the structural factors that influence the successes and failures of social movements (della Porta and Diani, 1999: 169). I now turn to the work of three representative figures in this tradition, Charles Tilly, Doug McAdam and Sydney Tarrow.

A clear extension of the resource mobilisation tradition pervades Charles Tilly's historical analysis of collective action, in his pivotal text *The Contentious French* (1986). Tilly's study considers the influence of political conditions as it explores the relative success and failures of historical protests in France. Throughout much of his wider work, Tilly's persistent theme was the search for causal mechanisms that regularly influence diverse collective actions. Tilly's theory calls for a focus on causal mechanisms like 'political opportunities ... mobilizing structures, framing processes, and contentious interactions' (Tilly, 1999: 58). An ambition behind this work was to lead us towards a 'grand-theory' of social movements, in which we can anticipate suitable and unsuitable conditions for collective action (Tilly, 2002; see also Tarrow, 2008: 228).

The Contentious French (Tilly, 1986) embodies this project. In it, Tilly pays specific attention to the level of interaction that movement actors have with powerful elites and the wider political environment (1986). He finds that mid-seventeenth-century French protesters, for example, 'rel[y] heavily on patronage' by a local aristocratic elite to achieve their goals. By contrast, mid-nineteenth-century protesters construct their goals with respect to mechanisms available under the auspices of the nation-state. Tilly argues that local elites were no longer as influential as they had been in the mid-seventeenth century (1986: 391). Instead of local elites, protesters could secure their political demands via the national legislature – by influencing electoral campaigns, public assemblies and meetings (1986: 395–396). He concludes that as the capitalist state expands, new institutional avenues increase the options available for collective action to be mobilised.

Doug McAdam's *Political Process and the Development of Black Insurgency, 1930–1970* (1982), similarly focuses on social movement collectives interacting with changing political conditions. His work explores the interaction between civil rights activists in the USA, and the 'expanding political opportunities' available to them at the time (1982: 2). His extensive study looks at the role pre-existing networks within the black community – what he refers to as 'indigenous resources' – play during the mobilisation of the movement (McAdam, 1982: 128). Focusing on the way in which civil rights groups recruit and then interact within changing political circumstances, McAdam demonstrates that the National Association for the Advancement of Colored People (NAACP), and black churches and colleges, were instrumental in the mobilisation of the movement's opportunities (1982: 128–129).

Tarrow's *Power in Movement* (1994) also concentrates on political opportunities, with a specific focus on the protest cycle. For Tarrow, it is not strictly the social and political conditions themselves that create movements; instead, it is the changes to these conditions that encourage movement mobilisation, whereby 'people join in social movements in response to political opportunities and then, through collective action, create new ones' (Tarrow, 1994: 17). As a result, Tarrow (1994: 101) sees much political action as responsive to external circumstances largely controlled by the state and authorities. Accordingly, most of what makes up a social movement, such as movement solidarity and movement networks, is created in response to the fluctuating opportunities and constraints put in place by the state (1994: 101–103). Therefore, if we develop our understanding of 'when' political opportunities expand, this will help us account for 'why' political action occurs (Tarrow, 1994: 17).

Studies examining the relationship between the political environment on the one hand, and high-profile social movements and those partaking in 'less conventional forms of action' on the other, have certainly strengthened our understanding of the struggles and conflicts faced by social movements (della Porta and Diani, 1999: 10). While these approaches are an advance over the simplicity of collective behaviour models and the narrowness of resource mobilisation models, political process theory still has some serious weaknesses. For Jeff Goodwin and James Jasper, political process theory is not worthy of its status as the 'hegemonic paradigm among social movement analysis' (1999: 28). Others agree that political process theory is vulnerable to a number of criticisms (Gamson and Meyer, 1996; Jasper, 1997, 2010; Opp, 2009).

To begin with, there is a presumption of group homogeneity that comes from concentrating on collective action as a final construct. We find this in the work of Tilly, McAdam and Tarrow. Their research neglects the diverse identities within movement collectives, as well as the intense negotiations that occur within the decision-making processes of collectives. As Jasper observes, such an 'approach ignore[s] actors' choices, desires, and points of view' (2010: 966). For example, just because a collective participated in an action, we cannot assume that everyone agreed on the action; dissent can be as revealing as agreement. Without that information, it is difficult to have meaningful discussions about what is occurring within social movements and collectives (Melucci, 1985: 800). In addition, it strips social movement actors of their individual agency, consuming all within this unified notion of a collective. Such a presumption is particularly problematic when applied to openly heterogeneous collectives, like Athenian anarchists and anti-authoritarians. To paraphrase Emile Armand, the margins or the minority views also need to be embraced, lest they be contained, governed or asphyxiated by the decisions of the majority (2005 [1911]: 146). Their work is therefore unsuitable for my research, and indeed most work on anarchist collectives, as it pays scant attention to the internal dynamics of a movement.

Political process theory also assumes that movements are beholden to external factors; as if movement actors have formed their opinions, are ready to participate, and are merely waiting for the right opportunities to arise (Jasper, 2010: 966). While it is wise to explore myriad exogenous factors that influence the existence of social movements and collectives, it is unhelpful to do so at the expense of exploring their internal differentiations and dynamics (Gamson and Meyer, 1996). When McAdam (1982) usefully explores the political opportunities available to the civil rights movement, he subsequently ignores the complexities and intricacies within the movement itself, assuming that anything not immediately visible cannot be studied. A limited embrace of human agency, as well as an obsession with external factors, creates a blinkered, structurally reductive approach (Taylor and Dyke, 2004: 273).

This denial of agency is so addictive within political process theory that the external factors influencing social movements are themselves denied human agency. In Tilly's French study (1986), for example, a large number of his observations come from looking at movements interacting with elites, and later the state. In fact, the successes of different periods of struggle depend on the outcome of these interactions. In this work, the state itself is treated 'as a unified actor – a "structure" – rather than as a complex web of agencies and authorities, thoroughly saturated with culture, emotions, and strategic interactions' (Goodwin and Jasper, 2004a: 16). This again diminishes the value of the paradigm, by narrowly focusing on structural mechanisms in order to account for collective action and its successes and failures.

In 2001, McAdam, Tilly and Tarrow published *Dynamics of Contention*. Their intention was to develop political process theory and to engage with some of the critiques levelled against their earlier work (Jasper, 2010: 967).

Importantly, it would entrench the broader shift away from resource mobilisation, 'stressing dynamism, strategic interaction, and response to the political environment' (McAdam et al., 2001: 15–16). As a result, political opportunities were understood in a broader, more encompassing sense. There was acknowledgement that the political process approach had previously created a limited image of collective action and social movements. Hinting at change, research would no longer produce 'still photographs of contentious moments.' Rather, it would instead create 'dynamic, interactive sequences' (McAdam et al., 2001: 18). Writing on the tenth anniversary of the study, McAdam and Tarrow summed up their intended new direction: 'We were calling neither for the staunch structuralism of the social movement tradition nor its rejection in the name of agency, but for attention to the mechanisms that link structure and agency (2011: 4).' It appeared that an 'open-ended, strategic and cultural perspective' on social movement research was to be the paradigm's new direction (Jasper, 2010: 967). As one of their primary antagonists hoping for a shift in direction noted, however, *Dynamics of Contention* 'widely disappoint[s]' (Jasper, 2010: 967).

Any suggestion that agency was to have a heightened consideration with respect to structure seems in stark contrast to the realities of the final product. From its outset, *Dynamics of Contention* continues the theoretical focus on how structural factors shape agency and account for a movement's success or failure (McAdam et al., 2001: 5). Still, their work was also given a new comparative twist. McAdam, Tilly and Tarrow insist that 'the static, individualistic, and often reified character of previous analyses – including our own – bars the door to dynamic, interactive analyses of mobilization and demobilization' (2001: 73, 123); the new call was to look for mechanisms and processes that movements share in common with each other. Movements were to be situated in the light of other moments of contentious politics, such as wars, industrial conflicts or the rise and fall of nationalism (McAdam, et al., 2001: 313–314). To put their work into context, they would be far less concerned with the specifics of the December 2008 uprising in Athens and associated anarchist and anti-authoritarian militancy, than the comparability of this event to, say, the 2005 Parisian riots, or the Rwandan genocide in 1994 (see McAdam et al., 2001: 337; see also Bevington and Dixon, 2005: 188).

Clearly, this theoretical focus can be richly rewarding for students of social movements. Nevertheless, it comes at the expense of considering other key aspects of social movements (Goodwin and Jasper, 2004a: 4). Take, for example, McAdam, Tarrow and Tilly's call to ignore the 'internal social relations' of social movements (2001: 5). Despite acknowledging that 'much of politics' takes place in this arena, the pioneers of political process theory argue that 'there is no collective public struggle' at this level (McAdam et al., 2001: 5). My experiences in the streets and squats of Athens suggest that it is negligent to ignore localised interactions. Internal politics are a critical location for research on social movements, and a highly political location of struggle (see Chapters 5, 6 and 7). Even if we were to follow McAdam, Tarrow and Tilly's strict lead and only concern ourselves with collective public struggles, our insights on those struggles are themselves enhanced and strengthened through a better understanding of what is happening at the local level. Take the negotiation of a speaker's list in a small meeting. Here, anarchists and anti-authoritarians suggest a progressive speaker's list, in which potentially marginalised groups of people are pushed up the list so they can be heard. This 'internal social relation' is negotiated, tested and fine-tuned within a localised confine. These processes can be telling, shedding light on a whole host of significant political interactions regarding diversity, marginalisation and power. This progressive speaker's list is then employed elsewhere, in a general assembly, or in the middle of an Athenian street-protest as activists sit on the road exploring tactics. The local becomes public. These localised 'internal social relations' and processes are catapulted into the public arena, having been first refined at the local level. According to McAdam, Tarrow and Tilly (2001: 5), we should limit the study of social movements to moments of political interactions occurring in public. However, this tells us nothing about the impetus, negotiations and conflict that led to this public act. By ignoring the internal complexities and nuances of social movements, political processes theory excludes so much from possible study and unnecessarily 'narrow[s] the research agenda' (Gould, 2001: 16).

By focusing on the public manifestations of social movements, McAdam, Tarrow and Tilly's work overlooks the human dimension of social movements (Goodwin and Jasper, 2004a: 23; see also Jasper, 1997).[1] In the day-to-day functioning of a collective or a movement lays intense human interactions, where cultural concerns like symbols, rituals, forms of communication and historical narratives, intertwine with emotions, giving life to the movement. Resource mobilisation and political process theorists were so at pains to repudiate the irrational baggage of the collective behaviour school that rationality became the cornerstone of the new paradigm and all collective action was considered thoughtful and 'with reason' (McAdam et al., 1996b; McAdam et al., 2001; McCarthy and Zald, 1973, 1977). This focus on creating a rational actor meant other important elements of social movements were misplaced.

Political process, culture and emotions

Given this history and entrenched theoretical assumptions, political process theorists only belatedly began to consider emotional stimuli and cultural influences on movements (Ferree, 1992: 30; Gould, 2001: 161; Melucci,

1996: 71). While an occasional rogue resource mobilisation study considered them in some way or another, these were largely exceptions (see Gerlach and Hine, 1970; Gurr, 1970). It was not until new social movement theorists like Alain Tourain (1985) and Alberto Melucci (1989) started writing about the importance of cultural factors such as symbols and later emotions, that we witnessed an expansion in cultural analysis within North American social movement research (Johnston, 2009).

The most common approach incorporating cultural and emotional aspects into political process theory is undoubtedly the framing process (Williams, 2004: 93). In their 1986 journal article 'Framing alignment processes, micro-mobilization, and movement participation', David Snow, E. Burke Rochford Jr, Steven Worden and Robert Benford observe that as political circumstances change, sometimes traditional forms of collective action are unsuitable for making the most of new environments (1986: 466–468).[2] Analysing the field of opportunities through a cultural lens provides new options for social movements (Snow et al., 1986: 467). Here the *framing* concept is central.

Essentially, the framing concept is a tool to help explore and enhance group mobilisation, identity, unity and participation. Snow and Benford define a frame as 'an interpretive schemata that simplifies and condenses the "world out there" by selectively punctuating and encoding objects, situations, events, experiences, and sequences of actions within one's present or past environment' (1992: 137). By focusing on framing, the focus shifts to looking at how groups deploy certain 'cultural' strategies in order to bolster movement participation and movement support.

To help this process, the 'world out there' is divided into three central collective action frames: prognostic frames, which look at how actors select strategies and tactics; diagnostic frames, examining how tactics and strategies are deployed; and motivational frames, which explore how individuals decide to participate in movements (Benford and Snow, 2000: 613–618). The theoretical impetus behind this project suggests that as frames align, we can more accurately establish how successful groups are at adapting to changing opportunities; the more time and energy invested in frame alignment, the greater the likelihood that mobilisation will occur (Benford and Snow, 2000). For a body of theory that had neglected non-structural concerns, this was a distinctly new attempt to resolve previous flaws.

Despite the promise of this approach, the attempt to understand cultural influences within this paradigm is problematic (Goodwin and Jasper, 2004a). The epistemological framework that drives this approach still asks questions within a resource mobilisation and political process theoretical context (Benford and Snow, 2000; Williams, 2004). Culture is incorporated into research, insofar as it is considered another structure that can influence mobilisation (see Peterson et al., 2012). Subsequently, however, it is treated as a rigid social object rather than an ongoing and dynamic process informing collectives. Recently, for example, Daniel Blocq, Bert Klandemans and Jacqueline van Stekelenburg use the frames premise to explore mobilisation in relation to anger (Blocq et al., 2012: 330). Similarly, Yulia Zemlinskaya considers framing and gender in social movements, while separately Katja Guenther and Timothy Gongaware use frame analysis to study various aspects of movement collective memory and its impact on mobilisation (Gongaware, 2011; Guenther, 2012; Zemlinskaya, 2010). In all these studies, culture and emotions become yet another opportunity to be deployed rationally by the movement in order to maximise their goals; they are 'subsumed' as a political opportunity, where the 'meaning and fluidity' is washed out of 'strategy, agency, and culture' to the point that culture looks like structure (Goodwin and Jasper, 2004a: 4–5).

Notwithstanding the thrust of my discussion, I have not closed myself off from the work of the previously discussed scholars. While the projects undertaken by the different theoretical camps are remarkably different in terms of their epistemological starting point, I am more than happy to lean on their empirical observations and theoretical leads, albeit cautiously. As Goodwin and Jasper suggest, political process theory is less of a paradigm to launch a theoretical analysis than a 'set of important causal mechanisms' that can facilitate studies (2004b: 84). I agree with this sentiment and in later chapters dip into political process approaches, particularly framing work on culture and emotions (see Blocq et al., 2012; Groves, 2001; Gongaware, 2011; Guenther, 2012; Zemlinskaya, 2010). Nonetheless, the instrumental bias of the political process model precludes an adequate understanding of the complexities of a group's internal dynamics and collective identity. Such an understanding is better pursued through the lens of new social movement theory.

New social movement theory: the early years

As resource mobilisation theorists were responding to collective behaviourists in North America, European early new social movement theorists began challenging the perceived inadequacies of their forerunners – particularly Marxist and Marxist-inspired analyses of social movements. In the *Communist Manifesto*, Marx and Engels provided both a political manifesto for proletarian revolution, and a summary of their materialist conception of history, according to which such a revolution was inevitable (1972 [1848]: 72, 92, 94, 104–105). Notwithstanding the many tensions, nuances and contradictions in their work – which would subsequently give rise to many different forms of Marxism – the basic arguments were clear. They argued that the capitalist mode of production was characterised by a key structural divide between capital and wage labour, defined by ownership and non-ownership of the means of production. In their view, the contradictions entailed by this structural divide would create conditions necessary for its own transcendence (Marx and Engels, 1972 [1848]: 4). Those conditions included both periodic economic crisis, and the creation and growth of a class that was the agent of revolutionary change – the proletariat. In order for the proletariat to create a society where the producers of wealth collectively shared the fruits of their labour – rather than having those fruits concentrated in the hands of a tiny ruling class minority – they would first have to overcome the violent resistance of the bourgeoisie and its state (Marx and Engels, 1972 [1848]: 8–9). Consequently, this change would be revolutionary, it would most likely be violent, and it would be a conscious political act led by the proletariat.

Later Marxists would develop these arguments in multiple directions (Gimenez, 2001). Be that as it may, they typically shared the assumption that social class provides the key to understanding political struggle and progressive social change, even if in 'the final instance'. Despite the undoubted insights of the Marxist tradition, developments in the late 1960s rendered this class-reductionist framework increasingly inadequate (Laclau and Mouffe, 1985; Melucci, 1985; Touraine, 1971).[3]

When, for example, over a million people marched through the streets of Paris on the 13 May 1968, their grievances were not restricted to economic, class-based domination. Their struggles were also concerned with cultural power and control of contemporary systems (Singer, 2000 [1970]: 67). Furthermore, the demonstrations were inspired by decentralised student collectives rather than by left-wing trade unions and/or the Communist Party (Eley, 2002: 342). Writing in response to this famous social unrest, Touraine (1971) identifies a new form of struggle that could not be understood in rigid class terms. In *An Introduction to the Study of Social Movements*, Touraine (1985: 789) begins to see social movements as more socio-cultural than socio-political phenomena, facing challenges around the production and control of culture and meaning. As such, 'macro' new social movement theory emerges as a challenge to the rigidity of the strict class-based collective analysis of Marxist theory (Fominaya, 2010a: 394).

Extending this development, social movements are viewed as struggles against what Jürgen Habermas[4] calls the 'colonization of the life-world' (Habermas, 1981: 37; Touraine, 1985). As society's private realms are 'colonised' by the state and ever-expanding transnational corporations, control and initiative are stripped away from individuals. Habermas argues that as advanced capitalism and the state's intervention into the personal arenas of life increase, post-industrial societies introduce new forms of social control (Habermas, 1981: 37). These new forms require equally novel forms of protest, dissent and organisation to counter their intrusive consequences (Habermas, 1975: 196). 'New' social movements, such as the women's and environmental movements, proliferate, raising what Melucci calls 'cultural challenges to the dominant language, [and] to the codes that organise information and shape social practices' (1995a: 41). Shifting away from struggles primarily around the distribution of economic resources, new social movements are an attempt by individuals to regain personal autonomy in areas formerly of private concern. As a corrective to strict class analysis, the early macro-level work in this school is a welcome shift, indicating the significance of other locations of struggle.

After four years of fieldwork looking at social movements in Milan, Italy, Alberto Melucci (1994) began to question the value of this new approach. He raised three principal concerns. First, like much of political process theory, this earliest phase of 'macro' new social movement theory fails to consider the diversity of actors within movements. Instead, it concentrates on the way in which social movements respond to 'new' historical circumstances, assuming that collective action is an empirically unified act. In doing so, it reifies and homogenises collective action (Melucci, 1995a: 42, 55). Melucci argues that this 'may contribute, even unwittingly, to the practical denial of difference, to a factual and political ignorance of that complex articulation of meanings that contemporary movements carry in themselves' (1996: 79; see also 1995a: 55).

Second, while Melucci agrees that colonisation of the life world is 'an observable trend in complex society', he is doubtful that this is a necessary precursor to collective action (1989: 195). Structural preconditions alone, he argues, cannot account for individual and collective actions (Melucci, 1989; see also Scott, 1996: 84). Melucci's final concern with 'macro' new social movement theory is that while Habermas and Touraine could explain some of the structural conditions in which social movements occur, they could not account for the way in which movement actors sustain and develop their collective action (Melucci, 1989: 195). At their core, they fail to address the meso-level of collective action, the lifeblood of movements, where individuals interact with each other to create a collective. It is at this level that I locate my own research.

Without overstating the significance of Melucci, contemporary new social movement theory owes much to the way in which he overcame these earlier shortcomings. To develop his response, Melucci (1995a) presents the idea of collective identity, not as a fixed conglomeration of individual identities, but as a process whereby political actors themselves produce meanings and negotiate decisions on action. To do so, he rejects the idea of collective action 'as a unified datum' (Melucci, 1989: 25). No longer is a social movement the starting point for research, with its presumptions of homogeneity; instead, he turns to focus on the ways in which it becomes a movement. The spotlight shifts to the way in which actors 'negotiate, understand and construct their action through shared repeated interaction' (Fominaya, 2010a: 395). Melucci refers to this as the process of collective identity (Melucci, 1995a).

The process of collective identity: a tool

Melucci uses the 'notoriously abstract concept' (Fominaya, 2010a: 393) of collective identity as a tool to untangle the 'interactive and shared definition produced by several individuals (or groups at a more complex level) and concerned with the orientations of actions and the field of opportunities and constraints in which the action take place' (1995a: 44).

In this definition, collective identity is *interactive*, making it a dynamic and reflexive process, constantly negotiated and constructed within groups. This is particularly useful when discussing anarchists and anti-authoritarians, who are forever renewing their political projects. Moreover, it is a collective process distinguished from the individual identities of those participating in social movements. These individual identities are 'the wholly personal traits that, although constructed through the interaction of biological inheritance and social life, are internalised and imported to social movement participation as idiosyncratic biographies' (Laraña et al., 1994b: 12). That is not in any way to suggest these individual identities are unimportant. In fact, there is plenty of room for more individual identity research like that proposed in Olivier Fillieule's (2012) study on the psychological effects of participation in demonstrations, and even studies about brain activity and neural pathways during protests. In terms of understanding collectives, however, an aggregation of individual biographies conceals the essentially communally negotiated component of collective identity construction. At the same time, a movement's collective identity is also different from its public identity, which is more concerned with the 'influences that the external public have on the way in which social movement adherents think about themselves' (Laraña et al., 1994b: 18). Like individual identities, any external influences will ultimately be negotiated and considered at the group level of identity construction.

Moving on from the definition, Melucci's three components of the process of collective identity are more telling. First, collective identity is a process involving 'cognitive definitions concerning the ends, means, and field of action' (1995a: 44). In this sense, 'language' encoded within sets of rituals and practices partly define collective identity, which is perpetually constructed through negotiation, conflict and compromise (Fominaya, 2010a). Consequently, seemingly benign practices and rituals are critical as they ultimately reflect a series of collective, potentially fragmented voices. These collectively constructed (but not necessarily unified) voices represent an active language involved with the means, ends and negotiation of the action field. This component allows us to get at the hidden and subtle elements that contribute to collective identity construction. In particular, it encourages us to uncover dissent or points of contention within collectives. As I will show in Chapter 6, this was immensely useful in Athens where some of the most insightful conversations revolve around conflicting views on violent forms of direct action, otherwise hidden in the grander spectacle of collective action.

Second, Melucci defines collective identity as a process that recognises the importance of the dynamic 'network of active relationships' between actors (1995a: 45). The organisational structure and form, and the avenues and methods for group communication, are all encompassed within this component. Here though, Melucci is not suggesting a return to the structural functionalist approaches, where networks and active relationships were studied as a unified entity, in order to create generalising claims about social movement participation and action (1996: 300). Rather, he suggests adhering to the constructivist approach, in which social relationships and networks are constructed and reconstructed within a field of action.

To contextualise this point, let us consider the nature of affinity groups within the Athenian anarchist and anti-authoritarian space. These voluntary, non-hierarchical and self-regulating political and social networks are a central element of the Athenian milieu. To operationalise Melucci's paradigm, we should not limit research to mapping the relationships between affinity groups. This would tend to treat them as homogenous entities. It is far more fruitful to view affinity groups as social relationships within which negotiations unfold about violence, actions, solidarity and politics. These relationships and networks are part of a process that contributes to the construction of a fluid collective identity.

The third and final component of Melucci's approach to collective identity is emotional investment, 'which enables individuals to feel like part of a common unity' (1995a: 45). Apart from highlighting the need to investigate emotions within his processes of collective identity, Melucci's work is rather limited on this topic, neglecting to delve into the nuances and subtleties of emotions. Instead, we are left with a broad set of tools for future research. In Chapter 7, I develop this work, showing how emotions are very significant influences on the Athenian anarchist and anti-authoritarian space. There, I present insights into intense feelings like hatred, trust, empowerment, revenge and rage. I show how all these emotions intertwine to give meaning and substance to the space. In lieu of Melucci's lack of detail, my work on emotions is guided by Jasper's social-constructivist typology of protest-related emotions, in his article 'Emotions and social movements: twenty years of theory and research' (2011). My research specifically focuses on three types of emotions: reflex emotions, long-term emotions and moral emotions (Jasper, 2011: 287).[5]

Processes of collective identity: emotions

According to James Jasper, reflex emotions are responses to our social and political surroundings that are 'usually quick to appear and to subside, and accompanied by a package of facial expressions and bodily changes'

(2011: 287). These emotions include reactions to moral shocks and injustices that occur before our eyes, producing feelings such as hatred and anger. Alongside these emotions, I look at long-term emotions, which include feelings of affinity and revenge, as well as affective loyalties such as 'love, liking, respect, trust [and] admiration' (Jasper, 2011: 287). Ethnographic research is particular fruitful here. Inasmuch as these emotions can play out during a street-protest, they can also develop and materialise at other times. Finally, I also discuss what Jasper calls moral emotions, the 'feelings of approval and disapproval based on moral intuitions and principles ... such as compassion for the unfortunate or indignation over injustice' (Jasper, 2011: 287). These emotions can include feelings of pride, liberation and empowerment.

Initially, it was Melucci's call for heightened 'cultural analysis' (1996: 68) that attracted me to new social movement theory. I was only intending to explore emotions as a minor point, as opposed to the rituals and coded language in the Athenian anarchist and anti-authoritarian milieu. Emotions were to be a relevant, albeit peripheral concern of the book. While in Athens, though, I became acutely conscious that emotions were contributing to the dynamics of the movement and informing a temporary unity within the space. My focus then shifted to a shared concern for cultural influences and emotions. Melucci's process of collective identity provides a suitable epistemological framework and set of tools with which to pursue this research agenda. Still, his work needs to be read alongside a host of scholars who have more intently explored the empirical manifestations of emotions within social movements.[6] It is within the new social movement paradigm, where the internalities of social movements and collectives are given due research focus; I do not believe this is the case for political process theory.

Revisiting the collective behavioural models in order to set up my claim, their earlier studies viewed emotions as irrational and hence incompatible with rationality, creating 'the false dichotomy of emotions and rationality' (Aminzade and McAdam, 2002: 107). Emotions were seen as 'natural sensations' where people were 'seized' by feelings such as passion, anger and disgust (Jasper, 1998: 154). They were bodily symptoms that consumed rational thought processes, overwhelming the mind. Seen through an irrational-deviance lens, they were considered physical responses rather than cognitive.

Somewhat understandably, resource mobilisation and political process theorists 'banished' emotions from social movement study (Calhoun, 2001a: 48). Resource mobilisation and political process theorists sought to extricate all notions of irrationality from social movement analysis, to show that collective action was a positive act by rational individuals. To some extent, I think that the idea was to valorise these political activities, and disarm opponents of particular social movements. This was an important corrective to the characterisation of movement actors as deviant and irrational (Gould, 2001: 161).

The result though, as Deborah Gould argues, is a narrowing of the 'research agenda' (Gould, 2001: 161). So much of what makes up a social movement is abandoned in this stampede to 'rationality', as political process theorists neglect stories of the passion, emotions and feelings of movement actors (Gould, 2001: 156). In no small part, this body of theory became fixated with factors that 'facilitate protest and on questions of movement emergence and decline', subsequently ignoring accounts and narratives of emotion and beliefs, as they become 'irrelevant to such inquiries' (Gould, 2001: 156).

I noted earlier that the irrationality attributed to emotions in the collective behaviour approaches was largely an attempt to devalue the importance of emotions, superficially thought of as feminine characteristics (Ferree and Merrill, 2004: 251; see also Zemlinskaya, 2010). The 'politically charged image' of the rational actor (superficially associated as a male character) as 'unemotional, calculating, individually self-interested, dominant, [and] hierarchical' overwhelms the literature (Ferree and Merrill, 2004: 251). In contrast, Melucci argues that emotions, such as '[p]assions and feelings, love and hate, faith and fear' contribute to the meaning and action dynamically constructed within a social movement, bringing it to the fore of new social movement theory (1995a: 45). This approach encourages us to observe the ways in which emotion can facilitate the process of collective identity.

Despite advances, there are still problems when political process theorists deploy the idea of 'framing' in their analyses of emotions. Most significantly, such analyses prescribe the investigation of emotions in ways that do not engage with the complexities of emotions as they relate to group identity. When Robert Benford (1997) analyses emotions within the political process 'frame' approach, for example, emotions are viewed reductively as structural factors to be employed as resources. The rational lens of political process theory asks how these emotions can be 'produce[d], orchestrate[d] and strategically deploye[d]' (Benford, 1997: 419). More recently, the same sort of issues arise in Blocq, Klandemans and van Stekelenburg's (2012) research on anger in social movements. They explore the way in which leaders of social movement organisations construct political messages with respect to anger. Using quantitative research, they find that leaders of social movement organisations who are less embedded in the political system are more prone to mobilise using anger than leaders who are more embedded. Further, non-embedded activists were angrier than embedded activists (Blocq et al., 2012: 330). While it is an insightful analysis, their predilection for political process theory compels them to turn emotions exclusively into a resource. Investigations turn to how movement organisers 'evoke different emotions while informing or appealing to their members' and how 'particular frames trigger emotional responses' (Blocq et al., 2012: 331–332). These same themes permeate Jorge Cadena-Roa's work on emotions and frames in Mexico City's urban movements, and in Douglas Schrock, Daphne Holden and Lori Reid's study of transgender communities in the USA (Cadena-Roa, 2005; Schrock et al., 2004). In all these studies, the way in which emotions inform the group during the process of collective identity formation is lost. As a result, we 'produce a flat, thin caricature of protesters' stripped of the characteristics that make them human (Gould, 2001: 161). This is, then, an unsuitable theoretical paradigm for unravelling the internal complexities in the Athenian anarchist and anti-authoritarian space.

Partly as a response to these shortcomings, some theorists reintroduced the study of emotions, but on a different footing (Goodwin et al., 2001a; Gould, 2001; Jasper, 1997; Melucci, 1985, 1995a; Polletta and Jasper, 2001). These scholars argue that, to greater or lesser degrees, emotions are created, defined and interpreted within a cultural context, and are as much rational as they are irrational (Calhoun, 2001: 47; Jasper, 2003: 155). This results in consideration of emotions as reflexive and dynamic responses to the social world, intertwined with beliefs, morals and assumptions (Jasper, 2003: 155). Movement actors are motivated by passion, love, affection or disdain (Gould, 2001: 156), and driven by pride, indignation, joy, intuition, obligation or instinct (Jasper, 1998). In my research, I show how emotions and intense feelings like hatred, trust, empowerment, revenge and rage inform affinity and militancy, unity and disunity. As a result, there is no question that emotions 'are intimately connected with both the values and ideas of movement actors', which once unravelled can significantly enrich our understanding of collective action (Ferree and Merrill, 2004: 252; see also Fominaya, 2010a; Simiti, 2012).

To sum up, Melucci's understanding of collective identity as an ongoing and reflexive process is a critical contribution to the study of social movements. It provides me with the necessary theoretical tools to understand that Athenian anarchist and anti-authoritarian collective identity is informed by a sense of emotionally sustained unity produced in militant protest actions, not just by various anarchist ideas and ensuing conflicts regarding praxis. Melucci encourages researchers to investigate beyond the public expressions of social movements and to engage with the meso-level of movements, previously neglected in alternative theoretical paradigms. In his work, collective identity is transformed from a thing, to a 'process that is generated through the interaction of movement members as they attempt to mobilize for a shared goal' (Fominaya, 2010a: 394). In doing so, movement actors are rightly attributed with agency, and research focuses on the self-reflexive and negotiated 'ability of a collective actor to recognize the effects of its *actions* and to attribute these effects to itself' (Melucci 1995a: 46, emphasis added). This is undertaken without losing the essentially political nature of movements – and without ignoring the structured economic and political circumstances within which they operate – as the use of 'actions' in the quotation implies.

Process of collective identity: applicability

Despite moments of temporary unity, one of the more evident aspects of my research on anarchists and anti-authoritarians is that a homogeneous, shared and static collective identity is very unlikely for activists who embrace 'free initiative, free action, [and] free association' (Kropotkin, 1993 [1896]: 1). This mirrors what Joshua Gamson identifies within the queer movement as an 'impulse to blur, deconstruct, and destabilise group categories' (1995: 402). So, does the absence of a unified collective identity render Melucci's tools useless for such movements? To some extent, Kevin McDonald (2002) pursues this question in his work on protesters at the Asia/Pacific regional meeting of the World Economic Forum in Melbourne 2000 (s11) and in Burlington before the Quebec City FTAA Summit in 2001. Here, McDonald rightly challenges the notion of homogeneity in autonomous activist collectives (see also Polletta and Jasper, 2001: 294). His exploration of some affinity groups during these protests, demonstrates an ephemeral solidarity at best, but more so a clear lack of a shared collective identity amongst activists. One of the strengths of McDonald's work is that it provides a practical example of the need to challenge assumptions of collective unity and collective identity. In concluding, he calls for a new paradigm of collective identity, 'where action instead needs to be understood in terms of a shared struggle for personal experience' (McDonald, 2002: 124–25).

Despite being a useful corrective to some other approaches, McDonald loses sight of the importance of collective identity formation as a process; illustrating what Cristina Flesher Fominaya refers to as a confusion between '"product" and "process"' (Fominaya, 2010a: 397). As Fominaya's (2007) research on Madrid's anti-capitalist networks demonstrate, the processes involved with collective identity formation, even for heterogeneous social movements, continue to yield interesting results. But this only works if collective identity formation is considered a process, not a static product.

In this light, it is not surprising that one of the strengths of the process of collective identity is its pliable applicability. Indeed, this concept had been variously applied to the women's movement (Maddison, 2003; Whittier, 1995), the queer movement (Gamson, 1995), the environmental movement (Apoifis, 2008; Seel and Plows, 2000), and the anti-capitalist movement (Clough, 2012; Fominaya, 2007). It has also been applied to issues of solidarity (Downton and Wehr, 1997; Hirsch, 1990) and movement symbolism (Helman and Rapoport, 1997; Juris, 2005). Indeed, as Fominaya accurately observes:

> As we have seen, although collective identities can be understood as (potentially) encompassing shared interests, ideologies, subcultures,

goals, rituals, practices, values, worldview, commitment, solidarity, tactics, strategies, definitions of the 'enemy' or the opposition and framing of issues, it is not synonymous with and cannot be reduced to any of these things. (2010a: 398)

At its core, then, the process of collective identity is actually a set of tools that can be used in a variety of ways to assist our understanding of social movements.

New social movement theory: critics

New social movement theory and Melucci's process of collective identity are, of course, not without their critics. As I have already noted, Melucci's work is rather limiting when it comes to discussions of emotions. A component of this book engages with this shortcoming. Other criticisms are dismissive of the whole research agenda. Snow (2001), one of the pioneers of 'framing' (discussed earlier in this chapter), is particularly critical of the reification of the *process* of collective identity over the *product* of social action (2001). While he acknowledges the benefits of looking at collective identity, Snow argues that we should analyse it according to its historical aggregation, prevalence and frequency, rather than studying the forces involved in its production (2001: 4). Writing in the political process tradition, Snow relies on the same epistemological rhetoric that has framed the paradigm and, like McDonald's conclusions on autonomous activist collectives, Snow focuses on the end product rather than the process itself.

This critique continues the oversimplification of collective identity, viewing it as an empirical object. This denies the inherently constructive nature of collectives – with all the dissent, conflict and diversity that goes with it. For example, if we focus only on the product of a social action in Athens, say the protest, we are vulnerable to making false assumptions about the space and we may miss the intricacies of gender politics or varying nuanced attitudes on violence within the milieu. These are points I discuss in Chapter 6. On top of this, a focus on the final product ignores the intense negotiations that make up collective action.

A different and more prevalent critique comes from the rejection of the 'new' classification in the term 'new social movement'. Social movements of the late 1960s are as concerned, if not more so, with forms of struggles around cultural power and control of contemporary systems, as they are with more traditional economic, class-based conflicts (Melucci, 1994; Touraine, 1985: 789). Generally, the counter-argument runs, there is nothing new in what these movements espouse. Tilly, for example, asserts that these so-called 'new' movements, like the women's, peace and environment movements are similar to movements in earlier historical periods. Comparing the action-forms undertaken by historical and contemporary movements, Tilly asserts that they have 'met, marched, formed associations, petitioned and demonstrated' in much the same fashion (1988: 13). For Tilly, there is nothing novel about 'new' social movements.

Michael Young's (2002) study of the temperance and anti-slavery movements in the 1830s similarly concludes that cultural politics were a major component of these movements. Their goals were also about personal and social transformation, 140 years before Melucci's movements. Along the same lines, Bernd Reiter's (2009: 52) genealogy of black Brazilian organising suggests that identity-based mobilisation during slavery was evident as far back as the 1530s. Concern over identity politics within this movement highlights that there is nothing new about the shift away from mere class-based organising (Reiter, 2009). As a result, Reiter finds the 'new' in new social movement so problematic he is willing to repudiate the whole theoretical paradigm (2009).

Nick Crossley raises the point that even if we accept the 'newness' of these movements, such is the nature of a relative notion that the term new social movements itself 'is rapidly approaching its sell-by date' (2003: 149). In Richard Day's *Gramsci Is Dead* (2005), he provides exactly this example, by arguing it has already happened. Day observes that most 'new' social movements traditionally challenged for state-based reforms and concessions (2005: 70). In his work on anarchic trends in contemporary social movements, Day sees more recent groups orienting themselves to alternative forms of direct action, 'pushing beyond the possibilities and limits of liberal reform' (2005: 8; see also Feixa et al., 2009). In that sense, social centres and groups like Indymedia and Reclaim the Streets, are all operating non-hegemonically rather than counter-hegemonically, seeking radical change 'but not through taking or influencing state power' (Day, 2005: 8). This challenge to the very logic of hegemonic desires for state control differentiates these *newest* social movements from Melucci and Touraine's *new* social movements.

I am very sympathetic to this line of critique. Melucci's (1995a: 41) argument that there has been a general shift away from strict class-based challenges to the existing order is fair enough. But his related claim that the shift is towards more cultural and symbolic challenges to the existing order, and that these represent a clear break with the past, is more problematic. As Tilly (1988), Young (2002) and Reiter (2009) have suggested, cultural and symbolic challenges to power have always been a feature of movements pressing for change. Even Day's identification of anarchist currents within the most contemporary radical social movements as novel, is historically imprecise – a point he readily acknowledges (Day, 2005: 9). Pursuing social and political change without trying to take control of state power, acting *non*-hegemonically, has been a feature of anarchist movements as diverse as Spanish anarcho-syndicalists in the 1930s, to the German Autonomen current in the 1980s. Rather than any claim that a non-state focus is a historical novelty, what Day is really suggesting is that the *newness* represents 'the ongoing displacement of the hegemony of hegemony' – a lineage that extends to classical anarchist thought (2005: 9).

In this light, Melucci's concept of 'newness' should be understood as a *relative notion*, which draws attention to an important but not an absolute transition point in the history of social movements. It is premised on an observation that many of the social movements under observation in the late 1960s and thereafter were structurally different from traditional working-class movements (Melucci 1995b: 109). Irrespective of whether or not his idea of newness is accepted, Melucci's process of collective identity is still sound and is not designed to produce any universal claims regarding the history or the genealogy of social movements. Rather, it provides us with a set of useful analytical tools.

The process of collective identity sets out an approach to address the failure of alternate theoretical paradigms to consider the meso-level of collective action (which I referred to earlier as the lifeblood of movements), in which individuals interact with each other to create a collective. The fact that the movements and collectives it was designed to study may be viewed in different historical contexts does nothing to diminish its usefulness, as my own research demonstrates. With this in mind, it is quite surprising that established academics such as Tilly continued to focus on this 'newness' critique, apparently searching for a simplistic critique to rid themselves of a challenging alternative paradigm.

An alternative approach? Hardt and Negri

Before concluding, I briefly pause to discuss a different approach to social movement theory, a body of work that does not identify itself within the North American or European paradigms. I engage with the work of Michael Hardt and Antonio Negri's *Multitude* (2004), largely because of the interest it aroused amongst the anarchist and anti-authoritarians I came into contact with in both Australia and Europe. Not often esteemed or venerated amongst my respondents, it nonetheless generated, dare I say, a multitude of conversations on its broader themes. Here though, I touch on the reason I did not employ it as a theoretical pillar for my research.

In *Multitude*, the authors propose a framework in which to conceptualise the largely heterogeneous resistance to capitalism (Hardt and Negri, 2004). They argue that alongside the shift from industrial to post-industrial societies has come a transformation in the dominant forms of labour, from the material labour of industrialism to immaterial labour (or biopolitical production – like work within communications and social relations) (Hardt and Negri, 2004: xiii). As global capitalism expands and its intrusions become more obvious, counter-forces develop within the actual networks that perpetuated the changing forms of labour – what Hardt and Negri call the multitude. The multitude is 'an open network of singularities that links together on the basis of the common they share and the common they produce' (Hardt and Negri, 2004: 355). The 'multitude based on the common', the authors stress, is very much heterogeneous in nature and 'composed of radical differences, singularities, that can never be synthesized in an identity' (Hardt and Negri, 2004: 355).

This image of the multitude aligns with anarchist and anti-authoritarian principles like diversity of thought and practice. Some Athenian anarchists and anti-authoritarians spoke to me of their solidarity with anarcho-syndicalists in Spain, for example, and at the same time stressed substantive differences. As Hardt and Negri note, the multitude does not imply 'unification' of ideas, or 'subordination of differences', but instead celebrates the heterogeneous nature of resistance to capitalism (Hardt and Negri, 2004: 355).

In this context, Hardt and Negri's image of the structure of resistance to capitalism, with its diversity and individuality, balanced by its common struggles against hierarchy, is a reasonable meta-sketch. While actors within recent resistance movements like Occupy and the *Indignados* share hostility to elements of contemporary capitalism, for example, they are equally characterised by their points of political difference (Graeber, 2011a). I have incorporated Hardt and Negri's notion of the common into my discussion on the anarchist and anti-authoritarian space. Nonetheless, I see their work more as an insightful broad analysis of advanced capitalism and its antagonists, rather than providing any particular tools with which to research the said resistance. In contrast, new social movement theory provides exactly that – a set of tools to guide research.

Theoretical tools in need of fieldwork: a conclusion

I have made the case throughout this chapter that new social movement theory – in particular Melucci's process of collective identity – is best suited to my research, where the goal is to unravel internal complexities within social movements and their collectives (or affinity groups). Melucci's approach problematises contentious assumptions about internal homogeneity within collectives; assumptions that come from treating collective action as an empirical object. With this as a starting point, the process of collective identity is presented as a set of tools facilitating a more penetrative understanding of the dynamic, reflexive and negotiated processes of identity construction relating to the 'field of opportunities and constraints offered to collective action' (Melucci, 1985: 793). Still, this is a set of tools whose usefulness for understanding social movements is only made manifest through fieldwork and engaging with the activists themselves.

To this end, later chapters put these conceptual tools to work, providing a lens through which to gain a better understanding of the Athenian anarchist and anti-authoritarian movement. Before discussing those more concrete findings, however, it is necessary to consider some core issues involved with 'militant ethnography.' Thus, the next chapter provides a meta-analysis of my fieldwork methods at the Athenian coalface. Returning to my introductory anecdote, inasmuch as Melucci's set of tools helped me to understand the nuances of the flags, navigating the riot that followed required a more practical set of methods.

Notes

1 See also Calhoun, 2001; Goodwin and Polletta, 2001a; Gould, 2001; Jasper, 1997; Melucci, 1989, 1996.
2 This was an adaptation of Erving Goffman's work in *Frame Analysis: An Essay on the Organization of Experience* (1974).
3 For a spirited defence of the Marxist approach to social movements, see Verity Burgmann (2003), who argues that a class-based analysis is more relevant than a cultural approach to understanding social movements. The latter she views as an unfortunate by-product of postmodernist thought (2003: 22).
4 Habermas adopted the concept from the phenomenological tradition of philosophy.
5 Here, I am not referring to emotions that come from what Jasper calls urges, like the 'urgent bodily needs that crowd out other feelings and attention until they are satisfied: lust, hunger, substance addictions, the need to urinate or defecate, exhaustion or pain' (2011: 286).
6 I engage with these scholars in my 'emotions discussion' in Chapter 6; see Calhoun, 2001; Clough, 2012; della Porta, 1995; Gould, 2001, 2009; Groves, 2001; Ferree and Merrill, 2004; Fillieule, 2012; Flam, 2005; Fominaya, 2010; Goodwin et al., 2000, 2001b, 2004c; Gould 2009; Grindon, 2007; Jasper, 1998, 2011; Nepstad and Smith, 2001; Peterson et al., 2012; Polletta and Jasper, 2001; Risley, 2011; Ruiz-Junco, 2013; Simiti, 2012; Sitrin, 2013; Taylor and Whittier, 1995; Turner and Stets, 2005; Wettergren, 2005; Wood, 2001.

3
Militant ethnography and taking notes in a furnace

'Καλώς ήρθατε στην αθήνα'
[welcome to Athens]

As I prepared for my trip to Athens in late 2010, a colleague convinced me to read *Letters from the Field; 1925–1975*, by pioneering anthropologist and ethnographer Margaret Mead (1977). In a collection of correspondence sent to her friends from the field, Mead offers counsel on the inconsistencies of fieldwork research. Poignantly, she advises, 'one must be continually prepared for anything, everything – and perhaps most devastating – for nothing' (1977: 25).

Reading Mead's insights and feeling nervous about the challenges of my own fieldwork, I went about fastidiously preparing in order to avoid her latter point, a data-less yield. I began like an addicted hoarder, stockpiling meticulous day plans with scheduled visits to known squats, social centres, suburbs, squares and meeting places. Through contacts in Australia, North America and Europe, I compiled lists of names, emails and phone numbers of Greek anarchists and anti-authoritarians. I wanted to avoid using these contact lists (for reasons discussed later in this chapter), but if pressed, I would resort to them if nothing fruitful was coming from my time in Athens. I even planned to travel up north to Thessaloniki – another anarchist and anti-authoritarian stronghold. Very early on, it became apparent that the first part of Mead's quotation was more relevant. Rather than being prepared for nothing I had to be ready for 'anything [and] everything' (1977: 25). It was within less than three hours of my first jet-lag-free night in Athens that I realised I might have wasted my time formulating alternative plans.

It was close to 11:30 p.m. on my first night in the field. Christo and I were mid-way through a conversation on the side of the road just on the fringes of Exarcheia. I had approached him cold, offered a rolled-up cigarette and commenced my first 'fieldwork' conversation. I was like a nervous teenager on a first date – thoughts on what to say, how to say it and playing it cool kept running through my head. A navy blue police van was parked on the footpath opposite us with grills obscuring the windows. It formed part of a network of police outposts surrounding Exarcheia, giving the neighbourhood an embattled feel of limited autonomy, the likes more consistent with a colonial territory. The police looked young, boyish and perhaps in their early twenties at best – certainly not like the wild men of the MAT (Μονάδες Αποκατάστασης Τάξης, the Greek riot police).

Suddenly, our conversation was broken when six hooded characters popped out of nowhere, pelted rocks at the police and their van, and then scurried away into one of the darkened lanes. One policeman had blood pouring from his forehead and another was holding his shoulder in pain. Unfazed – as if he had seen it all before, which he probably had – Christo began to educate me, speculating it was retaliation for some violent police abuses of anarchists earlier in the week. I never found out the specifics though. As he was talking, I began naively jotting some observations down in my note pad until Christo quickly shoved it back in my pocket: 'You don't want trouble', he warned me, 'do it later.' I nodded like an obedient pupil as we backed up into an alley, lit another cigarette and watched the blood now percolating from the policeman's head.

A few moments passed before police came from every direction with their sirens polluting the night air. Agitated, Christo whispered that it was not a good time to be on the streets. He said his farewells and with a smile added, 'καλώς ήρθατε στην Αθήνα' – welcome to Athens. I sat down at a coffee shop and penned a recollection of what had just happened. I realised that I needed to cede control of my research to the events and people around me and follow Edward Hedican's research dictum to 'go along with the flow of events' (2006: 21). I had a quick laugh at the expense of my now-redundant, meticulous plans. The city was too alive for that.

Incidents can occur rapidly and chaotically in the field. As such, it is necessary to embrace a research paradigm that encourages adaptation and flexibility to attain useful data effectively. At the same time, it must conform to an ethical and theoretical framework consistent with the broader research project (Goetz and LeCompte, 1984: 4–11). The eclectic and holistic characteristics of militant ethnography satisfy these concerns.

In this chapter, I discuss the benefits of using militant ethnographic methods to capture the stories, experiences and emotions of the participants in these collective actions. Jeffrey Juris's (2007) concept of militant ethnography is a combination of politically engaged participant observation and ethnography, premised on intense reflexive collaboration between ethnographers and activists, in which, as much as possible, researchers assume the role of active political practitioners. Importantly, it aims to produce politically applicable knowledge from within movements. It required me to 'get my politics on' and actively participate in anarchist and anti-authoritarian praxis throughout my time in Athens.

Further, upon the consistent recommendations of my collaborators, I disseminated fieldwork insights in numerous anti-fascist, anarchist and anti-authoritarian forums in Australia. The following discussion details some of the strengths, functional issues and nuances associated with my preferred qualitative research approach. I finish the chapter by looking at some of the consequences of militant ethnography and researching militants, including issues of ethics, illegalities, anonymities and violence. Before moving on to these considerations, I briefly present some practicalities of my fieldwork experience in order to contextualise some of the forthcoming discussions.

Setting the scene: Athens

I was initially in Athens from the beginning of January through to late March 2011 (and then again in late 2013). For the better part of those first three months, I stayed in squats or shared housing with Athenian anti-authoritarians and anarchists. On the odd occasion I needed a break from the intensity of research, I would spend a day or two at a hostel. I used this time for writing up field notes and emailing them to various accounts to avoid having data on me in the field.

When I arrived in Athens, my Greek language skills had been refreshed with some lessons in Sydney, but I still felt a prisoner to time with a language I had not properly engaged with since I was a child. As a third-generation Greek-Australian, I spoke Greek at home when I was younger but over the course of three decades, its familiarity slipped away. Further, my family left Greece just after World War II, so the Greek I was taught sounded a lot different to the street slang prevalent in today's radical-left Athenian milieu. Such is the nature of immersion that within a short period in Athens, something in my brain was set free and the language of my childhood rushed back. Pepper Glass observes that an ethnographer's data is both 'enhanced and limited by their personal and demographic characteristics' (2009: 528). Whereas Glass's data was limited by his lack of fluency in Spanish, my proficiency in Greek enabled me to communicate readily with all willing respondents.

Naturally, there were moments in which I was uncertain about the accuracy of my translation. In these instances, I merely asked my respondents to explain themselves more simply, or we would collectively construct a suitable translation (see Colectivo Situaciones, 2007: 73). Although I recognise the importance of relating to activists in their native tongue, and the subtle, nuanced differences you pick up during translation, I could have got away with only limited Greek as many activists had at least some basic grasp of English.

On my first days in the city, I went straight to the neighbourhood of Exarcheia, occupied ground for the anarchist and anti-authoritarian community, 'where the very presence of police ... is treated as an intrusion' (Vradis and Dalakoglou, 2011: 40). I hung around the main square and in the liberated park (the one I mentioned earlier where locals had successfully resisted the development of a car park in the heart of Exarcheia, converting the space into a communal park). Here, I was constantly going up to people to explain my presence and my research. After I had established a number of personal connections, I was offered various spaces on floors or some bedding in small squats in Exarcheia and beyond. At the same time, I was getting involved in as many political actions as possible, hearing of these events at assemblies, on posters, on flyers, or from my 'squatmates'. I was also invited to watch less publicised direct actions that necessitate a degree of discretion on my part.

By the end of my time in Athens, I had squatted and participated in assemblies, meetings, intense protests and other direct actions, all the while conversing with activists. Over the more than 80 days, I was involved in about 90 formal interviews/conversations with 30 activists – formal in the sense that I took accurate, quotable notes. On the advice of activists, I did not electronically record any of the conversations, a point discussed later in the chapter. With all but 12 of the respondents, I was able to confirm face-to-face my handwritten recollection of the conversation, encouraging their edits and clarifications. In some instances where I was conducting interviews during protests, however, I never saw the individual again, usually because tear gas dispersed the crowd before I had had a chance to arrange another meeting. In addition, there were also hundreds of informal conversations that took place casually and without written records. As the lines of researcher and participant blurred, I sometimes found it was too burdensome to be constantly note taking. In addition, it is worth noting that my research was informed by a handful of conversations and interactions with the police.

Before moving to my discussion on militant ethnography, I provide some final points about making contacts in the field and my interviewing style. In terms of sampling, I made the point in my introductory anecdote that before I left Australia I had a list of contacts that I preferred not to rely on. I wanted to avoid actively seeking interviews with people of note, like those who had produced written work or had travelled to talk about Greek anarchism (see also Razsa and Kurnick, 2012: 240). When chance had it that I met authors or noted speakers I took the opportunity to chat, while respecting their anonymity within my book. Despite this, I was driven by a desire to capture a cross-section of Athenian anarchists and anti-authoritarians.

Reading the informative text on Greek anarchists and anti-authoritarians, *We Are an Image*, it struck me that the selection process for articles and interviews coming from within complex movements invariably relies on networks (Schwarz et al., 2010; see also Vradis and Dalakoglou, 2011). In *We Are an Image*, an insider's selection process is privileged, whereby those known to the authors and their comrades are given space to contribute in the book. I do not think that there is anything necessarily wrong with that process, but for my work I did not want to rely only on prominent voices. I wanted as many different voices as possible to inform my project. Alongside the benefit of enriching the book with an array of diverse perspectives, this also gives due respect to the anarchist and anti-authoritarian organising principles of my respondents, by subtly challenging informal hierarchies and authorities (Razsa and Kurnik, 2012: 240).

As such, I initially made the most of 'convenience sampling' (Bruce, 2013: 10), by approaching individuals for a chat who were either at a protest, general assembly or sitting around in a square in Exarcheia. I had some problems with this approach at first, which reflects my insecurities at that time about intense fieldwork. I found a useful method was to find someone having a cigarette, ask for a lighter and then spark up one of my own, reconnecting with a habit I had long since discarded. For one, it is harder to find someone who does not smoke in Greece, so the initial premise of this plan had merit. And second, what I found was that people were more than happy to share a random conversation with a stranger because they knew that it had an end. Once that cigarette went out, we could say our goodbyes and leave our brief chat at that. With that outlet available, my experience was that people were willing to have that initial chat and more. The cancerous ice-breaker worked.

By approaching them myself, I avoided being overly reliant on those who were 'immediately eager to talk', as I was searching for hidden voices as much as dominant ones (Paulsen, 2009: 516). From there, alongside some much-appreciated goodwill and generosity on the part of activists, my ability to demonstrate levels of competency when discussing anarchist politics resulted in extended conversations. This led to invitations to squat and participate in direct actions and protests. A degree of snowball sampling was also present, where one activist referred me to another and so on (Atkinson and Flint, 2001).

I relied on minimally structured, open-style interviews for most of my longer conversations in Athens (see Hoffmann, 2007: 339). Driving this decision was a desire for the research agenda to be set by my respondents, as I wanted them to inform me of their topics of interest. From there, I used my experience with interviews to mine their knowledge. At times, particularly in squats, public squares or over a coffee, these interviews were less interviews than meandering, organic and near-epic conversations. Occasionally though, I was more proactive in setting the initial question. Sometimes in the heat of a protest I needed to know immediately what had happened and why, or I wanted to establish someone's emotional response before we lost contact in the protest melee. These moments required more direct questioning. Informing these fieldwork tactics was a commitment to militant ethnographic methods.

Militant ethnography

In a research furnace fraught with tensions and complexities, a militant ethnography facilitated my fieldwork. Jeffrey Juris's (2007) concept of militant ethnography is a combination of politically engaged participant observation and ethnography. At its core, it requires researchers to demonstrate participation and political solidarity with their subjects, alongside a commitment to share knowledge after the research is completed, in an equally politically minded fashion. In many ways, militant ethnography conforms to the more traditional aspects of ethnography (Juris and Khasnabish, 2013b). These more customary facets include a mixed-methods qualitative approach to research including participant observation and interviews, and emphasis on the personal experience of the researcher through reflexivity and elements of auto-ethnography (Ellis et al., 2011; Green, 2002; Hallett and Fine, 2000; Reed-Danahay, 1997). Further, it incorporates a strong regard for the written output of the research, the final product, while showing concern for issues of representation (Juris and Khasnabish, 2013b). Nonetheless, militant ethnography also aims to produce politically applicable knowledge from within movements (Juris, 2007). Its militancy is derived from the vigorous pursuit of, and dissemination of, partisan insights.

Militant ethnography deliberately blurs the distinction between research and political activism. In doing so, it reflects the way contemporary activists, particularly within anti-corporate and anti-capitalist movements around the world, procure relevant knowledge: as insiders producing politically applicable work (Juris, 2007: 164–165; see also Casas-Cortés et al., 2013: 201; Gordon, 2008: 8; Russell, 2014: 1). Maribel Casas-Cortés and Sebastián Cobarrubias (2007: 114) extol this approach, where '[r]esearch becomes a political tool to intervene in the processes that are moving us towards a neo-liberal world'. It reminds researchers sympathetic to movements and collectives challenging neo-liberalism that obligations as activist-researchers extend beyond the life of the fieldwork experience. As an activist-researcher, I have mirrored this process by collaboratively producing knowledge that is applicable within *as well as* beyond the confines of the academy. Aside from this book, I have vigorously shared my Athenian experiences and insights, with numerous anti-fascists, anarchists and anti-authoritarians, in multiple forums.

Juris (2007) develops his methods in 'Practicing militant ethnography with the Movement for Global Resistance in Barcelona'. Here, he calls for the empowerment of activists through 'a politically engaged and collaborative form of participant observation carried out from within rather than outside grassroots movements' (2007: 164). For Juris, it is not enough for researchers to take on the role of what George Marcus calls the '[c]ircumstantial [a]ctivist' (Marcus, 1998: 98; Juris, 2007: 165), nor should researchers assume that participant observation is political, by mere virtue of its participatory characteristics (Russell, 2014: 4). Instead, militant ethnographers should strive for participatory *and* politically informed involvement so that the logic used by activists becomes accessible (Juris, 2007: 165). Bertie Russell (2014: 1) describes this process as the 'disavowal of positivist knowledge and the construction of situated partisan knowledge(s)'. The idea is part of a broader push to overcome detached analyses that can stem from so-called objectivist research paradigms (Bryman, 2012: 33–34; Juris, 2007: 164–165; Staller, 2013: 13), in which researchers are encouraged to remain passive.

Militant ethnography is part of a historical tradition of militant research that extends as far back as Karl Marx's *Workers' Inquiry* (1880), the *operaismo workerist* research in Italy from the 1950s (Wright, 2002), and the Johnson–Forest tendency of the same period (Woodcock, 2014). More contemporarily, it builds on Nancy Scheper-Hughes's (1995: 409) 'politically and morally engaged' notion of militant anthropology, and Charles Hale's (2006) activist anthropology, by demonstrating its relevance for ethnographies on the anti-authoritarian Left. In that latter sense, it shares many similarities with the inspiring work of the Colectivo Situaciones in Argentina (2011). Further, it extends Paul Routledge's (2013: 251) 'activist ethnography', by entrenching the dissemination of knowledge in non-academic contexts. While the modes of inquiry are different, militant ethnography also shares a lineage with other research approaches celebrating the importance of collaboratively produced research between activists and researchers, such as participatory action research and co-operative inquiry (Borda, 2001; Reason and Bradbury, 2001). This historical lineage is generally informed by an 'emancipatory ethos', fostering the 'creation of valuable knowledge and practice amongst equals' (Feyerabend, 1970; Freire, 2000 [1970]; Gordon, 2008: 8; Touraine et al., 1983). Militant ethnography is also a continuation of the types of 'disrupted ethnographies' discussed by Mirka Koro-Ljunberg and Thomas Greckhamer (2005), where the openly ideological goals of the ethnography actually 'shape the process of doing [the] ethnography' (p. 287).

With this in mind, an openly political approach like mine may leave the resulting research susceptible to claims that it appears as a political manifesto, lacking in objectivity. Yet, as Victoria Sanford (2006: 14) points out: 'all research is inherently political – even, and perhaps especially, that scholarship presented under the guise of "objectivity", which is really no more than a veiled defense of the status quo'.

This mirrors Max Weber's (2011b [1949]: 61) advice that, '[t]he very recognition of the existence of a scientific problem coincides … with the possession of specifically oriented motives and values'. The moment we pay attention to a research agenda or concern, we imbue it with our own subjectivity, simply by giving it attention. To that end, militant ethnography is a contemporary contributor to a rich history of fieldwork advancements challenging sexist, racist, homophobic, colonialist and imperialist biases that once lay hidden in the shelter of objectivity.

A fusion of politically engaged participant observation and committed ethnographic research, militant ethnography expands upon recent trends researching anarchist and anti-authoritarian spaces in the English language. While very few academics engage with these collectives, the ones that do favour participant observation, ethnography or an amalgam of the two. These studies include Russell's (2014) militant research into the radical climate and climate justice movement; Chris Dixon's (2012) work on anti-authoritarian currents in Canada and the USA; David Graeber's (2009) ethnography on anarchists at the Free Trade Area of the Americas' (FTAA's) 3rd Summit in Quebec City; Polly Pallister-Wilkins's (2009) ethnography on Israeli anarchists and Palestinian villagers; Gordon's (2008) extensive participant observation on anarchists more broadly; Juris's (2007) militant ethnography of anarchists in Barcelona; and Cristina Fominaya's (2007) participant observation with Madrid's autonomous anti-globalisation networks. I locate my research within this methodological current.

Practicalities of militant ethnography: on the streets and in squats

Political participation in the field is a core component of militant ethnography. It can take various forms. According to Juris, some avenues for political involvement include running workshops, organising political actions, facilitating meetings, suggesting tactics and developing political positions (2007: 165; see also Dixon, 2012). In my case and for three main reasons, I found pursuing these suggestions fraught with complexities to the point at which I had to develop my own strategies to participate politically.

First, because of time restraints I was unable to establish the credentials and degrees of trust necessary for taking on particularly overt roles, such as those suggested by Juris. The Athenian anarchist and anti-authoritarian movement is a complex network of loosely connected affinity groups, bound by friendship and trust forged in countless collective actions. It requires years of participation in the movement and a close circle of dependable comrades to gain enough respect and trust to suggest political actions. Stressing the point, Christo implied that it was common practice to refrain from calling well-known activists 'anarchists' until after two or three years of involvement in the movement. Any time less than this indicated that they had not demonstrated enough commitment to warrant the term. In a climate of open warfare against the state and evidence of police torturing activists, it is completely understandable that outsiders are treated with trepidation. A recent incident involved Greek police torturing arrested anarchists, and then 'photo-shopping away' the brutality of the images sent to the media (Amnesty International, 2013; Margaronis, 2012). This is hardly a conducive environment for ephemeral researchers to be gaining trust and suggesting political tactics (Paulsen, 2009: 509; see also Bruce, 2013: 7).

In her ethnography on UK 'eco' direct action collectives, Alexandra Plows relied on her 'autobiography as an activist turned "insider researcher"' to facilitate relationships (Plows, 2008: 1524). Unfortunately, my experiences in Athens differed. No one was able to confirm my activist experiences and no one knew me previously. During one particularly physical protest at night and after a barrage of tear gas, I lost sight of the people I began the evening with and could not find anyone who knew me by name or face. With eyes watering, I found some comrades and tried to initiate dialogue so I could continue protesting with them (I did not want to be in a violent protest without a core group on which to rely if the situation became especially dangerous). In a similar experience to that of Graeber in Quebec, Canada, in which he found himself amongst affinity groups that did not recognise him, I too found myself in a sea of unwanted glares by suspicious militants unsure of my identity (2009: 181). I quickly moved on. In this environment, my commitment and subsequent involvement in praxis was always going to be limited as I simply lacked long-term exposure in Athens.

I overcame this to some extent by demonstrating a degree of expertise on anarchist politics, discussing complex anarchist theory and demonstrating an understanding of anarchist praxis throughout history. Elizabeth Hoffman's insights on showing competency were particularly useful (2007: 337). Hoffmann was interviewing coal miners when one asked about the specifics of a 'dosco' mining blade, essentially to test her. Once she was able to demonstrate her knowledge on the topic she had a far more enriching conversation with the respondent because she had established her competency (Hoffmann, 2007: 337). In my case, despite demonstrating knowledge, establishing trust was a constant battle often requiring exhausting effort.

The second restriction on my political involvement stemmed from an often-present hostility towards academics. In agreement with ethnographer Kathleen Blee's observation that far-right groups 'tend to regard academics as untrustworthy or hostile', the same can be said for some Athenian anti-authoritarians and anarchists (2007: 121). This hostility limited the number of people willing to converse with me. One of the more humorous conversations involved Pari, a friend of Christo (with whom I had my first conversation in Exarcheia). When I asked Pari if he would like to talk to me about Athenian anarchism, he punished me for wasting his time with a ferocious 'Οχι!' [No]. I gingerly persisted, asking why not; for which I was lectured for about 10 minutes on his justifications for hating what I was doing in Greece. He finished by referring to me, in heavily accented English, as a 'bourgeois puppet'. After the tension had settled I asked Pari why – if there was so much hostility – he had bothered to berate me. 'I am Greek', he responded, '[w]e love to talk' and then hugged me somewhat apologetically.

The final restriction relates to consent. I felt ethically obliged to obtain oral consent and make clear that I was conducting fieldwork for a book (Hesse-Biber and Leavy, 2010: 63–65; Stein, 2010: 565). Over time, I noticed that prefacing my questions with a consent statement or mentioning that this was part of a university research project, was limiting my pool of respondents. I note that at least 20 conversations halted once it was clear I was doing academic research. Interestingly, in the occasional time I brought it up after establishing a decent rapport with the individual, the conversation never stopped. It makes it difficult to build relationships in an environment where there is a degree of mistrust towards academic researchers. In spite of this, the fact that no one stopped talking to me when they found out I was researching after a relationship was already established, suggests personal connections have a way of overcoming some hostilities to academics. Certainly, my decision to pursue oral rather than written consent was also desirable. There was no way anyone had any interest in signing a piece of written consent, with their names forever marked as fighters against the state and the police.

In the face of these restrictions, I had to demonstrate political participation in other ways. One way was to squat or dumpster-dive with a number of activists. Sharing food and lodgings with others entails intimacy and is helpful for breaking down barriers (Squatting in Europe Kollective, 2013). This was particularly rewarding for my research. Some of the more insightful discussions came in the early hours of the morning after a night of talking politics in a small, squatted room. I found that in this environment people trusted me much more. After all, I was engaging in political praxis while living with them and sharing a beer and some food. It was in this setting, after one particularly exhausting but very open conversation about older Greek anarchist history, that we collectively concluded what I convey in the next chapter: that many Athenian anarchists had severed nearly all emotional, theoretical and practical links with nineteenth- to early twentieth-century Greek anarchist history. My insights into gendered hierarchies and housework, which I discuss in Chapter 6, also came while squatting.

Another way I 'got my politics on' was by participating in protests and direct actions, which Juris refers to as 'putting one's body on the line during mass direct actions' (2007: 165). This is an excellent way to establish trust and develop emotional connections by chanting together with fists raised in the face of armed police firing tear gas (Ferrell, 2009: 88; Juris, 2007: 166). Importantly, it also led to many of the discussions and insights on emotions and concepts of violence that punctuate the forthcoming chapters. Beyond the emotionality and physicality of the protest, directly participating in actions helped form my insights into anarchist and anti-authoritarian politics in action. Some of the less physical direct actions, such as feeding the homeless by setting up food banks, writing a letter to a political prisoner or attending assemblies in a square or squat, also helped illuminate examples of insurrectionist, prefigurative politics.

In addition to these important benefits of militant ethnography, my constant political participation meant I was incessantly talking politics with anarchists and anti-authoritarians. From one of these many conversations, as we waited for a 'poster run' to begin, I learnt of the importance of using both the categories 'anarchist' and 'anti-authoritarian' when referring to the anti-state, radical left-wing milieu in Athens. Revisiting the point I raised in Chapter 1, for a variety of reasons not all anti-authoritarians call themselves anarchists or even see themselves as anarchists, despite numerous similarities in beliefs and practices. A significant issue for some within the space, it highlights the need to engage in extensive fieldwork in order to represent adequately respondents' concerns. As a point of contrast, a recent publication neglected to do so.

In 2012, Seraphim Seferiades and Hank Johnston published *Violent Protest, Contentious Politics, and the Neoliberal State*, a collection of articles on social movements that engage with violence and militancy with four of the 14 chapters devoted to Greece. Although certainly a welcome addition to recent Greek political history, Seferiades and Johnston's collection of edited articles is not based on ethnographic fieldwork that actively engages with the actors in question (Johnston and Seferiades, 2012; Kanellopoulos, 2012; Kotronaki and Seferiades, 2012; Lountos, 2012). Perhaps as a result, the authors tend to refer to protesters involved in the 2008 Greek insurrection as anarchists, rather than as both anarchists and anti-authoritarians (neither they nor I are suggesting it was limited to activists of the anti-state Far Left). While Kostas Kanellopoulos (2012: 181) and Loukia Kotronaki and Seferiades (2012: 164) show awareness of anti-authoritarian politics more broadly, they do not justify their labelling of all radical anti-state leftists as anarchists. Arguably, this disempowers activists by inadequately representing their politics. Militant ethnographic methods, by contrast, encourage researchers to engage fully with the political nuances and subtleties of their collaborators which may help avoid similar shortcomings (Juris, 2007; Juris and Khasnabish, 2013a; Routledge, 2009).

From my own experiences in Athens it was their failure to communicate with the subjects of their research that led to this shortcoming. This incorrect labelling would have been rectified almost immediately had it been put to an activist in the field. Importantly then, social movement research that is concerned with movement actors should at the very least interview participants. More extensively, militant ethnographic tools help to avoid similar shortcomings.

Practicalities of militant ethnography: after the streets and the squats

Alongside political commitment in the field, militant ethnography calls for ongoing political commitment after the fieldwork context (Juris, 2007: 171). One aspect shows due concern for the written component of the research. Juris suggests that while it is important to pursue research that breaks down the distinction between researcher and activist in the field, the same sort of commitment needs to be followed through in the written aspect, and in the distribution of the work. Here, the concern is that academic, stylistic concerns, and the desire for academic publication, can fracture the power equality that reflexive activist-centric research is aiming to produce.

With this in mind, I have throughout this book tried to make it as accessible as possible. I am also mindful that a power imbalance exists between my collaborators and myself as the author. I am the holder of some of their knowledge and the way I present that information can ultimately inflict harm upon the representation of their ideas. In other words, the final product must reflect a commitment to challenging power imbalances between my privileged position as a writer and the activists who have committed to my research project. The most obvious way to attend to this is with reflexive interactions with respondents. This method involves clarifying observations and conversations with respondents while in the field. As I wrote earlier, I tried to achieve this wherever possible.

The second method aimed at continuing the (politically minded) sharing of ideas came about from a conversation with Yianni, where we established that political participation could and should continue beyond the ethnography's limited time frame. This became a common suggestion from my collaborators and a critical component of my militant ethnography. I promised to disseminate the insights produced in Athens with other anti-fascist, anarchist and anti-authoritarian milieux. This continues the process of knowledge-sharing that was gifted to me in the field. In that way, the research is not simply for the academic archives.

I have presented these collaboratively produced fieldwork insights and fieldwork experiences in anti-fascist, anarchist and anti-authoritarian forums and workshops in Australia. During these forums, I would emphasise how varying shades of anarchic tendencies and ensuing ideological and practical disagreements are, for the most part, overcome in street-protests and other forms of direct action. In the collective discussions that interjected or followed my talks, much was made of the significance of these insights in relation to Australian anarchist and anti-authoritarian activism. For one, by raising this idea of overcoming political differences through the lived experience of direct action, I was helping to verbalise experiences that activists had themselves felt.

The sharing of political insights from Athens encouraged participants in the forums to reflect on their own activist experiences and develop strategies and courses of action accordingly. My role was simply to present findings from within the world's most active and militant anarchist and anti-authoritarian space, and leave it for others to explore the applicability of these practices in different contexts. The conversation became particular boisterous as we discussed political violence, but were far more nuanced than calls for a blind replication of Athenian repertoires. Domestic political and social contexts were seen as critical to the choice of tactics and forms of direct action, and this was certainly what my respondents in Athens had often mentioned was key: localised contexts. I see my activity in these forums as an extension of Juris's notions of political participation, continuing anarchist international solidarity beyond the period of participation and the life of the project.

Ethics, illegalities and anonymities

Despite its many benefits, militant ethnography raises ethical issues regarding the study of violence and involvement in activities that fall foul of domestic legislation. A growing trend in social movement studies has academics 'consciously' and 'loudly' taking on the position of activist-scholar, which raises concurrent issues regarding the use of research (Bosi and Giugni, 2012: 34; Gillan and Pickerill, 2012: 135). Anchoring the following discussion is Alissa Cordner, David Ciplet, Phil Brown and Rachel Morello-Frosch's (2012: 171) description of research ethics as 'a series of responsibilities that researchers have to the multiple publics which their research may impact'. On this basis, I have an ethical obligation to provide an accurate account of my experiences in Athens to the academy as well as to activist collectives, to protect the identities of my respondents, and to ensure I can return to Greece in the future without fear of incarceration.

It should be evident by now that I have witnessed unlawful activities. This raises the question of whether, by sharing these experiences, I am passively or perhaps even consciously advocating some sort of violent revolution. Here a recent episode in American intellectual life is instructive. Lorenzo Bosi and Marco Guigni describe Francis Fox Piven's recent experience with elements of the political Right in the USA (Bosi and Giugni, 2012: 34; see also Dreier, 2011). In her article in the *Nation*, 'Mobilizing the jobless', Piven explores the validity and effectiveness of militant actions like 'angry crowds, demonstrations, sit-ins, and unruly mobs', in procuring real results for the jobless in America (2010). This led to condemnation from elements of the Right claiming she was advocating illegal activity and violent revolution (Dreier, 2011).

It is clearly the case that discussing violent activity does not necessarily connote support. Bosi and Guigni remark that analysis of political violence is not an attempt to 'legitimize this repertoire of action, but rather an attempt to systematize ... thinking about its payoffs and its social effects in terms of politics, culture and individual biographies as part of the broader enterprise of social science' (Bosi and Giugni, 2012: 34). While this position exonerates researchers from any critique that they are violent revolutionaries, it also may mask the potentially political nature of research.

As with my own research, sympathy and partisanship drive many of the contemporary studies on anarchist collectives (Feixa et al., 2009; Gordon, 2008; Graeber, 2009; Juris, 2007). Bosni and Guigni's claim flies in the face of contemporary research on anarchism where researchers are identifying with the movement they are researching, and taking sides in a political or social conflict (Waters, 2008: 73). Douglas Bevington and Chris Dixon argue that the 'researcher need not and in fact should not have a detached relation to the movement' they are studying (2005: 190). For better or worse, my book unapologetically embodies this political commitment.

In short, this book is humanising respondents involved in illegal activities. I am bringing to the fore the insights expressed to me by activists involved in illegal squats, supermarket raids and protest violence against cops and fascists. I am writing from their perspective and it would be dishonest to suggest otherwise. As long as I am attempting to produce accurate knowledge supported by extensive fieldwork, then it is ethical to write positively of a political action. My position just happens to publicise and present respondent-driven justifications for illegal activity, which is perhaps a question of law rather than ethics. These legal concerns must be weighed against the value of obtaining information that can enrich our understanding and politically challenge oppressive and discriminatory economic and social paradigms.

I am far more concerned with my ethical obligation to protect the identities of my respondents, who face a high risk of repression as a consequence of their illegal activities (Gillan and Pickerill, 2012: 133). Arlene Stein's caution that 'vivid ethnographic descriptions can clash with the ethical injunction to protect the privacy of our informants', is particularly relevant to my research (2010: 555). On the other hand, Nancy Scheper-Hughes has come to a different conclusion about anonymity. After writing *Saints, Scholars and Schizophrenics*, an ethnography on high rates of mental illness in a small Irish village, Scheper-Hughes was criticised for violating community privacy (Scheper-Hughes, 2000, 2001; Stein, 2010). Evidently, members of this small community were able to establish who was who, regardless of Scheper-Hughes's pseudonyms. Returning to the village 20 years later, she sees pseudonyms in a different light. For Scheper-Hughes, pseudonyms can lead to work that is discourteous and lacking in empathy because the researcher is able to hide behind the cloak of a respondent's anonymity.

While using people's actual names means 'less poignant, more circumspect ethnographies', she argues, a commitment 'to do no harm' to informants, demands that researchers sacrifice anonymity and write less 'brutally frank sketches of other people's lives' (Scheper-Hughes, 2000: 128). But if the stated concern is to be mindful of harming informants, then, anonymity may need to be preserved to the same extent. The bonds of trust I established with my respondents compel me to protect their identity and safety.

I have been guided by Graeber's approach, which avoids real names and changes minor details to protect respondents (2009: 8–13). For this reason, I have not included any of the locations of the squats at which I stayed, nor the locations of the direct actions, lest they suggest a pattern. Moreover, I have changed all the names of my respondents and have not included any identifiable physical descriptions or idiosyncrasies. For anarchists and anti-authoritarians, this latter point is hardly a break from contemporary practices; most writers will use pseudonyms for security, but also as a political point that emphasises their ideas rather than the personalities. As George Katsiaficas writes, this compels readers to 'consider arguments on their own merit rather than for the prominence or ideological allegiance of their authors' (2006: 192–193).[1]

It was also suggested to me a number of times in Athens that it would not be prudent to record any conversations. This posed a number of challenges but also allowed me unfettered access with no pauses to turn off the recording when things became particularly sensitive. Finally, I ceased all communication with respondents once I left Athens and destroyed all email addresses and contact phone numbers. This was a personal safety issue as much as it was for protecting my respondents. Early on in my project at an intra-departmental presentation of my work, a senior academic from my university's Policing, Intelligence and Counter Terrorism Centre approached me to say that he would love to get his hands on my data when I returned from Greece – to then share with the Greek police. The experience of sociologist Rik Scarce in the USA reminds us of the inherent dangers of researching movements hostile to the state. Scarce was jailed for 159 days for not revealing the names of interviewed animal rights activists to a grand jury (Bevington and Dixon, 2005: 200). In this light, I saw it as prudent to cease and destroy all communications upon returning to Australia.

Researching violence

Part of the militant ethnography also brought me face to face with the reality of political violence; namely, watching people inflict some serious harm on other people. As will be shown in the forthcoming chapters, the brutal violence we see in war zones does not define Athens. Nevertheless, there are many examples of violent, physical confrontations and, on occasion, homicidal incidents. I was witness to a number of bloody beatings in the midst of protests, mostly on activists by police and occasionally the other way round. For me, it was sickening to watch people being beaten up and was an uncomfortable part of the fieldwork. I noticed there was a real intensity to the hand-to-hand violence from all parties, which to me went beyond the confrontations I have witnessed in other physical protests involving anarchists (for example, in Sydney, Melbourne and Montreal).

To take one penetrating example from the midst of a protest melee, I saw three policeman charge at a teenager who was disorientated by a dense smog of tear gas. I was some 10 metres away hunched over, coughing and retching. From my relatively safe position I saw the police shove him to the ground, proceed to kick him in the ribs and belt him with a baton. I noticed a few times in Athens that when someone is being assaulted on the ground, they find it very difficult to resist or get up and run away. Most just curl up in the foetal position in what looks like an instinctive primal defence mechanism protecting internal organs. They then wait for the onslaught to finish.

In this instance, it got to the point where the young man was clearly unconscious, a point recognised by one of the policeman who held out his hand to stop his workmate. For good measure, the other two policemen continued to punish his now flaccid body for at least another 30 seconds. In that moment, I got a real sense of the intensity and even hatred that characterises these confrontations; after all, the protester was unconscious for the second half of his beating so what was the point of continuing?

What followed confirmed these observations regarding the intensity of this political struggle, but this time it was from the group I was studying. I was helped to my feet by Sofia, who urged me to join her to stop the beating, overtly distressed by this possibly lifeless body. Then, five activists charged towards the offending police and began reciprocating the violence bestowed upon the teenager. The savagery to which they took to the police was astounding and involved using the 'flag-poles' that were mentioned in the previous chapter, relentlessly barraging the uniforms. The white helmet belonging to one of the policemen – Greek helmets look like the old colonial pith helmets – fell off his head and landed on the ground to great cheers from a few onlookers. A pole landed swiftly and deliberately on the now-unprotected head and blood flowed out of the wound. Before Sofia and I could get in and help the teenager, some others came in and slid him away.

I turned to Sofia and watched her willing the revenge attacks on, mimicking the blows with her clenched fist, celebrating the violence. My face must have conveyed judgement or at least shock at Sofia's actions because she barked at me: 'Αλλα ειδες τι έκαναν πρωτα τα γουρουνια? [Did you see what the pigs did first?]' A tear gas canister exploded before I could respond and in the ensuing haze a swarm of police quickly claimed their troops and returned to their line. Almost as swiftly, everyone around me went to check on the teenager, saw he was breathing and then moved on.

Leaving aside the political discussions regarding the use of violence and the depth of emotions at play until the forthcoming chapters, I raise this example as a way of discussing the practicalities of researching and producing an ethnography in this climate. To begin with, Goodwin's 'Introduction to a special issue on political violence and terrorism' in the journal *Mobilization*, offers some particularly insightful suggestions when researching political violence (Goodwin, 2012). One observation is to consider political violence as one form of contentious politics, amongst others. Research should include consideration of these other forms too (Goodwin, 2012: 1). Hence, my research also includes a multitude of data collected and observed in other locations, not just in violent street-actions. Goodwin also stresses the importance of considering the individual reasons for violence rather than merely aggregating collective reasons. At the same time, he asks us to engage with respondents who eschew violence, not just those in favour of violence. Analysis of these respective motivations is considered within the context of the networks within which individuals interact (Goodwin, 2012: 1). I have taken a similar approach in my research.

Equally, I share Kevin Avruch's appetite for ethnographies that convey an unsanitised version of the fieldwork experience – violence and all (2001). In his work on ethnographies that have come out of 'conflict zones', Avruch concludes that despite ethnographers' exposure to violence and conflict, these accounts rarely appear in the final product of the research (2001: 638–639). Ethnographic accounts of violence are significantly less prevalent than one would predict. To counter this trend, Avruch suggests that when writing ethnographies that include violence, the violent component should be discussed rather than left as war stories for the pub (2001: 638). I echo his sentiments and hence include the violence I witnessed. My intention is not to romanticise the heroics of militants, but to convey the reality of an important part of Athenian anarchist and anti-authoritarian praxis – violent confrontations.

In a similar vein, Tessa Diphoorn's ethnographic work calls for research to include emotions evoked by the researcher during violent events in the field (2013). Whereas Avruch sees the necessity of discussing violent incidences in general, Diphoorn suggests that is also important to consider our emotions at the time these events were occurring. Considering my focus on the emotions of my respondents in Chapter 7, Diphoorn's work is particularly pertinent. In her study of private security officers in South Africa, she observed that emotions coming from our fieldwork experiences 'influence the way we as researchers act in the field and are therefore imperative in understanding the violence that we research' (Diphoorn, 2013: 202; see also Davies, 2010). Therefore, it is important to recognise these emotions for what they really are: 'crucial empirical data' (Diphoorn, 2013: 203).

Beyond recognition of researchers' emotions, Diphoorn also calls for their analysis. In order to more adequately consider emotions, she employs a concept referred to as 'the emotionality of participation' (Diphoorn, 2013: 203). This is a heuristic framework (a created device used to investigate or solve a problem) that loosely categorises degrees of participation and associated emotional influences. In a way, this is a form of 'after the fact meta-analysis', to explore how emotions influence the analysis of data when in the field and, more specifically, the choices we make when in the field. I agree with Diphoorn's primary concern for the need to consider and convey the emotions that we feel as researchers. As Jeff Ferell argues, 'it is emotional subjectivity that makes good research; without it researchers may observe an event or elicit information, but will have little sense of its meaning or consequence' (2009: 80).

Part of what I am trying to convey in my book is the vibrancy of the Athenian milieu with all its colour and vivacity, an approach reflected in my fieldwork vignettes. I often colour my observations with actual emotions I was feeling at the time. If an incident was confronting or disturbing then my language conveys that sentiment. Equally, when I was motivated or euphoric I have also tried to get that language across in the book. This deliberate ethnographic technique involves constant note taking. Such was the intensity of many events that it made writing detailed field-notes quite difficult. But I consistently tried to add 10 or so quick words about the events. Often I chose emotive adjectives, so I could remember how I felt, knowing I could expand on them later.

Ryan Moore uses a very similar method in his fieldwork on punk gigs (2007). He writes: 'Not wanting to be conspicuous while I was in the venue, I would only write keywords in my notepad that would help jog my memory, usually sneaking off to the bathroom stall or a relatively unpopulated corner of the club to do so' (2007: 443).

I too found myself moving to the side of an event and later writing more accurate extensions of my initial observations. Often, after a particularly intense conversation in a squat, I would retire to my mattress and elaborate the notes I had scribbled during the conversations. As I mentioned earlier, I have relied on these allegoric and metaphorical expressions of my emotions to convey the scenes I witnessed.

Evidently, while I agree with Diphoorn that the emotions associated with fieldwork are noteworthy and valuable, I am less enamoured with the idea of a post-analysis of the way in which my emotions influenced my behaviour in the field. I argue this for two reasons. First, in as much as a significant chunk of fieldwork involves hectic frenetic interactions, even more time is spent sitting, talking and reflecting. After a protest or a direct action, there is a significant debriefing process, which not only assesses tactics and politics but also looks at emotions. I believe these experiences have positively informed my writing.

My second concern regarding analysing my own emotions is that this project may then slide into solipsism, where it becomes about observing me. Any ethnography by its very nature promotes an authorial voice and it is not my intention to make this disappear (Davies, 1998: 16). At the same time, I am conscious about not leading my work into what Pierre Bourdieu would call 'observing oneself observing' (2003; see also Juris, 2007; Wacquant, 1992). The theatre in Athens, with all its politics, stories and dramas, is far more interesting. While my reflections add 'context and layers to the story', my experiences were not the central focus (Ellis, 2004: 62; see also Beatty, 2010; Ellis et al., 2011). They are a secondary consequence of an interventionist research method – militant ethnography.

Home from the field

As much as I have here abstractly extolled the virtues of militant ethnography, the remainder of my book adds flesh to these arguments, highlighting the strengths of this approach, through observations, interview quotations and insights into the space. From my first experience watching a stealth attack on police with Christo, over the next 80-odd days I collected more than enough data to unravel some of the complex internalities within the Athenian anarchist and anti-authoritarian space. As noted in the previous chapter, one of the points I raised was that internal movement diversity is often concealed by collective action. While it is important to consider the obvious manifestations of anarchist and anti-authoritarian politics, such as the protest and insurrectionist violence, it is equally important to examine other aspects of the movement. For example, a component of anarchist and anti-authoritarian political praxis involves skill sharing on topics as varied as Spanish language classes to dancing lessons. Guided by militant ethnography, I was encouraged to participate in these examples of anarchism in action, as much as I was inspired to join street-protests. In both cases, my participation cultivated greater openness on the part of activists while providing me with an insider's mindset. Katherine Bruce identifies a concerning trend in social movement empirical research whereby 'scholars view tactics as having the sole purpose of claiming political power' (2013: 4). An engaged ethnography in which one lives with collaborators, daily witnessing their emotions, tactics and struggles, opens up a raft of different avenues for research. Consequently, I looked at other less visible facets of anarchism and anti-authoritarian politics, played out in a host of venues like general assemblies, squats and social centres, as well as within affinity groups and activists networks. As all these venues and social interactions collide, they inform the movement's shape. Militant ethnography provided conducive and fertile field methods to pursue this research.

Concurrently, politically engaged participant observation and committed ethnographic research such as militant ethnography serves another purpose. It celebrates the importance of converting reflexively created movement information into knowledge accessible beyond the academy. This can take the form of a particularly activist-centric written output and/or a commitment to extensively share findings amongst activist networks.

The Athenian anarchist and anti-authoritarian space is a constantly changing network of socially constructed interactions. Accordingly, I have chosen methods to support an approach more likely to illuminate the complex interrelationships that are alive within social movements. As a social phenomenon, in which social actors continually redefine meanings, it lends itself to a constructivist epistemological framework such as militant ethnography. This is borne out in the next two chapters, in which interpretations of Greek anarchist history are adapted and negotiated within networks to produce new realities that inform the Athenian space.

Note

1 Of course, the cult of personality or personalities can also follow a pseudonym, as in the case of the 'CrimethInc' collective.

4
The early years of Greek anarchism: 'it just doesn't mean anything to me'

Repudiating links: old and new

From the beginning of nationalist struggles for autonomy against the region's colonial master, the Ottomans, to its current neo-liberal turmoil, explosive political ruptures have punctuated Greece's modern existence. These fractures have been fuelled by ideological and militarist violence in the grapple for state power and control. From royal rulers, foreign occupations and a military dictatorship, through to a fascist junta, a civil war and kleptocracies, political contention and metamorphosis has been a constant in Greece's history.

The region's fertile anarchist and anti-authoritarian history shares this constant contention and metamorphosis in its own evolution, albeit while spurning the clamour for state power. Greece's anarchism has shifted between currents since surfacing as a social movement in the 1860s.[1] The focus of this chapter is on the period between the 1860s and World War II, which was dominated by social anarchist currents including anarcho-collectivism, anarcho-communism and anarcho-syndicalism. Since the early 1970s, anti-authoritarian and insurrectionist anarchist currents have prevailed, which I leave as a discussion for the following chapter.

The anarchist currents introduced above all share an antipathy to the state, capital and oppression, while embracing class warfare to fight political hierarchy and domination in all forms. Despite this, most of the Athenian anarchists and anti-authoritarians I spoke to had severed nearly all emotional, theoretical and practical links with the region's early anarchist history.[2] The pre-1970s anarchist history is granted only marginal significance by contemporary anarchists and anti-authoritarians.

In discussions on the region's anarchist history, there was more than a prevailing trend amongst activists to flagrantly repudiate links between the anarchism of the past and the Athenian anarchist and anti-authoritarian currents of today. Many respondents were either ignorant of or indifferent towards the earlier history of anarchism. As Andreas told me: 'Our historical consciousness begins in the 1970s, the other is a story for the library. It all comes down to this ... it just doesn't mean anything to me.' For Sofia: 'I am simply not an anarcho-syndicalist. I am anti-authoritarian. My history is anti-authoritarian. My history is after the Junta [1974]!' Similarly for Christo: 'Bakunin and Kropotkin are dead, we move on. We create our own stories and history.'

My interviewees were mostly apathetic to the old history, clamouring instead to discuss the more recent history – even when specifically asked about the past. The social anarchist traditions of anarcho-collectivism, anarcho-communism and anarcho-syndicalism, although rich in history and full of militancy and direct action, are rarely embraced, celebrated or discussed.

Despite this, I open this chapter by exploring the older history. This is because that earlier history helps in the appreciation of more recent developments, but also because a few respondents did in fact have distinctive interpretations of and insights into that history. It is apposite here to restate one of the shortcomings of political process theory and 'macro' new social movement theory: these theories tend to reify the homogeneity and unity of collectives at the expense of examining internal differences and conflicts (Melucci, 1995a: 55). These internal differences and conflicts tell us much about movements. The book is ultimately strengthened, then, by exploring the different historical perspectives on pre-World War II anarchism.

This chapter relies on the works of ethnohistorians to empower the voices of my interviewees. Ethnohistory is an approach that springs from the wells of anthropology, ethnography and history. In a break from traditional historical methods, ethnohistorians use source materials 'like folklore, oral traditions, maps, paintings and artefacts, as well as written sources', to present historical narratives (Green and Troup, 1999: 175; see also Axtell, 1979: 3–4). It aims to understand a culture on its own terms, a major premise of this chapter (Chaves, 2008). In part, it was developed as a method in the 1940s, in which oral testaments as well as folklore were used to support the land claims of Native Americans during the US Indian Claims Commission (Harkin, 2010: 113). It is the affirmation of folklore as a useful source of material that attracted me to this body of work. I was additionally attracted to ethnohistory because it empowers marginalised groups who are unable to get across a particular historical narrative in the face of a more powerful and dominant account (Green and Troup, 1999: 176). While the anarchist community falls into this category more generally, I am specifically using ethnohistorical methods to give voice to the minority views within the Athenian anarchist and anti-authoritarian space itself.

With its embrace of oral history, ethnohistory appears similar to the oral research tradition. To distinguish between the two, David Henige (quoted in David Cohen's article) posits that 'strictly speaking, oral traditions are those *recollections of the past* that are commonly or *universally known* in a given culture. Versions that are not widely known should rightfully be considered as [e]thnohistory' (Cohen, 1989: 9, emphasis added). The stories I collected were not 'recollections of the past' and they were from people who had most certainly not lived through the times in question. In addition, they are stories not 'universally known'. Instead they are a collection of stories that make up a particular folklore. For these reasons, the way in which I have embraced folklore as a way of collecting historical stories, conforms to the ethnohistorical method. In that sense, I was buoyed by their embrace of alternative methods of constructing histories and have relied upon it here.

What follows then is not an encyclopaedic history of Greek anarchism. It is a pre-World War II history primarily informed by contemporary Athenian anarchists and anti-authoritarians themselves, but also drawing on secondary sources. It fills an English-language void that comes from the absence of oral history projects and ethnohistoric approaches to the region's anarchist history from a contemporary activist perspective.[3] I begin this chapter with some background on Greece's transition into statehood. This is followed by a history of early Greek anarchism that is largely informed by Tina, Yianni and Vasili, my three respondents with extensive knowledge of this period, and is primarily supported with clarifying evidence from Paul Pomonis' *The Early Days of Greek Anarchism* (2004).

Political turmoil from the outset

After almost 400 years of Ottoman rule and a long, bitter, protracted war for liberation, Greece moved towards limited political autonomy in the early 1830s. Backed by Russia, Britain and France, and in the hands of its first head of state, Ιωάννης Καποδίστριας (Ioannis Kapodistrias), the former Ottoman colony launched an intense modernisation programme aimed at improving the living standards of its largely agrarian peasant society (Koliopoulos and Veremis, 2002: 32–34). In a precursor of events to come over the next 180 years, however, the Kapodistrias administration stalled in convening the national assembly and began acting despotically. Other elites began to resent Kapodistrias' centralisation of power, at the same time yearning for their own share of power (feeling that it was deserved given their role in struggle for national liberation). Hostility from these sources would finally deal the Governor a mortal blow when he was assassinated by a bullet in his head (Koliopoulos and Veremis, 2002: 34). Rebellion, discontent and revolt were to become prevailing themes in the region's post-Ottoman era.

Hostility was further fuelled when – under the London Protocol in August 1832,[4] signed by Britain, Russia and France – the Greek state was transformed into a Kingdom led by the Bavarian regent Βασιλεὺς Οθων (King Otto). Despite the protocol, large sections of Greece's borders remained transient and conflicted, with sporadic secessionist violence against Ottoman rule in the north, the east and on numerous islands of the Mediterranean (Clogg, 2002: 17). In Athens, King Otto centralised power, continuing a trend set by the Kapodistrias administration. This period was similarly marked by protests and uprisings. In September 1843, as a response to growing nationalism and demands for greater popular representation, the army led a bloodless coup, forcing the regent to establish a written constitution. This act created the national bicameral assembly and by 1844 Greece had been transformed into a constitutional monarchy (Spyropoulos and Fortsakis, 2009: 38).

In contrast to the impressive socialist and libertarian-informed movements that would flourish in the late 1800s, popular politics between 1843 and the early 1860s could hardly be described as revolutionary. Even the bloodless coup involved soldiers passively chanting under the King's window, pleading for a constitution, rather than demanding the overthrow of the monarch or any form of internal state upheaval (Spyropoulos and Fortsakis, 2009: 38). In the two decades after the 1843 coup, there was a level of relative contentment that a parliament had been created and a Greek prime minister had been appointed. The next 19 years came to be dominated by a form of nationalism known as the Μεγάλη Ιδέα (Big Idea) (Clogg, 2002: 47). Nationalist sentiment swept the region as the constitutional monarchy sought to extend its borders and reconnect with the wider Hellenic Diaspora.[5] During the same period, much of Europe was dominated by the revolutions of 1848, with political refugees pouring into Greece from Italy, Poland and Hungary. Yet, Greece remained largely immune from the radicalism of the time (Margaritis, 2009: 1439). Despite the occasional strike and demonstrations in the mining region of Λαύριο (Lavrio) (about 60 km east of Athens), working-class solidarity and associated socialist ideas failed to penetrate (Margaritis, 2009: 1439–1440). It was not until the early 1860s that anarchist ideas began their ascent in Greece.

Anarchism as a social movement, 1860–1900: reading the φως (light)

In the 1860s, both propaganda and political action heralded the arrival of anarchism in Greece. The first anarchist publication written in Greek is the September 1861 lead article in the daily newspaper Φως (Light), entitled

'Αναρχία' (Anarchy) (part 1) (Pomonis, 2004: 1). Flavoured with anti-authoritarian rhetoric and initially anonymous,[6] its publication resulted in a raid of the newspaper's offices by offended police, which prevented publication of part 2 (Pomonis, 2004: 1–2).

Supporting this new propaganda, 1862 saw Greek and Italian anarchists join an anti-royal insurrection in downtown Athens. According to the only three respondents who had anything to say on the old history, it marked the first anarchist action in Greece.[7] For the first time in Greece, according to Tina, Yianni and Vasili, some of the insurrectionists unfurled a red, anarchist-inspired banner. While textual evidence supports the presence of anarchists in the protest, and indeed that they 'erected their own barricade', there is some conjecture as to whether or not the banner was specifically anarchist, socialist or simply the 'red banner of the revolution' against the monarchy (Pomonis, 2004: 1). The action itself is not in question, merely whether or not anarchist symbolism was present.

This is more than a moot point. If true, the presence of anarchist symbolism in a protest as far back as 1862 highlights the longevity of Greece's anarchist history, making it all the more significant that it is a history from which contemporary activists are alienated. While we cannot be certain, I suggest that the red banner was probably an anarchist inspired banner, for three reasons. First, in 1862 red was the colour of anarchist flags. Anarchist symbolism had not embraced the more iconic contemporary images of black or red-and-black flags and banners (McKay, 2009). It was not until October 1876 that the red-and-black flag was first used by the Italian section of the First International (the International Workingmen's Association). As to the black flag, this appeared in 1882 with Louise Michel and other French anarcho-communists, marking the anniversary of the Paris Commune (Mckay, 2009).

Second, the banner was unfurled by anarchists[8] Εμμανουιλ Δαουδογλου (Emmanuel Daoudoglou), Παυλος Αργυριαδις (Pavlos Argyriadis) and Italian Amilcaire Cipriani, who joined other anarchists in the protest (Pomonis, 2004: 1). This is the same Cipriani who later, in 1871, would fight for the Paris Commune alongside Μαρια Πανταζι (Maria Pantazi) (Pomonis, 2004: 1). According to Vasili, Pantazi was the first Greek female anarchist, and probably the only Greek female anarchist to fight in the Commune (for further details on the Paris Commune, see Edwards (1971)). Presumably then, as militant anarchists, they would have been aware of the significance of red flags and banners, giving further credence to the claim that it was an anarchist symbol on display. Third, Tina, Yianni and Vasili were all adamant that the red banner was the first symbolic display of anarchism in Greece. Encouraged by ethnohistorians, I have given weight to alternative methods of historical insight such as passed-down folklore – in this instance passed down amongst activists (Axtell, 1979). Combining all this evidence supports the claim that anarchist symbolism was on display during the 1862 insurrection against King Otto.

In the light of these two early manifestations of anarchism, how did these ideas spread to Greece? When pressed on the practical transfer of anarchist ideas there was a general view amongst interviewees that anarchism arrived in Greece via Italian merchants and Italian refugees, such as Cipriani. According to literature and my respondents, while an anti-state and anti-authoritarian consciousness would certainly have existed in the post Ottoman society, actually naming ideas as *anarchist* and organising accordingly first surfaced in Greek regions closest to Italy (Fragos and Pomonis, 2004; Sotros, 2004, 2005). In the mainland port town of Πάτρα (Patras) and the Ιόνια νησιά (Ionian islands) on the south-western coast of Greece, for example, Italian radicals fleeing the War of the Two Sicilies[9] arrived with anarchist ideas after 1848.

Yet Vasili, one of my three history buffs, expressed unwillingness to endorse this historical account. He was almost at pains to stress to me the importance of including the story of the early Greek anarchist Μηχαλις Αβλιχως (Mixalis Avlichos). According to Vasili, in the late 1860s while Avlichos was studying in Bern, Switzerland, he met the popular anarchist theorist Mikhael Bakunin. Vasili passionately argued that Avlichos's experiences shed a different light on the dominant body of thought that stresses the early Italian influences on Greek anarchism. While this may be the case, there is conjecture as to whether Avlichos was an anarchist before he met Bakunin, or only came to his political position after meeting the famous anarchist (Βαγγέλης, 2003). While Avlichos's interaction with Bakunin suggests that anarchism may have also trickled into Greece via non-Italian sources, this incident is an exception to the prevailing thesis. At any rate, it is a testament to the early embracing of libertarian, socialist politics in the region that a Greek anarchist was interacting with such an important theorist as Bakunin by the end of 1860s.

It was in the south-western pocket of Greece where anarchism continued to flourish with the founding of the Δημοκρατικος Συλλογος Πατρας (Democratic Club of Patras) in 1876. Tina called the club 'the third pillar of older anarchism; after propaganda and action, come organisational frameworks'. This is what the anarchist Democratic Club of Patras represented. To Tina, it seemed to be a place for discussion, the planning of tactics and a mechanism for the distribution of propaganda. For Vasili, it was a means for other anarchist-inclined groups throughout Greece to learn about resistance to authority (see also Pomonis, 2004: 2–4). Considering the limits of communication methods available at the time, a network such as this was a critical tool for the development and dissemination of anarchist ideas.

In 1876, the Democratic Club of Patras took the significant step of affiliating with the Jura Federation (Pomonis, 2004: 5 ; Vradis and Dalakoglou, 2009: 126). The Jura Federation was an anti-authoritarian and anarchist section of the First International (International Workingmen's Association), originally associated with watchmakers in Switzerland and then more generally with workers in Switzerland and France (Marshall, 2010: 280).[10] This affiliation gives an indication of the politics of the Club, and a rare insight into the anarchist tendencies of this collective. To put 1876 into context, at the time the anarchist movement was in the midst of intense discussions about the relative merits of old and new tendencies (Marshall, 2010: 7–8). By 1876, European anarchism was in the throes of a metamorphosis. The Proudhon influenced mutualism that had dominated the anarchist and anti-authoritarian elements of the First International up until the mid-1870s, had given way to and was remoulded and enriched by Bakunin and other anarcho-collectivists (Marshall, 2010: 7–8; McKay, 2009). For the Democratic Club of Patras, their affiliation to the Jura Federation reveals their endorsement of anarcho-collectivist principles. Broadly, these principles were as follows: the pursuit of 'a free federation of associations of producers and consumers to organize production and distribution' (Marshall, 2010: 8); the collectivisation of the means of production and common ownership of land; and the retention of a wage-based system, with labour being remunerated in accordance with the value of work performed.

Affiliation though was not just about expressing a political identity. Affiliation also internationalised anarchism as it developed in the Greek region. Tina, who was emphatically unsympathetic towards the syndicalist strand of anarchism, was nonetheless supportive of this affiliation: not so much for the relationship established with or the politics of the Jura Federation, but as a step in escaping the insularity of small group politics. For Tina:

We need as many voices as possible – this broadens diversity. Otherwise, we limit the pool of ideas. I've talked about this affiliation at [public] assemblies. I understand the irony in that this is an organisational structure and I have a tendency to be hostile to formal organisational structures. But this affiliation was a great idea because you share ideas with, at the time, the rest of Europe. I really like that.

In 1877, the Democratic Club of Patras continued the 'federating' organisational strategy synonymous with anarcho-collectivism and syndicalism by forming a regional federation; what Tina called the broadening of diversity. Called the Δημοκρατικός Σύνδεσμος (Democratic League of the People), it included groups from outside the Ionian Islands and was the first anarchist organisational framework in the region. Anarchists joined from the Κυκλάδες (Cyclades) islands in the Aegean Sea, south-east of Athens, as well as anarchists from Πελοπόννησος (the Peloponnese), the large area of mainland Greece west of Athens. In addition, the club began publication of Greece's first anarchist newspaper, Ελληνικη Δημοκρατια (Hellenic Democracy) (Pomonis, 2004: 6–7; Vradis and Dalakoglou, 2009: 126).[11]

So, were the early days of the region's anarchism restricted to publishing and federating?[12] 'As far as we know', Vasili told me, 'it was dominated by this, yes.' But he also talked of numerous strike actions spread across Greece that he believed were anarchist-inspired. Unfortunately, he could not name any particular island or town where these occurred. The only specifically anarchist-inspired action I could find around that time was an anarchist collective's role in a tannery and shipyard strike in 1879, on the island of Σύρος (Syros), in the Cyclades island chain (Vradis and Dalakoglou, 2009: 126). When I asked Tina and Yianni about this broader issue (my other two historical gatekeepers), their responses were not too dissimilar. From what they were told and what they had read, Tina and Yianni believed that between 1860 and the late 1890s, explicitly anarchist direct actions were almost non-existent. Note the disclaimer here though: explicitly *anarchist* direct action. Pressed, both referred to the general presence of anarchists in the continuing broader struggles against the Ottoman empire, in particular the Greco-Turkish War of 1897 (also known as Black '97) that was fought for the control of the island of Κρήτη (Crete) (Koliopoulos and Veremis, 2002: 111).

Tina also cited this war as a nod to the continued Italian influence on the early days of the Greek anarchist movement, highlighted by the presence of Giuseppe Ciancabilla. An Italian anarchist who fled to the USA towards the end of the nineteenth century to continue his political activism, he identified with the insurrectionist tendency of the anarchist movement and wrote supportively of it in a pamphlet titled *Against Organisation* (Ciancabilla, n.d.). He was to later edit the Italian-American edition of *La Questione Sociale* (The Social Question), an influential publication for Italian anarchism (Wilful Disobedience, 2003). Ciancabilla's presence in Greece was quite a jolting claim by Tina, implying a noteworthy link between Greek anarchists and the celebrated insurrectionary anarchist movement coming out of Italy. This is the same movement that informed the likes of Errico Malatesta, Luigi Galleani, Pietro Umberto Acciarito and later Ferdinando Nicola Sacco and Bartolomeo Vanzetti (Marshall, 2010: 446–452; Woodcock, 2004: 327–355). Returning to Tina's specific claim, while Ciancabilla may well have fought in Greece against Ottoman occupation at some time, written evidence suggests that he was 18 when he was fighting in Greece (Wilful Disobedience, 2003). However, he was born in 1872 which would have made him 25 years old during the Greco-Turkish war of 1897, not 18. Nevertheless, while it is unclear whether Tina's assertions regarding Ciancabilla are specifically correct, what we do know is that an important Italian insurrectionary anarchist had been in Greece around the mid-to late-1890s.

Anarchist activity in the period between 1860 and 1900 was largely limited to organising and writing. This changed in the early 1900s, as a current within the region's anarchism took on militant, direct action tactics. While some retained the pro-organisational strategies of anarcho-syndicalism, other anarchists were repudiating formal organisational strategies and instead pursuing tactics more in line with the insurrectionist anarchist politics associated with anti-organisational platforms (Pomonis, 2004: 20–21; Schwarz et al., 2010a: 5; Vradis and Dalakoglou, 2009: 126). There were propaganda campaigns alongside propaganda by the deed.[13] This is illustrated most vividly by Οι Βαρκάρηδες της Θεσσαλονίκης[14] (the Boatmen of Thessaloniki, also known as the Assassins of Salonika) and the assassination of Γεώργιος 1 Βασιλεύς των Ελλήνων (King George I of Greece) by Αλεξανδρος Σχινας (Alexandros Schinas). I turn first to the Boatmen of Thessaloniki.

Bullets, bombs and boatmen: the 1900s

The Boatmen of Thessaloniki were an anarcho-nationalist, pan-Slavic-influenced Bulgarian militant group, active in Θεσσαλονίκη (Thessaloniki) between 1898 and 1903 (Megas, 1994). Now the second largest city in Greece and increasingly a hotbed of anarchist and anti-authoritarian activity, Thessaloniki at the time was still under the rule of the Ottoman Empire. It was not until 1912, when the Ottoman garrison surrendered the city to the Greek army, that the ethnically diverse Thessaloniki became part of Greece (Clogg, 1986: 103–104). It is interesting to note that Bulgaria also had its eyes on capturing the city for its own territory. For this reason, Bulgarian militants were particularly active in the city in hostilities against the Ottomans. Moreover, Bulgarian anarchism has a rich history in its own right (see Grancharoff, 2013). It is in this context that the Boatmen of Thessaloniki staged their attacks against the Ottoman forces.

Most daring during 1903, their targets were diverse. At various times the group were involved in kidnaps and attempted assassinations of Turkish officials and wealthy elites. They were also involved in a host of other violent attacks, including ones against an Ottoman bank office, railway lines, hotels, theatres, a café and the city's water and gas pipes (Dakin, 1993; Megas, 1994; Vradis and Dalakoglou, 2009). Prolific, deadly and consumed with insurrectionary vigour, the Boatmen of Thessaloniki acted in the spirit of 'propaganda by the deed' (Vradis and Dalakoglou, 2009: 126). In brutal retaliatory actions, the state violently targeted innocent Bulgarians in Thessaloniki and executed nearly all of the Boatmen. With no literature or platforms left to us by the Boatmen, we are simply left with the stories of their insurrectionist violence.

It is because of the militant, insurrectionist strategy of the group that some contemporary anarchists have passed down their stories in oral folklore. While the case of the Boatmen of Thessaloniki is intrinsically poignant and instructive – because it provides details about tactics used by a group of militant anarchists in the region – it is also noteworthy because a number of interviewees talked about them, unprompted. This is significant considering that pre-1900 historical awareness of the region's anarchism was quite limited. Where other historical anarchist events remain largely unknown amongst contemporary Athenian anarchists, the Boatmen's violent repertoire of tactics and militant direct action is acknowledged in some oral folklore and narratives.

In a very similar manner, the assassination of King George I of Greece by Alexandros Schinas celebrates revolutionary strategies based on militant and violent direct action (Schwarz et al., 2010b: 5). It was well known to many of my respondents that anarchist Schinas assassinated King George I of Greece on 18 May 1913, while the King was travelling in Thessaloniki. Schinas was immediately arrested after shooting the King, and was tortured and found dead outside the Thessaloniki police station shortly after. According to police and media reports, he committed suicide by leaping from a police station window, albeit while chained in police custody (Kathimerini, 2006). This scene bears a striking resemblance to anarchist Giuseppe Pinelli's death in 1969 in a Milan (Italy) police station, which is the premise for Nobel Prize winner Dario Fo's play, *Accidental Death of an Anarchist* (Fo, 1992; Stampacchia, 2009: 1204–1205). As Aleko quipped to me, 'it is remarkable how unsafe police custody can be for enemies of the state, regardless of the jurisdiction, and health and safety concerns of the authorities'.

Aside from the suspicious circumstances of his death, Schinas's assassination of the King leaves unanswered questions about his motives. His varied motives have been attributed to supposed insanity (Clogg, 2002: 57, 241, although this author provides no evidence to support the claim), to either Bulgarian, Ottoman or even German desires to end the reign of an Anglophile King, or simply that he asked the King for money and the King refused (Kathimerini, 2006). Alternatively, according to Vasili and Tina his life and death suggest a more politically motivated chain of events leading to a calculated assassination. Schinas had been involved with the creation of a school influenced by anarchist thought and practice. In separate conversations, Vasili and Tina both believed that not long before the assassination the school had been shut down and some of the organisers had been arrested and charged. These charges related to the dissemination of anti-state and anti-monarchist propaganda. It appears that Schinas somehow escaped the arrests and shortly after assassinated the King, in front of the King's men.

Anarchists attempting assassinations of heads of states were not uncommon at the time (Gordon, 2008: 80). In 1892, Alexander Berkman tried to assassinate industrialist Henry Clay Frick; in 1894 Santo Jeronimo Caserios stabbed to death President Sadi Carnot of France; in 1900 Gaetano Bresci assassinated King Umberto I of Italy; and in 1923 the Spanish anarchist group Los Solidarios assassinated Cardinal Juan Soldevilla y Romero (Marshall, 2010: 393–394, 438–439). Trying understandably to counter the popular image of anarchists as 'bomb-throwing crazies', Graeber writes that these assassins 'almost invariably turned out to be isolated individuals' with fleeting connections to anarchism (2009: 212). Further, he adds that he is 'not aware of any actual assassin during this particular period [1875–1925] who actually was a product of ... anarchist organizations, much less were their actions planned or sponsored by them' (Graeber, 2009: 212).

The example of Buenaventura Durruti and his Los Solidarios companions murdering a Spanish Cardinal for his complicity in the murder of anarcho-syndicalist Salvador Seguí (Paz, 2007: 38–46), shows us Graeber may be off the mark with his observation. In addition, Berkman (Marshall, 2010: 393–395) and Bresci (Steven, 2007) could hardly be described as having limited ties to anarchism. According to Vasili and Tina, we can also add Schinas to this list. They were both under the clear impression from conversations passed down from older anarchists and anti-authoritarians, that Schinas strongly identified with anarchism (in particular anarcho-syndicalism), and was part of a wider organised network retaliating against the closure of the anarchist-inspired school. The oral history passed down amongst activists implies a clear political motivation for Schinas's act and suggests he may not have been acting alone.

In as much as the pursuit of historical authenticity is a worthwhile endeavour, the acceptance of these valorised histories amongst interviewees is telling. For the most part, contemporary anarchists and anti-authoritarians rarely celebrate anarchist-inspired historical events prior to the 1970s. When they do, it is typically events with a violent and spectacular theme, be it the Boatmen or the King's assassin. As movement actors discuss and negotiate historical events, it appears that violent episodes are granted greater importance over other actions. Before I speculate on the reasons for and consequences of these processes, I present some more examples of this propensity to ignore historically less violent anarchist actions.

Anarcho-syndicalism in Greece

Anarcho-syndicalism's Κωνσταντίνος Σπέρας' (Konstantinos Speras) role as a pioneer of the Greek working-class trade union movement is one such case (Leonardos, 2006; Uncreative, 2011; Vradis and Dalakoglou, 2009: 126). Speras was hardly talked about by my respondents and again it came down to Vasili, Yianni and Tina to tell the story of this influential anarcho-syndicalist figure in the development of anarchism in Greece (Leonardos, 2006; Uncreative, 2011).

In 1907, Speras was a tobacco worker in Egypt, where he met anarchist immigrants from Greece and Italy. Radicalised, upon returning to Greece he was involved in a number of tobacco workers' strikes that ended with his arrest and imprisonment. On his release in 1916, he was asked by a group of miners from his native island of Σέριφος (Serifos), in the Cyclades chain of Greek islands, to help them set up a workers' union and fight for better labour conditions (Uncreative, 2011). In a brutal struggle against the mining company who were assisted by the royal police and troops, four workers and four policemen ended up dead. Speras was once more imprisoned for his participation in the strike action. Again, upon release, Speras continued his political activities and in 1918 he was actively involved in the anarcho-syndicalist current in the first congress of the Γενική Συνομοσπονδία Εργατών Ελλάδας (Confederation of Greek Workers (GSSE)) (Uncreative, 2011). The GSSE is an organisation that to this day remains the peak body representing labour unions in Greece, and is routinely critiqued by anarchists and anti-authoritarians for its betrayal of workers' interests, and its 'undermining role' during the December 2008 Athenian insurrection (The Children of the Gallery, 2011: 124).

For the next 12 years, Speras was repeatedly jailed, the same fate suffered by many communists, socialists and anarchists under the ιδιώνυμο (idionymon) laws of the time. This was a law that criminalised most forms of labour mobilisation where there was a suspicion of an insurrectionist agenda – although this was often extended to include strikes, and resulted in arrests and beatings (Koliopoulos and Veremis, 2002: 116). Enforcement under these laws was politically motivated, aimed at entrenching Ελευθέριος Βενιζέλος' (Eleftherios Venizelos) government and preventing anti-capitalist forces from stifling bourgeois democracy.

After jail, Speras was again involved in union organising, radical writing and other anarchist activism, as a tobacco worker and then a railway worker. In addition, he was part of a broader struggle against the Κομμουνιστικό Κόμμα Ελλάδας' (Greek Communist Party's (KKE)) rapacious power-centralising within the GSSE. Ultimately, this last struggle would cost him his life when, in 1943, he was murdered by a KKE member (Uncreative, 2011). 'Again the communists, the authoritarian communists, murdering anarchists', Vasili despaired.

To my surprise, I found my participants had limited knowledge about Γιάννης Ταμτάκος (Yiannis Tamtakos); another example of greater historical awareness by anarchists involved in physical acts of violence as opposed to non-violent direct action. Tamtakos, originally a Trotskyist, was heavily involved in the shoemakers' union of Thessaloniki and as an organiser and militant unionist in the 1930s (Ταμτάκος, 2003; Vradis and Dalakoglou, 2009: 126). Attracted to anarchism in the 1940s this, as Tina drily observed, 'put him in a rather precarious position during the war [World War II], despised by the communists, the collaborators and the Germans'. This predicament led to his fleeing Greece and eventually ending up in Australia for 15 years. He returned to Greece in the mid-1960s and became active within Thessaloniki's anarchist and anti-authoritarian movement. Only

Vasili, Yianni, Andreas and Tina talked about Tamtakos, although Kosta knew that he was from Thessaloniki and had been involved with the movement in the last decade.

This theme of a limited embrace of non-violent anarchist history is not just restricted to individual anarchists like Tamtakos and Speras. Most startling, it also applies to knowledge of militant strike actions involving anarchists. There was marginal in depth awareness about the vibrant strike actions of the 1930s. A particularly volatile period for class conflict, strikes involved communist and anarchist workers pitted against a hostile government trying to smash the union movement. Some of the biggest industrial actions were the 1934 strike in Καλαμάτα (Kalamata), which ended in a 'full scale riot', but it was almost a mere procession compared with the wild scenes of the 1936 strike in Thessaloniki (Vradis and Dalakoglou, 2009: 126; see also Tsiliopoulos, 2008). Here, over 25,000 people joined a general strike over wages, culminating in the death of 12 workers. This was a period of violent Greek history exacerbated by the liberal and radical lefts' battles with the new prime minister-cum-dictator of Greece, Ιωάννης Μεταξάς (Ioannis Metaxas) (Tsiliopoulos, 2008). Although anarchists were vigorously involved in these mass mobilisations and militant direct actions against capital and the state, these historical accounts are unfamiliar to some of my respondents, while others do not consider these events part of their movement's history.

Written work, same trend

The same theme is infused within contemporary texts from the region's anarchists and anti-authoritarians, such as *We Are an Image* and *Revolt and Crisis in Greece* (Schwarz et al., 2010a; Vradis and Dalakoglou, 2011). *We Are an Image*, a text I discussed in the Introduction, is a collection of articles exploring the December 2008 insurrection in Athens (I explore the complexities of this event in the next chapter). In the entire collected work there are no more than 10 paragraphs documenting pre-World War II anarchist history (Schwarz et al., 2010b: 5–6). There is general awareness of this period of anarchist history in some of the articles, but this information is always used to stress a distinction between historical anarchism and contemporary trends (Alkis 2010; Kalamaris 2010; Schwarz et al., 2010). In one of the articles, Panagiotis Kalamaras writes that while he acknowledges the existence of a 'big [anarchist] movement' before the 1940s, he insists that '[i]n Greece there is no influence of traditional anarchism because with us it started in the 70s' (2010: 16). Similarly, for Alkis:

the birth of anarchy in Greece, as a movement, does not refer so much to traditional anarchism – with its most significant moment being the Spanish Revolution and its main expressions the anarchist federations and the anarcho-syndicalist organizations – but mainly to the anti-authoritarian, radical political waves of the '60s. (2010: 8)

This is taken further in *Revolt and Crisis in Greece*, a collection of recent articles about Greek anarchism written by anarchists and anti-authoritarians in Greece and London. In this work, there is no engagement with pre-World War II anarchism at all – not even to demonstrate a historical distinction (Vradis and Dalakoglou, 2011). The book is a collection of in-depth articles about historical factors leading to the December 2008 insurrection as well as housing conversations on the direction and dilemmas faced by the movement. But no mention is made of Greek anarchism before the 1970s. It is noticeably absent from the introductory chapter by Dimitris Dalakoglou and Antonis Vradis,[15] and in Alex Trochi's piece, where the authors talk about the creation of the modern Greek state (Trocchi, 2011; Vradis and Dalakoglou, 2011).

To be clear, this is not to suggest ubiquitous hostility or shame towards Greece's historical anarchist tradition. The first anarchist current that appeared in Greece in the late nineteenth and early twentieth century bears only a small resemblance to the anarchism alive on the streets of Athens today. Largely influenced by Bakunin, Proudhon and the anti-authoritarian elements of the First International (Graham, 2005: 189; Pomonis, 2004: 2–3), this first period is characterised as social anarchist in rhetoric and action. Included here are the usual suspects: the mutualist, collectivist, communist and syndicalist, anarchist currents (Alkis, 2010: 8; Uncreative, 2011; Vradis and Dalakoglou, 2009: 126). This all changed in the 1940s, however, when a rupture of sorts appeared within the trajectory of anarchist politics. Activity waned to a point of near inaction until, in the mid-1970s, an explosion of activity reintroduced anarchism and anti-authoritarian politics to the region, and cemented its place as a prominent radical force (Kalamaris, 2010: 15; Organise!, 1995).

No longer are repertoires of tactics focused on rank-and-file union mobilisation and the federating styles of the past. Instead, concepts such as autonomous zones, squats, assemblies, occupations and, more recently, Black Bloc tactics have become the prevailing praxes. Fuelling this explosion were small direct-action affinity groups more closely aligned with insurrectionist currents, who were influenced by the Situationists and the French, Italian and German autonomist strands of anarchism (Boukalas, 2011: 280; Organise!, 1995; Vradis and Dalakoglou, 2009: 116). Such was the rupture that emphasising a disconnect between the old and new histories is understandable. Nevertheless, it is something else altogether to be ignorant or apathetic to the region's rich anarchist history, which I found a constant theme in my interviews.

Attitudes to history: towards an understanding

So what is going on here? As I show in the next chapter, knowledge of the more recent history was sharp and informed. Taking into consideration the opinions of my respondents and incorporating them within my discussion, I suggest a number of linked hypotheses from my observations and interviews.

This clear historical repudiation may purely be a political choice of celebrating action over inaction, praxis over theory. This is a broader theme taken up by Peter Marshall who argues that historically, '[p]hilosophical anarchism has often been despised by militants' (Marshall, 2010: 7). An example of this might be on show in Athens, where some anarchist narratives are being ignored in activist folklore, because they are perceived to be less focused on praxis. The Democratic Club of Patras's attempts to produce propaganda, for example, may be considered *too theoretical* when viewed through the lens of revolutionary anarchist practice. As a result, somewhere along the line as the meaning of historical events was negotiated within activist folklore, the story of the Democratic Club of Patras became less relevant.

Similarly, historical indifference may be more closely linked to a rejection of certain tactics, a fenced boundary demarcating a preferred anarchist current. Perhaps the historical celebration of insurrectionist anarchists and advocates of propaganda by the deed, like the Boatmen of Thessaloniki, comes at the expense of other anarchist acts such as industrial actions and rank-and-file trade union militancy; acts usually associated with the tactical repertoire of the social anarchist schools. Some of today's Athenian anarchists and anti-authoritarians, steeped in the insurrectionist and Black Bloc tactics of direct actions and small affinity groups, may be hostile to formal organisations that focus on propaganda, and as such preclude them from historical narratives.

Certainly, this theme was evident in conversations with Tony. He was openly hostile to the benefits of anarchist rank-and-file unionism as part of his broader critique of notions of work. This is the sort of critique mirroring Bob Black's *The Abolition of Work*, where, in far greater detail than this memorable conclusion, he argues that '[n]o one should ever work. Workers of the world ... *relax*!' (Black, 1986, emphasis in original). Echoing this distinction between anarchist currents, Panayiotta told me that the old history is 'not our anarchism. We are not like the old fighters. They are not our stories to tell.' Likewise, and somewhat frustrated by my constant questioning, Helena insisted that she shares 'little with this history, what is there to eulogise?'

Antonio Vradis notion of 'riot-porn' sheds further light on the reasons for an apathetic attitude to history, except towards the more violent acts (SubMedia, 2012). The idea of riot-porn draws parallels between the sexual arousal experienced when watching pornography and the excitement that comes from hearing about and/or watching a riot or protest. This delicious phrase shared by Vradis in an interview with dissidentvoice.org, may provide the clearest insight into the celebration of some historical events over others, although not in the way intended by Vradis (SubMedia, 2012). In the interview, Vradis is talking about how the Greek state is abrogating its responsibilities to the poor and the working class as a result of its neo-liberal agenda. Some of this void is being filled – in a reconceptualised manner – by the anarchist and anti-authoritarian milieu. His point is that it is easy to miss the valuable work that they do – in the barter economy and neighbourhood assemblies, for example – because it is not as spectacular as a riot (SubMedia, 2012). In his example, he is alluding to a media fondness for riots to satisfy the masses yearning for theatre.

I agree with Vradis, as this is a fair indication of Greek corporate TV news and, to be fair, some of the propaganda coming out of the movement itself, such as the short film *The Potentiality of Storming Heaven* (2009). At the same time, riot-porn is an equally useful way to characterise what may be occurring in regard to the historical chasm I have been discussing.[16] Violent events are celebrated because they are more gratifying, more spectacular and observable. In other words, political arousal and satisfaction that comes from the theatrics and revolutionary fervour of insurrection, akin to sexual gratification from pornography, is leading to a particular historical narrative being ascendant. As the construction and negotiation of historical folklore and the creation of heroes and martyrs unfolds, it is arguably dominated by more emotionally and physically satisfying narratives. Vasilli, Andreas, Kosta and Yianni all believe, for instance, that there is a prominent historical place given to anarchist events that have openly challenged the state and capital. The most 'memorable' for Andreas 'are the most violent'. Yianni suggests that this is because the state is such a violent institution that 'nothing less than violence' in response should be focused on, and that 'that is why we remember the big shit'.

At the same time, another interpretation is altogether possible, where it is simply that theatrical and violent events tend to stick in our minds. Tina saw the historical separation as just a prevailing characteristic of human history and perhaps even human nature; that we do not remember 'the day-to-day, we just remember the spectacular. Here, violent spectaculars.' Tina advised me that she did not believe it was significant that the violent events are remembered. She directed me to concentrate on the broader picture: the fact that old Greek anarchist history was not embraced. As historical gatekeepers, I asked her, Vasilli and Yianni why they thought this was the case. I was met with the same sentiment expressed by Andreas in my introduction to this chapter when she told me, '[i]t all comes down to this ... it just doesn't mean anything to me.' Despite Yianni and Tina's extensive knowledge of history, they too did not identify with or embrace this history. Tina knew it because it was 'important to know your history' and for Vasilli, he said he just likes to read.

It may be that historical attitudes are simply driven by a demarcation between anarchist currents. Nonetheless, I remain unconvinced that the two particularly violent and theatrical events discussed above were merely celebrated because of their general theatrics, instead of any specific propensity to favour more violent insurrectionist actions. I write this with reference to the following chapter on activist's accounts of more recent anarchist and anti-authoritarian history, which are inundated with narratives extolling militant and often violent direct actions.

Whether it is a desire for theatrics and the exultation of violent acts (riot-porn), or a clear distinction regarding anarchist currents, a prevailing theme remains that, to a very noticeable degree, pre-World War II anarchist history is largely ignored by contemporary Athenian anarchists and anti-authoritarians. As these perceptions of history are negotiated and constructed within affinity groups, in publications and at assemblies, they inform the anarchist and anti-authoritarian processes of collective identity. One aspect celebrates violent insurrectionist action. Intertwined, another aspect features an acute distinction between anarcho-syndicalism on the one hand, and contemporary Athenian anarchism and anti-authoritarian politics and praxis on the other. Encoded within these group discussions and negotiations are particular attitudes that shape the contemporary manifestation and direction of the movement (Melucci, 1995a: 44). Specifically, perspectives on history and celebrations of particular anarchistic currents and forms of praxis are one of the phenomena producing a propensity for militant and often violent street-protest in Athens. Returning to a primary claim made throughout the thesis, despite tensions within the milieu it is these street-protests that contribute a temporary unity to the anarchist and anti-authoritarian space.

Conclusion: no lament, just not their history

In the absence of any English-language oral history projects on contemporary Athenian anarchists and anti-authoritarian perceptions of pre-World War II history, this chapter offers a rare insight into activist folklore. I have provided an activist-driven account of Greek anarchist history since the late 1800s until the early 1940s (plus the peripheral events, individuals and collectives associated with this history). Primarily, it is informed by contemporary Athenian anarchists and anti-authoritarians themselves, but I have also cautiously lent on historical texts as supporting evidence where clarification was required. Ultimately though, this is a history emancipated by contemporary anarchists and anti-authoritarians, and at the same time limited by them. Apart from the more obvious concern that they are the immediate inheritors of the anarchist history, my approach empowers the activists who facilitated my research, in line with my militant ethnographic methods and use of new social movement theory. In doing so, it provides a better understanding of the context in which the movement exists today, by highlighting factors informing the space's processes of collective identity construction. That is not to say that the historical narratives are factors that explain Athens' contemporary anarchic intensity. I strongly doubt whether preconditions and historical events can exclusively account for individual and collective actions (Goodwin and Jasper, 2004a: 4). More accurately and modestly, however, the chapter has aimed to provide better information about the history of a movement as told by some of its contemporaries.

One final point: I had a very difficult time finding anarchists in the street-protests of Athens who had an in-depth knowledge of pre-World War II Greek anarchism. Initially, incorrectly and probably judgementally, I perceived this as a sad weakness of the movement – to be so out of touch with their rich and vibrant history. I would understand the desire to smother historical narratives if they were marred with brutalities and hypocritically 'un-anarchist' politics, forged under the banner of anarchism. But no contemporary anarchist talked of lament or betrayal. According to the vast majority of activists willing to contribute to this project, they are histories with which contemporary anarchists and anti-authoritarians do not identify. The metamorphosis of anarchist currents is not only evident in the streets of Athens, but also in attitudes to anarchist history. These same attitudes are also evident in the more recent anarchist and anti-authoritarian history that has unfolded since the re-establishment of parliamentary government in 1974–75, to which I now turn.

Notes

1 Anarchism as a social movement is contrasted with what Peter Marshall refers to as 'anarchist sensibilities' – sensibilities that appear within classical Greek thought for example (Marshall, 2010: 4).
2 I use *the region*'s anarchism interchangeably with *Greek* anarchism to describe a historical period with changing borders.
3 For a Spanish- language version, see Rodolfo Montes de Oca's (2013).
4 Ratified in the Treaty of Constantinople 1832.

5 Ironically, this nationalist push was led by a head of state who was neither Greek nor of the Orthodox faith (King Otto was a Bavarian Roman Catholic).
6 The text was later attributed to journalist Demosthenes Papathanasiou (Pomonis, 2004).
7 An event amongst many others that year that ultimately led to the exile of King Otto in 1862–63, to be replaced by King George I in 1864 (Thomopoulos, 2011: 79).
8 I deliberately use the term 'anarchist', rather than also using 'anti-authoritarian', because that is what my interviewees called these activists in this period.
9 Also known as the First War of Italian Independence.
10 The Jura Federation was not invited to the International Workingmen's association conference in 1871, in line with the treatment of other supporters of Bakunian-influenced collectivist-anarchism. Bakunin was to refer to this as the establishment of the 'personal dictatorship of Marx.' In response, Marx labelled Bakunin 'a man devoid of all theoretical knowledge' (Marshall, 2010: 301).
11 Contrary to this assertion, according to an article on Libcom.org posted by Ed (2010), the first Greek anarchist newspaper was Επι τα Προσω [Forward].
12 These activities were nonetheless met with state repression.
13 I cannot answer the question, but I wonder then, whether the presence of Ciancabilla and perhaps other Italian insurrectionary anarchists helped to foster this shift in the repertoire of tactics.
14 I have provided the Greek translation of the name, in accordance with the way it was told to me.
15 This is interesting considering Vradis and Dalakoglou and discussed Tamtakos, and strike actions in their contribution on *Greece and Anarchism*, in *The International Encyclopedia of Revolution and Protest. 1500 to the Present* (2009).
16 I develop the idea of riot-porn in the following chapter by including a discussion of the fetishisation of a revolutionary identity, where more violence equates with more revolutionary spirit and commitment.

5
A contemporary history: 'Fuck May 68, Fight Now!'

Replicating repertoires, renewing repertoires

On a mild January morning in Athens in 2011, Helena's informal guided tour was as informative as it was physically exhausting. I had been invited on a hike through the streets of the ancient city, which started at Exarcheia and went then up to Πλατεία Ομονοίας (Omonia Square) and further, slowly looping round and back towards the Πλάκα (Plaka) and Μοναστηράκι (Monastiraki). For five hours, we weaved in and out of alleyways, roads and streets, down into metro stations and around squares, while Helena relentlessly pursued her objective: a comprehensive discussion and tour of the city's considerable political graffiti. Tactical and artistic outlets for political expression since the Nazi occupation, painted slogans, stencils, posters and murals (and football taunts), continue to adorn walls – a living outdoor political art gallery in the heart of Athens.

We passed by hundreds of circle-As and anti-authoritarian motifs, alongside wall after wall of painted rallying cries such as *Μπατσοι, Γουρουνια, Δολοφονοι* (Cops, Pigs, Killers) and 'Don't Live Your Life as a Slave, Riot Now!' One of these political slogans was of particular significance to Helena. Abruptly we stopped as she pointed to its large, bold, blood-red letters. Written in English, it said 'Fuck May 68, Fight Now!' 'Look at this, it is for me, everything' she began, pausing momentarily to roll her cigarette with the finesse and effortlessness of an addicted artisan:

> It asks us to move on from the past. To go beyond May 68 and Paris. But we must first know May 68, what happened, the struggles, the failures, the successes. History is important to us … to our movement. It shapes us. It influences. We learn from it. But then, listen, we must

fuck it. Fuck May 68! Fuck Spain![1] Enough talk of old revolution, we must create our own revolution ... our own insurrections.

Helena's words are emblematic of my respondents' general attitudes towards more recent anarchist and anti-authoritarian history, in two ways. First, where Helena talked about how important it was to 'know' the events of May 1968 and to 'learn' from them, other activists persistently conveyed extensive knowledge of modern Athenian anarchist and anti-authoritarian histories, and expressed a willingness to *learn* from these events. Violent historical episodes were particularly emphasised throughout conversations and appear to be regularly reproduced in the streets. Second, and much like Helena's call to 'Fuck May 68', contemporary activists feel no obligation to emulate historical repertoires. As a result, this chapter is bursting with examples of anarchists and anti-authoritarians frequently producing novel forms of direct action.

In this light, Chapter 5 presents two prevailing themes stemming from my oral history discussions on more recent anarchist and anti-authoritarian history. Athenian activists are well aware of contemporary Greek anarchist and anti-authoritarian history (since the 1970s), unlike the more limited knowledge of early anarchist history. As much as a plethora of political actions and events inform these contemporary historical reflections, militant, often-violent direct actions dominate the narrative presented in this chapter. Concurrently, insurrectionist anarchist and anti-authoritarian histories overwhelm discussions at the expense of other anarchist currents. These historical reflections help to construct a framework in which to gain a better understanding of the movement today (Gongaware, 2011: 51). As activists interpret and negotiate the meaning and significance of their region's anarchist and anti-authoritarian history, these processes help to give form and shape to the contemporary aspects of the movement.

In the second part of this chapter, and consistent with anti-authoritarian politics more broadly, I suggest that Athenian anarchists and anti-authoritarians are not restricted or limited by historical examples of praxis (Marshall, 2010: 6). While there is a clear pattern of violent direct actions, protests, riots and property damage, anarchist and anti-authoritarian practices are simultaneously refreshed with numerous diverse and novel forms of direct actions, such as supermarket expropriations and the creation of social spaces. This gives a sense of the dynamism and fluidity within the recent history of the space.

Let me make one final point before commencing. The purpose of this chapter is not to reduce collective identity to a rigid set of shared and agreed upon understandings and interpretations of history. The insights garnered below are best understood as some of the often-contested historical narratives informing the Athenian milieu.

1974–1983: Let sleeping dogs lie

For the most part, Greek anarchism lay dormant during World War II and the better part of the following three decades. There were anarchists and anti-authoritarians in Greece, but amongst interviewees, there was a consensus that overtly anarchist activity was stifled by life-threatening distractions. The mid-1930s until the early 1970s was a period of hellish conflicts for the Greek Left. After a rigged plebiscite in 1935, the exiled Γεώργιος II, Βασιλεύς τῶν Ελλήνων (King George II of Greece) was restored to the Greek throne. Within a year, the King bypassed parliament and appointed the Greek General Ιωάννης Μεταξάς (Ioannis Metaxas) to the position of prime minister. Shortly after, on 4 August 1936, Metaxas declared a state of emergency and disbanded parliament, setting up a fascist-leaning dictatorship. The Καθεστώς της 4ης Αυγούστου (the 4th of August Regime) would rule until 1941, aggressively suppressing leftist activity (Clogg, 2002: 118). Things became worse with the outbreak of World War II. Divisions within the Greek resistance organised along political lines, dividing between communist led forces and royalist forces. Aside from the immense brutalities of World War II and Nazi occupation, after the war these political divisions culminated in a bitter civil war (Thomopoulos, 2011: 141). Rumours of Stalinists murdering anarchists during the civil war exacerbated an environment of anarchist inactivity (Schwarz et al., 2010b: 6). With American and British support, the anti-communist, royalist forces eventually prevailed and a government was formed. Many leftists remained exiled or languished in prisons during this time. Hostilities towards leftists continued during a period of relative political stability, during which Greece were granted associate membership status to the European Economic Community. Circumstances took a turn for the worse for leftists when, on 21 April 1967, a military coup ushered in Το Καθεστώς των Συνταγματαρχών (The Regime of the Colonels) (Koliopoulos and Veremis, 2010: 143–153). Colonel Γεώργιος Παπαδόπουλος (Georgios Papadopoulos), a German collaborator during World War II, led the military junta. Under his rule, left-wing organisations were banned and leftists of all stripes were abused and tortured (Thomopoulos, 2011: 158).

In a climate inspired by waves of radical change throughout Europe and North America in the late 1960s, as well as challenges to Marxist orthodoxies in European social movements, anarchism awoke from its dormancy. Despite oppressive conditions under the military junta between 1967 and 1974, Greece's revolutionary circles came into contact with radical ideas coming out of the Parisian May of 1968, the Italian autonomous Marxists (*Operaismo*) and the Situationists. The spread of revolutionary materials challenging the status quo accelerated alongside greater awareness of anti-capitalist radicals. Militant groups such as *Brigate Rosse* (Red Brigade) and the *Baader-Meinhof* Gang (The Red Army Faction) became known to Greek anarchists and anti-authoritarians. Arianna captures the significance of circulating examples of radical militancy:

> Just hearing about revolutionaries gives you excitement, they don't have to be anarchist, any leftists will do, it makes you feel like there is potential and hope that anything is possible. Look, you then have to question their motives and things, but still. There they were these young Greek radicals – future anarchists, yearning for change, living under a military dictatorship and then they hear of some German-leftists blowing shit up and some Italians doing the same. It would have been liberating.

In 1971, Χρήστος Κωνσταντινίδης (Christos Konstantinidis) opened Διεθνής Βιβλιοθήκη (Diethnes Vivliothiki), a bookshop in Athens dealing in anarchist and anti-authoritarian literature. This was a widely known place. Konstantinidis was a celebrated identity amongst a number of my respondents. For many early Athenian anarchist and anti-authoritarian radicals, the bookshop was a gateway to anarchist literature, housing the classical anarchist texts by Kropotkin, Proudhon, Bakunin and Goldman, and the more recent Situationist and counter-culture literature. Of particular note, I was told many times that Diethnes Vivliothiki sold Guy Debord's *The Society of the Spectacle* (1967) when it was otherwise unavailable in Athens.

The year 1973 saw resistance to the military junta intensify, culminating in the Εθνικό Μετσόβιο Πολυτεχνείο (Athens Polytechnic, also known as the National Technical University of Athens) uprising from 14 to 17 November. This was a catalyst for the regime's downfall (Kallivretakis, 2004). The military junta would fall six months later after the dictatorship failed in their attempt to overthrow the Cypriot government, which led to Turkey's invasion of the island. Yet it is the specific events of 17 November 1973 that are memorialised in protest. The occupation of the Athens Polytechnic by students and activists protesting against the military junta came to a brutal end when an army tank crashed through the gates of the school. The number of dead is contested but a study by the Εθνικό Ίδρυμα Ερευνών (National Hellenic Research Foundation) suggests that upwards of 24 individuals were murdered during this short uprising (Kallivretakis, 2004). A truly infamous event in Greek history, it is commemorated each year on 17 November with a huge protest march from the Polytechnic to the US embassy. The march culminates at the embassy to protest the US's role in supporting and financing the military junta. Hostile attitudes to the American government continue to this day.

While anarchist and anti-authoritarian sentiment was only a very small part of this resistance, a commonly repeated anecdote has anarchists and anti-authoritarians attaching a banner to the Athens Polytechnic wall and displaying other anarchist banners during the uprising. In the prologue to *We Are an Image*, the editors imply that Konstantinidis (from the book shop Diethnes Vivliothiki) and his comrades were somehow involved with the banners, although this was not mentioned in my conversations (Schwarz et al., 2010b: 6). I was told of a number of different variations of the actual wording of the banners that were attached to the Polytechnic wall, but generally, it appears that they read: *Down with the State, Down with Capital, Down with Authority* (see also Schwarz et al., 2010b: 6).

One interviewee, Yianni, referred to this banner-event as the point of conception for contemporary Athenian anarchism and anti-authoritarian politics. Equally, Helena (who, as mentioned in the previous chapter, was annoyed with my focus on the older history because she was adamant that she shares 'little with [that] history') instructed me to begin my story here: 'Don't waste your time writing about the other rubbish', she said, '... this moment is the start of our history.' It may have been the first event of note, but in terms of what was to come over the next 40 years the overtly anarchist and anti-authoritarian politics presence in the uprising was minimal.

After the fall of the Junta in 1974, the Μεταπολίτευση (Metapolitefsi) era of Greek politics began, marking Greece's transition towards parliamentary democracy (Miller et al., 2009). While the traditionally militant Κομμουνιστικό Κόμμα Ελλάδας (Greek Communist Party or the KKE) enjoyed a similar transition into parliament, other groups took up armed resistance to capitalism. Around this time, Επαναστατικός Λαϊκός Αγώνας (Revolutionary People's Struggle, also known as Popular Revolutionary Struggle) commenced their armed campaign of violence against the state and capitalist institutions, while espousing anti-authoritarian, anti-imperialist and anti-capitalist rhetoric. Concurrently, the neighbourhood of Exarcheia started to become more of a radical leftist space in what was a precursor to its contemporary place as the seat of Athenian anarchist and anti-authoritarian activism. Notwithstanding the lack of specificity regarding actual dates from my respondents, it seems that this period was full of university occupations and street demonstrations.

But there was one date consistently mentioned by interviewees: 17 November 1980. Since 1976, the parliamentary parties, including the KKE, had agreed to a ban on the yearly 17 November march finishing up at the US embassy. During the march in 1980, some protesters ignored the ban and made their way to the embassy, which resulted in brutal clashes with the police and the death of two militants Σταματίνα Κανελλοπούλου (Stamatina Kanelopoulou) and Ιάκωβος Κουμής (Iakovos Koumis). According to Tina, there was talk of anarchist and anti-authoritarian ideas amongst activists in these protests; however, the anarchist and anti-authoritarian presence was again largely overshadowed by the Marxist–Leninist contingent.

1984–1998: riots, Molotov cocktails, unions and squats

This was to change on 6 December 1984 when, at a conference for Europe's Far Right (attended by the French National Front (Front National (FN)) leader, Jean-Marie Le Pen), Black Bloc tactics made their first confrontational appearance in Athens. In terms of significant forays into the public sphere, this left an indelible mark on a number of anarchists and anti-authoritarians, and was an event celebrated in most of my conversations. From many accounts, the scene was set earlier in the year when students occupied the Chemistry School at the Polytechnic, and throughout the year had fought hard against the gentrification of Exarcheia. In these occupations and actions, anarchist ideas and practices fermented and were refined. In fact, the action at the Hotel Caravel on 6 December displayed many of the more militant tactics deployed today, including the use of petrol bombs and the targeting of capitalist and consumerist icons in the surrounding area such as banks, car dealers and designer shops.

The event was a specific source of motivation for Georgia and James's militancy (despite the fact they were too young to have been involved), and is reflected in their zealous contemporary militancy with respect to fascists. Pondering the significance of this event, Georgia saw it as a milestone in which 'we announced our intentions, tactics and all, to fight capital, fascism and the state.' Echoing this tone, James added the following: 'In our country, you must understand, we have seen the face of fascism, we have seen it numerous times throughout our history. So when it comes parading at our door, we have an obligation to crush it.'

Both these quotations were delivered with a degree of pugnacity. This was a point I raised with both of my respondents in order to get a better idea of how an event three decades earlier has had such an effect, considering that neither of them were there. In response, both identified this as a celebrated moment in Athenian anarchist and anti-authoritarian history, passed down amongst activists through stories, public talks and presentations. As this event is discussed and its significance negotiated and celebrated, it becomes part of the active language defining the movement's biography and, in turn, informs contemporary rituals and actions.

In 1985, on the anniversary of the Polytechnic uprising, another event occurred that pervades the historical narratives. In huge riots during the 17 November demonstrations, police officer Αθανάσιος Μελίστας (Athanasios Melistas) shot dead 15-year-old Μιχάλης Καλτεζάς (Michalis Kaltezas) (Demotix, n.d.). All my respondents mentioned this murder with many, such as Anna, citing the 'tragic symmetry' with the death of Kaltezas and the 2008 police murder of 15-year-old Αλέξανδρος Γρηγορόπουλος (Alexandros Grigoropoulos). What followed Kaltezas's death was a repertoire of actions, fast becoming familiar, which included the occupation of the Polytechnic University and major rioting.

Of course, there is much more to this space than rioting and Molotov cocktails. The year 1986 saw a potentially watershed moment for anarchism and anti-authoritarian politics in Greece in the form of an anarchist conference aimed at unifying the various anarchist tendencies. Despite the best intentions, 'it failed miserably', Tina insisted, because 'they couldn't agree on shit!' Perhaps because of this fractured output, few respondents thought that this event merited attention, and a perception was conveyed to me that little came from it in terms of uniting the movement (although Mary was at least encouraged by the attempt). Vasili and Electra did note that the conference produced an Anarchist Union, which continued for a number of years. But they otherwise offered no further details (see also Schwarz et al., 2010b: 7). When I raised this point with Penelope, Stavro and Sam (all of whom I characterise as insurrectionist anarchists), they implied that they did not care about the product of the conference. To them, the conference itself came across as an attempt to federate, which is contrary to the anti-organisational nature of the temporary affinity groups synonymous with insurrectionist anarchism. Notwithstanding these activists interpretation, there is little to suggest that this was a premise of the conference, though some interviewees indicated hostility towards the possibility of an organisational framework resembling a federation or meta-structure. This attitude is consistent with some of my conversations in Athens – certainly with those who identified more with insurrectionary anarchism.

In contrast to attitudes towards the attempts at an anarchist union, there was celebratory praise for the commencement of *squats* in Athens, which became part of the scene in the 1980s. Squats had existed before in Athens. They became a more central part of the anarchist and anti-authoritarian tradition around 1987–88, however, when the squat Λέλας Καραγιάννη (Lelas Karagiani) was established, and again a couple of years later when Villa Amalias, Scaramanga and a whole host of other squats entered the scene. Many of these larger squats still existed at the time of my interviews, which was a source of great pride to all of those who talked about the history of the movement (however, after two decades, both Lelas Karagiani and Villa Amalis were raided and shut down by the Greek police in late 2012 and early 2013 (Indymedia Athens, 2012; Squat!net, 2013)). This pride was one of the rare times in which I found complete unity on any issue. Squats continue a political tradition at the heart of anarchist and anti-authoritarian praxis (see also Squatting in Europe Kollective, 2013: 28, 91). As anarchist and anti-authoritarian squats improved and as skills developed, they began to reflect the political aspirations of their inhabitants, becoming hubs for political action and organisation. Some were turned into social centres and disused lots nearby were converted into gardens and parks, with the occasional squat even generating its own electricity. For Dino, the beauty of squatting is that as 'one squat closes down, another opens up – that is what happens in Athens'. As I walked through the streets of Athens, I could see the way in which economic decline has shut down places of business and often these premises are boarded and empty. It is within this vacuum that squats appear.

Around the time that squats became more prevalent, the Athenian anarchist and anti-authoritarian space saw a burgeoning artistic and written political output develop. In 1990, the Void Network began its involvement by creating social spaces and artistic endeavours aimed at 'the radicalization of everyday life' (Void Network, 2013). Still active today, this autonomous cultural, political and philosophical network helps create political art and publications. Kyriako was quite forceful in his insistence that I include the Void Network, stating: 'It is not hard to smash up those ... ATMs, that is easy ... breaking things is easy, but it is hard, very hard, to create. We should rejoice in things we create.'

In the same year, the first edition of the magazine Τα Παιδιά της Γαλαρίας (The Children of the Gallery) hit the streets and continued to be published irregularly over the next 23 years (The Children of the Gallery, 2011; Τα Παιδιά της Γαλαρίας, 2013). According to the few respondents who were politically active at the time, other ephemeral publications and collectives also contributed to the increase in activity.

The Void Network and The Children of the Gallery reflected a growth in the activity of anarchists and anti-authoritarians in the 1990s. According to Christo and Pari, this was partly a result of the government's economic policies. In the early 1990s, Greece was in the grips of what Pari called 'privatisation-mania'. These reforms began enthusiastically under the centre-right New Democracy government, and continued 'more reluctantly' under the centre-left government PASOK from 1993 (Pagoulatos, 2001: 126). Regardless of the vigour with which they were pursued, neoliberal economic policies dominated the parliamentary narrative from the 1990s, with the government selling off state-owned assets, such as banks, shipyards and heavy industry (Pagoulatos, 2001: 126–127). In addition, privatisation attempts focused on changing the constitution to allow for the creation of private universities, as section 16 of the Greek Constitution does not allow for the operation of private tertiary institutions ('Constitution of Greece', 2013 [1975]; see also Kremmyda, 2013). Within this climate, militants and newly radicalised secondary and tertiary students began a series of occupations in over 1,500 education institutions (see also Schwarz et al., 2010b: 7). In the ensuing protests, Νίκος Τεμπονέρας (Nikos Temponeras) was bludgeoned to death by some 'centaurs', a youth militant group of the right-wing New Democracy party, which resulted in mass rioting in Athens. In the end, many of these privatisation attempts failed, including the attempt to allow private universities into Greece. Penelope describes the mood at the time:

Look, we were not, let's say anarchist then, we were school kids. We just knew there were big troubles. We had an idea that things were changing for the worse. And we knew it was the fault of authority. You see. Not of one party or the other. But everything to do with that filthy hole, there [pointing to where the parliament is]. So we were anti-authority. In a very pure understanding of the term. There was a feeling that we could do anything. And we learnt that our fights can succeed. Many lessons [were learnt].

Whereas Penelope talks of anti-authoritarian sentiment and feeling, Zizo's insights on the nature of the occupations amidst these protests convey a real sense of anarchism in action, and a renewal of organisational practices: 'The nature of the occupations changed. We were structured. We rotated tasks. We cleaned. We had assemblies. We respected the occupied χώρος [space], and at the same time introduced anarchist principles to the physical space, but also to the mentality of young radicals. It was a very expressive moment.'

With squats appearing, writing collectives forming, and students embracing these radical ideas, I consider the early 1990s a period in which Athenian anti-authoritarian and anarchist politics truly came into its own. This is a historical perspective that considers less that social movements are born and then die, than that they merge, separate or change shape (Cox, 2003). Once the student of Italian, French and German anti-state radicals, the Athenian anarchist and anti-authoritarian space was now an adult forging its own path. By the early 1990s, it was developing new traditions of direct action with its own martyrs, rituals, successes and failures. This does not mean that activists were unwilling to share and export their ideas or disinclined to participate in insurrectionist and organisational moments elsewhere. Instead of being insular about their experiences, Athenian anarchists and anti-authoritarians began to visit North and Latin America to give public lectures and establish themselves as regular participants in anti-capitalist protests throughout Europe. Within this period, the anarchist and anti-authoritarian space became Athenian. After this point, we can speak of a broadly Athenian anarchist and anti-authoritarian current in the same way we can speak of the anarchism of Catalonia. When I put this to Tina she tended to agree, but with a disclaimer:

Sure, in the 90s we can see a distinct character developing, a sort of autonomous anti-authoritarian character, let's say. But trust me. We only see this in hindsight. It is very difficult to see these things as they happen. And in the immediate years that followed it was even harder to see this fruition. Things became a lot harder again.

Despite the spike in activity discussed in the last few pages, the influence and presence of anarchist and anti-authoritarian politics dipped over the course of the next 10 years.

Regardless of its newly entrenched identity, the space was no less vulnerable to down-turns. Even with familiar repertoires of protests such as 17 November, May Day marches, sporadic antagonism with police and actions in support of political prisoners, a malaise set in. From conversations with activists, I sensed that the writing and dissemination of propaganda was not as prolific during this period. To be sure, there was still some activity during this period: in 1995, there was a large polytechnic occupation with symbolic Greek flag-burning and solidarity actions with prisoners at Κορυδαλλός (Korydallos) prison, resulting in mass arrests; in 1997–98, the anarchist militants Εμπρηστές Συνείδησης (Arsonists of Conscience) launched an extensive fire-bomb campaign; and throughout this period the anti-authoritarian *Alfa* newspaper was active. Nonetheless, these appear as exceptions to the general limitation on activity. If anything, this period is probably better known for tensions between anarchists and anti-authoritarians. Yianni recalls a number of incidences during the mid-1990s where ideological and sometimes personal conflicts would escalate into verbal and physical attacks.[2] Similarly, Tina remembered times where the choice of tactics and ideas around process would cause friction.

1999–2007: 'They don't mind throwing a brick'[3]

Things started to heat up again for the anarchist and anti-authoritarian space towards the end of the 1990s. The context or environment in which this occurred was important, though not in the deterministic way that political process theory might understand the external environment.

Taking an international perspective, the proliferation in Athenian anarchist and anti-authoritarian activity during the past 15 years parallels anarchist trends elsewhere. Mindful of Greece's already significant anarchist and anti-authoritarian history since the 1970s, a mobilisation of the multitude of networks within this community mirrors developments in the Americas and Europe of an escalation in anarchist-informed collective action. As Gordon observed of events in the last decade and a half: '[i]n case someone hasn't noticed, anarchism is alive and kicking' (2008: 3).

The Introduction to this book provided an overview of the economic reality in Greece today and it would be naive not to acknowledge the impact of these material changes for creating the preconditions for increased radical political activity. There is no doubt that the period in question, 1999–2007, coincides with an intensification of neo-liberalism in practice (Harvey,

2005). This economic policy had largely bipartisan support between the two major parties at the time, ND and PASOK. Some instances of collective action during the 1990s were directed at challenging, resisting and countering the reach and extent of this economic paradigm. In 2005 and 2006, the New Democracy government again sought to amend the constitution to allow for private universities. A part of the increase in anarchist and anti-authoritarian militancy was directed at these neo-liberal inspired reforms (Giovanopoulos and Dalakoglou, 2011: 109). These ultimately unsuccessful legislative and constitutional changes were attempts by the Greek government to implement the European Union's Bologna plan, as part of a scheme to standardise European educational services (European Commission, 2010; see also Schwarz et al., 2010d: 27). Over yet another coffee with an interviewee, Aris described this plan as 'neo-liberalising the education system. Economic values, greater competitiveness, all the usual capitalist criminalities'. Towards the end of 2006, Greek politicians were engulfed by a series of corruption scandals – most notably relating to bonds purchased by the state-run pension fund (*The Economist*, 2007) – which were at least partly responsible for inspiring political mobilisation (della Porta and Gbikpi, 2012: 92). That said, similar corruption scandals elsewhere, and similar economic and social conditions in other culturally and politically comparable nations in Europe (Portugal and Italy come readily to mind), did not give rise to the same degree of anarchist and anti-authoritarian-informed resistance. Hence, structural factors alone cannot explain the spike in anarchist and anti-authoritarian-inspired resistance in Greece.

Another aspect to consider is the globalisation of movement and the increasing ease of travel. Christos Giovanopoulos and Demitrios Dalakoglou identify the flow of anarchists and anti-authoritarians both in and out of Greece as a factor in the exchange of radical ideas within the region where, '[n]ew international points of reference were added to the logic of the Greek movement' (Giovanopoulos and Dalakoglou, 2011). Putting this into practical context, Arianna talked about the experiences of attending various protests outside of Greece ('summit hopping'):

> Sharing tactics is one thing and a beautiful part of the experience. I need to tell you that I also think it is crucial to make mention of the conversations that occur outside of the protest. [The ones] at night and in squats and tents. This is where you learn that capitalism is having comparable impacts throughout Europe. This is where you learn that the cops are savages throughout Europe. And this is where you learn that we are resisting in much the same way – with differences sure – but in much the same way we are fighting with the same anti-authoritarian essence.

The movement of people and the exchange of radical ideas may also be bolstering the increases in mobilisation.

The proposed visit by US President Bill Clinton to Athens in November of 1999, together with protests against that visit, marks a turning point for my interviewees, with many being active participants in this action and a large proportion of the events discussed hereafter. For Kosta, it was his first opportunity to participate in violent direct action and Black Bloc tactics. He remembered it with vivid intensity, recalling that anarchists amongst the Clinton protest took the opportunity to target a range of high-end shops and designer clothes outlets. 'We were angry for sure', Kosta explained, 'but it was more [than that]. The actions had meaning – they were political, anarchist!' Around that time, another anarchist/anti-authoritarian group called Μαύρο Αστέρι (Black Star) engaged in militant direct action by setting fire to US embassy cars and attacking pro-Zionist offices. They were a short-lived group and were never apprehended.

By the time protests against the International Monetary Fund (IMF) and World Bank mobilised at the end of 1999, Athenian anarchists and anti-authoritarians were already well versed in direct action and Black Bloc tactics. Aleko explained the emotional changes that come from experience within large protest mobilisations:

> Your heart still pumps hard in the insanity of the moment but experience gives you composure. The second time, the third time, the tenth time, your heart pumps but wiser, giving your mind fuel so it can make clever decisions. You watch, you take the time to think, to see. And you become smarter. Safer and, you see, you become a better fighter. We went to Prague with this intelligence.

In September 2000, a contingent of Greeks made their way to Prague, in the Czech Republic, as part of an endeavour to shut down the IMF meeting. Ultimately, the meeting was closed earlier than the organisers had planned (Connolly, 2000). For Yianni, it was his first opportunity to share Black Bloc tactics with activists from other geographical locations, and become part of a broader networking process prevalent amongst radical activists (Juris, 2008: 11). 'Look, it was a powerful experience', he fondly recalled, 'we learnt and we shared. It was good training for what was coming.'

Indeed, what followed Prague was a barrage of direct action, of militancy and protests dominating the collective memories of my respondents. In July of 2001, Greek anarchists and anti-authoritarians were active in the protests against the meeting of the G8 (Group of Eight)[4] in Italy, when over 200,000 activists hit the streets of Genoa (see Davies, 2008). 'That was a brutal demonstration', remembered Sofia:

> We are used to violence and police brutality here [in Athens] and I felt that the pigs had the same hatred for us as they do here. You know, something that makes them enjoy it, they despised us there. And when I heard about him, what was his name ... Carlos[5] [Carlo Giuliani],

it was devastating. Like when the cops killed Temponeras,⁶ Kaltezas, Grigoropoulos and more. These experiences, like Genoa, hardened us. They hardened me. You know that it is not a game. They will kill us. We must strike first.

After Genoa, a small group of Greek anarchists and anti-authoritarians protested at the European Union (EU) summit in Brussels, Belgium, in 2001. Then, with a huge contingent from Athens, Greek anarchists and anti-authoritarians inundated Thessaloniki in northern Greece for the meeting of the 2003 EU's West Balkans Summit, under the Greek EU presidency (Autonomedia, 2003). According to the numerous respondents who participated in the action, this was one of the largest bodies of Black Bloc they had ever seen in Greece, with over 3,000 people rioting and protesting. A number of Greece's anti-fascist militants also attended. Zizo offered the following insights on this protest:

Look, ok, it is not always about how many people are there [at demonstrations]. Sure, it is sometimes more important to look at the intensity and the commitment of people. But, Thessaloniki was something special. There were so many of us. Militants ... anarchists ... anti-authoritarians together. And many from our immediate region. So many of us. In all my years, and before December [2008], this was one of the more uplifting moments. You were not alone. You were more than not alone. You were with brothers and sisters!

As part of the planning processes for this protest the Αντιεξουσιαστικη Κινηση⁷ (Anti-Authoritarian Current or AK) was formed in 2002 – a further example of new anarchist praxis. 'See', Kyriako said to me with a big smile as we talked about AK, 'it's not all about [street] fighting.' A political network of anarchists and anti-authoritarians based on direct democracy and horizontal organisational principles, AK is an influential component of the anarchist and anti-authoritarian space throughout Greece. It is involved with the creation of social centres and organisational frameworks that participate in myriad actions, including supporting the occupation of factories by workers.

It is interesting to note that there was so much talk about AK's creation, as well as conversations on riots and protests, that few respondents brought up the creation of another important contribution to the anarchist and anti-authoritarian space – the establishment of Athens Indymedia, in 2001 (Indymedia Athens 2014). While not a specifically anarchist or anti-authoritarian collective, Indymedia operates on an anti-authoritarian model of participatory journalism and remains an important source of information for the radical Left in Athens. Indymedia played a huge role in the dissemination of independent, activist-inspired information during the 2008 insurrection, for example, and presented a constant challenge to dominant narratives conveyed in the mainstream media. It is such a threat to the Greek state that in April 2013 the government shut it down for weeks (Indymedia UK, 2013). It is telling that respondents at various other times raised the importance of Indymedia, yet in terms of its place in historical narratives, it barely garnered a mention. The penchant for riots and protests may account for this absence.

Athens held the Olympic Games in 2004; an event that was met with numerous protests and direct actions. Apart from typical attacks against the state, capitalist and corporate institutions, anarchist and anti-authoritarians set up solidarity campaigns with 'hyper-exploited immigrant workers' involved in the construction of venues and transport networks (Schwarz et al., 2010d: 27). In 2002, similar solidarity campaigns had been set up to support the Roma community, who were forcibly evicted from their camps located near future Olympic sites (Mivelaz, 2002). Another notable aspect of the Olympic Games protests was that it was the first time anyone had mentioned an eco-anarchist theme to me. Along the same lines, Tony observed that it was around this time that he first heard of the English word *ecotage* (*ecotage* is a combination of the word ecology and sabotage, to denote direct action environmentalism aimed at causing damage to the tools used in ecologically unsustainable practices). The rapacious consumption of parkland and foreshore development for Olympic projects along Λεωφόρος Ποσειδώνος (Leoforos Poseidonos) was cited as a particular concern.[8]

With familiar repertoires of riots, protest and property attacks thus far dominating the historical narrative, 2005 saw the emergence of a newer form of anarchist praxis with the entrenchment of a social space in Athens. The *Nosotros*[9] Ελεύθερος Κονωνικός Χώρος (Nosotros Free Social Space) in Exarcheia began as an autonomous space for a variety of anti-authoritarian and anarchist collectives and activities. The Anti-Authoritarian Current's (AK) associated collectives, which include the group involved with the anti-authoritarian newspaper Βαβυλωνία (Babylonia), predominantly occupy this space. They share it with a mixture of collectives including the Void Network (see also Nosotros, 2013). This is quite a well-known social space that runs language classes and skill-share exchanges. In addition, it regularly holds events (some of which I attended) such as live music and film nights.

To give an indication of where the space sits in the consciousness of some activists, I fortunately bumped into Sofia while I was disoriented in trying to find the building for the first time. I asked her where it was and she replied with one of my favourite lines from the entire ethnography. Pointing to a building, she said, 'the mainstream anarchist building is over there'. Some of the people who are involved with Nosotros interact with parts of the mainstream media and the parliamentary left and for this reason many insurrectionary anarchists would refer to them in a somewhat disparaging manner.

Another way of looking at this is that such is the depth and breadth of the movement that they have a significant 'mainstream'.

The period from 2005 to the time of writing continued with a flurry of direct actions. When we talked about this most recent period, Taki explained that, '[w]e were alive. We had a lot to say and we knew how to say it ... loudly and directly.' Acacia's words on that historical period reflect a similar slew of activity: 'We became obsessed with being more violent, more aggressive and therefore more revolutionary. We were performing over and over again, because that is how revolutions begin.'

One such event attended by Athenian anarchists was the No Border Camp on the Bulgarian and Greek border, which aimed at highlighting the lack of immigrants' rights in the region (Laure, 2005). Athens also hosted the European Social Forum in 2005, with more than 70,000 activists in attendance (Giovanopoulos and Dalakoglou, 2011: 109). In addition, anarchists and anti-authoritarians provided physical protection against threats of fascist intervention into Athens's first Gay Pride march (SubMediaTV, 2012).

Throughout 2006 and into 2007 there was an increase in demonstrations, riots and protests as students occupied university campuses, protesting against the government's plans to again try to allow for private universities. Also in 2006, the anti-authoritarian cell Αντικρατική Δικαιοσύνη (Anti-State Justice) fire-bombed a number of targets associated with the ruling ND party. In the summer of 2007, huge forest fires raged through Greece with 170 blazes and over 50 deaths (Itano, 2007). In response, activists hit the streets protesting against the government's lack of environmental concern.

Before turning to the momentous events of 2008, I note that alongside all the narratives presented thus far lie important examples of anarchist and anti-authoritarian praxis that were mentioned without specific dates. Mixed in with the hundreds of more traditional rallies fighting government reforms or memorialising a particularly important date (such as 17 November) were rallies in support of migrants and asylum seekers, the environment and solidarity actions with international anarchists. Alongside these demonstrations were regular confrontations with fascists and, more recently, neo-Nazis. A significant component of anarchist and anti-authoritarian energy also goes into supporting their comrades incarcerated in prison. This can take the form of protests, but can also include daily letter writing to prisoners as well as the creation and implementation of solidarity networks around the prison's physical location. Furthermore, what does not come across in a broad historical discussion are the individual cases of arrests, assaults and even torture at the hands of the police, which also forms and informs the historical context for contemporary activists (for recent examples, see Amnesty International (2013) and Margaronis (2012)).

Some of the other more novel examples of Athenian anarchist and anti-authoritarian direct action include activists providing free health-care services; the creation of food banks for the poor that have been stocked by dumpster-diving or supermarket expropriations, the former involving foraging through supermarket bins for unnecessarily discarded food; the liberating of a public space by turning a proposed car park into a communal park (in the heart of Exarcheia); and the creation of an extensive bartering network where services such as dance, self-defence, language, music and skill-sharing lessons can be exchanged for goods or other services without the need for money. Furthermore, there is the political graffiti discussed at the beginning of this chapter; a real commitment to showing political film screenings and holding political talks; acts of sabotage, like smashing transit ticketing machines; the occasional bank robbery; and, of course, the creation of thousands of pamphlets, flyers, posters and stickers. Finally, there was also a desire to share anarchist and anti-authoritarian ideas throughout Europe, and North and Latin America. As such, there is a noticeable network of information exchange involving the Athenian space and other activist communities.

2008: an insurrection

The year 2008 began with the sort of activity recognisable to the Athenian anarchist and anti-authoritarian landscape. The anarchist group Συνωμοσία των Πυρήνων της Φωτιάς (Conspiracy of Fire) fire-bombed a number of banks and car dealerships. Golden Dawn members tried to hold a rally in Athens and were met with violence from radical leftists, and a Greek industrialist Γιωργος Μυλωνας (George Mylonas) was kidnapped and ransomed by anarchists (see also BBC News, 2008). Within these actions there was nothing specific to suggest the insurrection that would occur at the end of the year.

There is a litany of work on the events of December 2008 with academics and activists inundating media, literature and film with their own insights into the events. In summary, these accounts rest on five overlapping assumptions. I again present them not as causes but as a background to the December 2008 insurrection. Yianni, one of my participants, began his recollection of these events with confronting language, pre-written on a scrap of paper pulled out of his wallet. It serves as an emotive and insightful summary of what precipitated the uprising:

> Buried beneath our stories, is the body of a murdered 15 year old boy. On the evening of the [December] 6th, a group of kids walking the streets of Exarcheia saw a police patrol. They disrespected them – as we must do. And this act was inordinately, disgustingly, deplorably countered by Κορκονέας, who shot at the youths, killing Γρηγορόπουλος. When word of the murder spread through our networks – [via texts, word of mouth, on Athens Indymedia] the streets began to fill.

What followed was the largest uprising in Greece since the Junta.

It is important to note that some of the participants in the insurrection had never – and perhaps still do not – identify with anarchist or anti-authoritarian politics. As my respondents' forthcoming quotes illustrate, some of those in the streets over the course of the week after Grigoropoulos's murder were 'active' for the first time. Certainly, some thereafter became involved in the space. Furthermore, some of the participants who chose to riot were migrants expressing their own grievances. Thus, the following scholarly accounts are very much broad-brush strokes lacking in the individual and group nuances that can accurately account for collective action (see Slater, 1998: 381). Nonetheless, if read as background context and some of the 'deeper social forces' involved in the political and social landscape, they may help us understand more clearly the December 2008 insurrection (Johnston and Seferiades, 2012).

Insofar as this event was but the spark that lit the fire, scholars have offered other explanations for this upsurge in militancy. Johnston and Seferiades discuss four of the five accounts that also appear throughout other literature. First, they note that neoliberal policies and associated harsh working conditions were a force at play (Johnston and Seferiades, 2012). At the same time, The Children of the Gallery (TPTG) are cautious in attributing too much focus on this policy and on its effects in the light of the fact that the uprising did not encompass organised labour. They do, however, concede that neo-liberalism is a force to consider (TPTG, 2011). Second, Johnston and Seferiades also raise the specific impact that Greece's economic decline has had on youths, citing the often-heard phrase in Greece that dissent stems from the €700 generation (2012). This refers to the average monthly income of recent university graduates in Greece, or at least the ones who can find employment. This observation accords with Michalis Psimitis's suspicions that the insurrection was primarily a youth revolt (2011). Third, corruption scandals may have led to forms of distrust that subsequently inform dissent (Johnston and Seferiades, 2012). Finally, for Johnston and Seferiades, Greece's protest culture 'and historical patterns of militancy' are viewed as another component contributing to the riots (Boukalas, 2011; Johnston and Seferiades, 2012; Kornetis, 2010). In addition, others have argued that militancy was a culmination of hostility towards the police and their tactics of harassment and abuse (Kouki, 2011: 178). Combined, these brief sketches offer an overall context. One thing is clear from my respondents: their participation was part of a commitment to anarchist and anti-authoritarian politics, revolutionary activism and solidarity with the slain Grigoropoulos.

It is hard to offer any detailed critique or wisdom on these scholarly works because to varying degrees they are all objectively correct, in that they are descriptions of the socio-political environment. Whether these factors ultimately led to the insurrection in December 2008 is an impossible question to answer without in-depth qualitative interviews, which are lacking in all the aforementioned studies. Alongside the expected superficiality of popular media, Donatella della Porta and Bernard Gbikpi note that analyses of this event in social science was done 'by citing socioeconomic and demographic characteristics of the actors and areas, rather than by listening to the voices of the participants themselves' (della Porta and Gbikpi, 2012: 91). Even my ethnography only looked at Athenian anarchists and anti-authoritarians who are but one element of the insurrection. From conversations with anarchists and anti-authoritarians, as angry as they were about holistic political issues, it appeared that for many of them participation was an act of solidarity with Grigoropoulos – a counter-attack against the police for their actions. Further, it is quite clear that there was no way they were going to miss an opportunity for an uprising. This is just one milieu within the insurrection. The questions about why migrants rioted, why middle-class suburban teenagers rioted, and why working-class youths rioted, must be answered with engaged qualitative research, and not by a book chapter or a journal article's worth of meta-analysis.

Vignettes from the streets

Returning to my research agenda, what follows now are vignettes from the streets. Of particular note is the fragmented, non-lineal way people spoke about December 2008. Many of the discussions on history thus far have more or less followed an ascending, chronological timeline. As well, many of the interviews on history I conducted, occurred in small groups and, up until this point, people let each other speak and finish what they were saying. For that reason, I presented events in a lineal format. Things completely changed when conversations turned to December 2008. The narratives became fragmented and people began speaking over the top of each other in what was a rapid-fire of information. I was met with short punctuated memories of incidences that were sporadically presented with little reference to a specific time within the insurrection. Along these lines, Andreas likened any project that aimed to tell the 'entire' story of 2008 as a 'misunderstanding of insurrection'. What he meant was that so much goes on in the explosion that is a revolt, that any attempt to wrap it up in a neat lineal and complete narrative fails to reflect what it is actually like to be in the middle of one.

Conversations on December 2008 resembled Elsa Barkley Brown's observation that history is 'everybody talking at once, multiple rhythms being played simultaneously' (1992: 297). For Brown, the presentation of history is analogous to a jazz concert where 'each member has to listen to what the other is doing and know how to respond while each is, at the same time, intent upon her own improvisation' (1992: 297). This is in contrast to the more traditional way of presenting history, as a form of classical music – scripted and tightly structured. Up until this point, my discussions are like a classical concerto that is lineal and structured, because I wanted to adhere to the way in which the conversations unfolded in the field. Considering the way the stories altered when we started talking about December 2008, the following conversations are presented straight after each other with no sense of time or narrative – but for the fact they are linked by December 2008.

Writing in the opening pages of an Athenian anarchist and anti-authoritarian book on 2008, Tasos Sagris provides a poignant statement based on a song sung during the military junta: 'The street has its own history. It doesn't need historians, it doesn't need intellectuals or sociologists to speak in its name. Nobody can write the History of December 2008 and we assure you that a project like this is beyond our capabilities or intentions' (2010: 1).

The following discussion echoes Andreas's approach. What is presented are historical fragments of insights fused together to create an image of December 2008 and the immediate months following.

> ANNA: You could tell it was the first time [in a riot] for some people, and the 50th time for others. You could tell. There were some in the assemblies who knew about process, others who had no idea. You had some targeting banks, car dealers, police stations, fashion shops, luxury hotels; yet others, I would say certainly first timers, smashing anything – like petite-bourgeois shops.
>
> ARIS: It was amazing to have 300 people helping you erect a barricade. Knowing that this was going on 20, 30 times over and over again in other parts of the city. When we'd conclude at an assembly, we'd flow onto the streets and we felt like anything was possible. We'd attack the pigs, and they'd run. There was a power in the streets. When word came through of the solidarity actions elsewhere, Patras, Thessaloniki, the islands, it was liberating.
>
> DINO: The intensity was like a drug high. Everything was occupied. The polytechnic, schools and government building. We hit hard. I saw a police station on fire. Police vans burning. Tear gas being propelled back at the cops. Those pigs running like the animals they are. They fired real bullets at us. Live bullets. So comrades responded by firing on a police bus in Ζωγράφου [Zografou].
>
> SAM: On the third night, the big [Christmas] tree in Πλατεία Συντάγματος[10] was burnt to the ground. What symbolism! We were shouting in passion, in anger at Alexis' murder, at the pigs for constantly fucking us! And at the vile shrine to consumption. Gone. Then we smashed government offices and banks. A department store. Everything was there to be destroyed.

GEORGIA: Sure, no revolution came from this. And it died down after, but people learnt how to act. What to do in an insurrection. I saw four boys, screaming hatred at police. Throwing rocks. Taunting the pigs. It was amazing. They had no fear. That is a lesson you never forget. That you can take them on. The lessons learnt from this event are the most important. Next time and the time after that and that one, we will have people who are not learning for the first time but as experienced militants causing revolution.

ACACIA: It became too intense. It was out of control. It wasn't just anarchists in the streets. Everyone was there. Assemblies became nonsense. It showed we need to be more ready in the future. Spread our ideas now, before the next one.

VASILI: The GSSE[11] had called a general strike on the 10th. They cancelled it, of course, to avoid inflaming the situation. Filth! 50,000 people marched anyway. In response some 500 people from base unions,[12] occupied the GSSE building in Athens.

KYRIAKO: It's amazing to have 20,000 people alongside you. Some old people too. Then to hear of prisoners refusing meals in protest against the death of Alexis. Then to hear of Roma attacking a police station.[13] Or Kuneva's[14] assault later in December and see people fighting back, showing their disgust, taking it out on the police and her bosses. It was immense.

The ferocity of discontent alongside the range of emotions that flooded the streets of Athens in December, extended beyond those felt for the death of a young man. To all respondents, unconditionally, the murder of Grigoropoulos was the spark that lit the fires of late 2008. To that end, it was a hugely emotive catalyst. Yet, they were also driven by a myriad of emotions, politics, and personal and shared experiences. Anarchists, antiauthoritarians, leftists and migrants came out in solidarity with Alexandros Grigoropoulos, but also to share and vent their grievances and claim the streets as their own – that much is certain.

2009–2011: more of the same, greater intensity

Returning to the lineal presentation of historical narratives, the eruption of December 2008 was followed by direct actions with greater intensity and frequency than the years before. Many of the people I spoke with talked of a collective reinvigoration after December 2008, as well as their own personal renewal in anarchist and/or anti-authoritarian politics. The years 2009 and 2010 included numerous occupations in universities, schools, trade union buildings, factories and even the National Opera Hall. There were also hundreds of often daily general assemblies, exploring issues as diverse as anarchist economics, strategies to confront the rise of fascism, and the role of social spaces. Alongside this were countless skill-sharing workshops as well as B-Fest, an anti-authoritarian festival of music, political speakers and activist workshops (see B-Fest, 2013).

At the same time, many of my respondents also characterised 2009 and 2010 in terms of the violent repertoires of direct action that went beyond the regular street-protests and confrontations with riot police. This led one participant, Anna, to describe 2009 and 2010 as a 'time of milk, honey, blood and fire'. Similarly, Deme saw this period as a time of 'assemblies and molotovs!' Some of the actions in Athens highlighted by interviewees during this time include: the murder of a counter-terrorism policeman (Kyriakidou, 2009); violent retaliations against police following the murder of Λάμπρος Φούντας (Lambros Fountas) in a shoot-out;[15] bullets sprayed at a few police stations and a TV station (Alter); plus the fire-bombing of government buildings, conservative think-tanks, the offices of New Democracy, financial firms, ATMs, luxury cars, banks, hotels, fast-food chains, police vans, the houses of security personnel and the Athens stock exchange. In 2010, the additional antagonism of Greece's €110 billion loan from the IMF and Eurozone countries – as well as the crippling socio-political aspects of the attached austerity measures – served to add fuel to militant fervour. By the time I arrived in early 2011, militant and violent direct action was well and truly ritualised.

Themes: rejuvenation and familiarity, riot-porn and fetishes

Returning to the points I introduced at the start of this chapter, my contemporary historical discussions illustrate two themes. First, Athenian anarchist and anti-authoritarian praxis is as much defined by new forms of direct action as it is by the perpetual replication of others. The Athenian anarchist and anti-authoritarian landscape is a regular site for novel forms of direct action like food banks and supermarket expropriations that constantly replenish the space. At the same time as new types of direct actions and tactics are renewing the space, familiar repertoires of violent direct actions concurrently pervade historical discussions. I saw very consistent repertoires of action repeating themselves, such as those of the violent anarchist cells, and the militant and violent street-actions and protests.

The second theme I mentioned at the start of the chapter related to the dominance of insurrectionist anarchist and anti-authoritarian historical narratives. For the most part, the remembered events, people and publications reflect an insurrectionist anarchist and anti-authoritarian theme. Libertarian-communist, anarcho-communist, anarcho-syndicalist, platformist and council communist histories are either ignored or unknown to Athenian anarchists and anti-authoritarians. The historical prevalence of these strands of anarchism are minimal in contrast to the histories already discussed in this chapter. Nonetheless, they do exist. Taki was the only respondent who mentioned anything about the numerous publications that have come from this tradition, including the libertarian-communist Eutopia project with its extensive written output and the anarcho-communist collective Tristero, who put out the magazines Νέα Τοπολογία (New Topology) and *Anares*. The work of the platformist Ομοσπονδία Αναρχικών Δυτικής Ελλάδα (Federation of Anarchists of Western Greece) and the loosely anarcho-syndicalist Ελευθεριακή Συνδικαλιστική Ένωση (Libertarian Syndicalist Union) were also not raised.

Bringing my two stated themes together, we see how historical narratives portray a space inspired by insurrectionist and anti-authoritarian events, which is full of violent militant direct actions. Inasmuch as the space is renewed by other examples of praxis, there is an unrelenting presence of riots and violence, so much so that the story of Athens Indymedia (despite its anti-authoritarian and anarchist framework) was side-lined. This brings us back to an idea raised in the previous chapter regarding an adaptation of Vradis's notion of 'riot-porn' (SubMedia, 2012): that amongst activists, the constant negotiations and discussions about historical events has produced a narrative that celebrates violence because it is gratifying, shocking and seductive – as pornography can be. As historical events, they are observed through the lens of time in the descriptions passed down in activist folklore. These stories then arouse contemporary activists and inspire them to produce new explosive acts.

This, in turn, leads us to the separate discussions by Christos Boukalas and John Karamichas of a revolutionary fetishism amongst contemporary activists (Boukalas, 2011; Karamichas, 2009). The term refers to the idea that revolution and its associated violence and militancy is held in unshakable reverence. Boukalas argues that Greek anarchy is consumed by an identity that fetishises violence, where '"more violent" equals "more revolutionary"' (2011: 282–284). In his footnotes, Boukalas acknowledges that to an extent his claim is a generalisation. He is adamant, however, that this reflects a 'general line of force' in contemporary anarchism and anti-authoritarian politics (Boukalas, 2011: 294). In much the same way, Karamichas talks of a revolutionary fetishism stemming from the rich and recent history of youth rebellion and street militarism in Greece (2009). Putting the analogies of riot-porn and revolutionary fetishism together, historical narratives celebrating the riot appear as foreplay where the *act* is talked about, alluded to or watched from a distance (the distance of time). The real act of coitus occurs in the street-protest itself, in the present. The climax being the frenetic, emotive and euphoric interaction with the police, the Far Right or pillars of capital.

As much as these analogies are useful in capturing the dominance of violent repertoires, they are limiting. They are based on the assumption that the street-protest or violent acts are premised on replicating an historical trend. Contemporary activity is certainly informed by these trends, but it is also imbued with the emotions and decisions of contemporary activists. Historical attitudes inform contemporary processes of collective identity, but they do not govern them. Contemporary activists are not beholden to continue a particular set of actions. That they do so is partly inspired by the dominant historical narratives, but it is also fuelled by contemporary realities. While notions of riot-porn or revolutionary fetishism may go some way to account for the dominance of violent repertoires of action, so too, for example, must the hostility and constant antagonisms of the police. Participants flooded conversations with stories of police oppression, harassment and violence. Adding to this, the more recent revelations that over one in every two Athenian police officers voted for the right-wing political party Golden Dawn, a party openly premised on fascist principles and hostile to anarchists (Το Βημα, 2013), it is not surprising that violence is deployed as a counter-response in Athens. Equally, Chapter 7 looks at emotions, which are another aspect giving shape to the movement.

Insofar as the influence of prevailing historical narratives are not governing, they are nonetheless telling. Historical folklore plays a role in building Athenian anarchist and anti-authoritarian collective identities today – in particular, the way violent tactics and violent collective identities contribute to the unity of the space (Melucci, 1995a: 45; 1996: 300). Activists' conceptualisation of history sheds light on a range of processes involved in giving shape to contemporary Athenian anarchist and anti-authoritarian politics. Evident, for a plethora of reasons, is the habitual presence of street-protests, riots, violent actions and property attacks. A predilection for these forms of direct action, both as historical incidences and as events ingrained and repeated in historical narratives, denotes their significance as forces informing the contemporary milieu. That these forms of direct action are continuously replicated, is testament to this fact (Gongaware, 2011: 39).

If violent direct action is a consistent aspect of the anarchist and anti-authoritarian space, this does not provide an explanation or tell us anything about its effects. In the following two chapters, I move beyond the empirical observation developed in this chapter to look at how participation in violent repertoires (such as in street battles, smashing up banks and other actions, and their associated emotions) coalesce to inform the movement's collective identity.

Notes

1. Helena is referring to one of the high points in anarchist history – Spain and particularly Barcelona in the mid-1930s (see Marshall, 2010: 462–463). An almost identical point is made by The Curious George Brigade, regarding their attitude to the Spanish Civil War (The Curious George Brigade, 2012).
2. 23.10 (the author's pseudonym) suggests that some of these issues revolved around the murder or suicide of anarchist Χριστόφορος Μαρίνος (Christoforos Marinos) and his subsequent character analysis by different groups (23.10, 2010: 10).
3. With apologies to The Clash.
4. The G8 is a forum for the leaders of Canada, France, Germany, Italy, Japan, Russia, the UK and the USA.
5. Carlo Giuliani was murdered during the Genoa G8 protests by an Italian Carabiniere. He was shot at point blank range but ballistic experts employed by the defence convinced the Judge that the bullet had ricocheted off some plaster. The Carabiniere was acquitted of the crime (Hooper, 2003).
6. Rather, and as noted earlier, Temponeras was bludgeoned to death by some 'centaurs', a youth militant group of the New Democracy party.
7. The literal translation of Κινηση is closer to the English word 'movement'. I was told a number of times, however, that it is more accurate to translate it as 'current' to reflect the context in which it is used by people associated with AK. On the other hand, I note that in an interview with two members of Thessaloniki's AK, Malamas Sotiriou and Grigoris Tsilimandos, the word 'movement' is preferred (Bray et al., 2013).
8. In hindsight, I wish I had asked more questions about Athenian anarchist and anti-authoritarian activism driven by environmental concerns. It was only when I was putting all my field notes together that my limited engagement with this issue became apparent. Nonetheless, this dearth creates an opportunity for future research in this area.
9. On all their propaganda and signage, *Nosotros* is written in English.
10. Syntagma Square, the main square of Athens, a few hundred metres from Parliament.
11. The Confederation of Greek Workers (GSSE) (Γενική Συνομοσπονδία Εργατών Ελλάδας).
12. Greek grass-roots workers unions organised on anarchist and anti-authoritarian principles of non-hierarchy and direct democracy.
13. A group of Roma attacked a police station in Ζεφύρι (Zefyri) Athens.
14. Κωνσταντίνα Κούνεβα (Konstantina Kuneva) was general secretary of the Panattic Union
15. Fountas was a militant involved with Revolutionary Struggle. He was murdered by police in a shooting.

6

The anarchist and anti-authoritarian space: tensions and tendencies

'Don't smash the ATM ... here'

There are flickers of antagonism that often precede that combustive moment when a protest march turns into a violent street-protest. These can take the form of catalysts like a chunk of marble crashing through a window here or a trunk of wood shattering an ATM (bank machine) screen there. For one particular protest, the explosion had to wait a minute, interrupted by a middle-aged woman calling from a balcony as the march passed by. 'Όχι εδώ' [Not here], she insisted to the hooded man dressed in black and poised ready to strike the ATM with a wooden pole. He stopped, turned to her, grunted and left the machine unharmed. He was outside one of the oldest anarchist squats in Athens and respected the woman's call, an understanding that smashing up the ATM in this location might bring unwanted attention from the police. I ran after him to talk. When I got closer, I saw it was Kosta, a guy in his late teens whom I knew from a squat. The following conversation unfolded:

ME: Hey man, what happened there?

KOSTA: Ah you know, I don't want to start any trouble here. But it is μαλακίες [bullshit].

ME: You don't agree? You're outside the squat, no?

KOSTA: Ελα εντάξει [Ok, sure]. I get their point. But I am sick of it. People like her, the oldies, fuck them. I am sick of it. Always telling us their hour-long opinions. In assemblies stumbling on about the right way to do things. That we should follow established methods. That their way is the best way. Κοίταξε [Look], I am sick to fucking death of this constant self-righteous behaviour. It is not just me either. Λοιπόν [So then], here

I respect the squat. But I refuse to be bullied by them. So it is. Ελα πάμε [Let's go], I can see the pigs!

This anecdote is illustrative of frictions within the space. It is a milieu brimming with varied opinions, tensions and disagreements giving shape to the movement.

This chapter explores some of the more prominent tensions within the anarchist and anti-authoritarian space. I discuss tensions around gender and sexuality politics; tendencies and currents; tactics and media engagement, as well as violence and solidarity. The processes of collective identity within the space are partly generated through negotiations and interactions around these issues, which are explored more fully in the following chapter.

Gender and sexuality

A constant tension within the movement relates to the politics of gender and sexuality. In her article on sexism in the Greek anarchist and anti-authoritarian movement, Sissy Doutsiou argues that we should not assume the space is going to be immune from sexist behaviour just because it is an anarchist and anti-authoritarian milieu. The actors within the space itself have, after all, been socialised within a sexist society (Doutsiou, 2010: 249). From a number of first-hand and second-hand accounts (from anarchists and leftists who had spent time in Athens), I had heard suggestions that the space had issues with sexism and homophobia (see also Doutsiou, 2010; Sullivan, 2004). During meandering late-night conversations while sprawled across couches in dreary squats, I identified no verbal indication of overt sexism or homophobia. Discussions reflected an ethical sophistication that eschewed these forms of discrimination and subjugation. Despite this, sexist and homophobic behaviour is definitely an issue within the Athenian anarchist and anti-authoritarian space, and is manifested in some obvious ways. The following discussion reflects my own observations and the insights of some of my participants.

I proceed by first conveying the initial 'ethically sophisticated' squat conversations. I have merged conversations into a narrative that conveys the colloquial tone in which these thoughts were expressed to me in the field.

If, as activists argue, the anarchist project is to challenge all forms of domination and hierarchy in society, then the annihilation of patriarchal structures is necessary alongside the smashing of capitalism and the state. Patriarchal systems are where inflated authority, privilege and power lies with men. They are systems that reproduce a dominant/submissive binary that ultimately subjugates women, leading to sexism and sexual violence.

Sexism at its core creates two rigid categories of gender – males and females – with power and authority vested in the former.[1] Institutional, cultural and socially constructed norms and behaviours enforce it (see Bornstein, 2013; hooks, 2004; Lerner, 1986).

With respect to Greece's socially constructed gender norms, respondents constantly talked of the entrenched sexism within the Greek Orthodox Church, nationalist folklore, the family structure and the historical division of labour in the private and public sphere. From the outset then, sexism is transphobic – a fear, hatred or strong dislike of transgender people. Gender identity is set within socially constructed parameters that lock in gender categorisations at birth. Any aberrations from these – such as transgender and intersex identities – are viewed as deviant (see also Serano, 2007). Simultaneously, sexism expresses and reproduces a system of power and domination by enforcing expectations of what it is to be male and female. These socially constructed assumptions ultimately reinforce the subjugation of women, through the legal system, political structures, as well as cultural, sexual and historical narratives. Some respondents made the additional point that patriarchal systems also subjugate anti-sexist men, by alienating and 'othering' their beliefs. Given the power of these assumptions to shape thought and behaviour, all respondents identified the struggle against sexism as an important and ongoing challenge for the anarchist and anti-authoritarian space.

Another aspect of patriarchal structures is the prescription of heterosexuality as the normal sexual orientation (see also Jung, 1993; Seidman, 1995: 116–119). Attitudes embedded in Greek society by dominant institutions consider deviations from hetero-normativity as illegal in the eyes of the law, immoral in the eyes of the church and unproductive in the eyes of a capitalist system (see also Butler, 1990; Warner, 1993). As pointed out by some of my respondents though, it is possible that the relationship between hetero-normativity and capitalism is changing, as some 'enlightened' capitalists and politicians come to appreciate that families with two male or two female parents can reproduce the next generation of labour just as well as their heterosexual counterparts. Indeed, some capitalists are positively predisposed to middle-class gay and lesbian relationships, because they see in them a relatively cashed-up market. Nonetheless, Greece is still far from realising even the limited gains that gays and lesbians have won elsewhere in the Western world. According to my participants, in patriarchal societies like Greece, homosexuality is not only deemed different to the norm, but it also seen as a sign of inferiority. Thus, heterosexism assigns superiority to heterosexual behaviour while discriminating against homosexual behaviour.

In response to discussions about patriarchy, my respondents repudiated normative assumptions about gender roles. 'Gender' is not a biological term, they proposed, it is instead a socially constructed notion describing certain characteristics. It is a concept fuelled by stereotypes and assumptions, like women–weak, men–strong, which serves to entrench a system whereby an entire category of people are deemed submissive and inferior (including transgender and intersex people). It strips women of their autonomy and instead prescribes expected behaviours. Some of the examples included women's roles in the labour market, in social settings, their responsibilities at home, their obligations to their family, and their submissive role within the Greek Orthodox Church. Furthermore, all my interviewees rejected hetero-normative assumptions that grant superiority to heterosexuality. Beyond the encouragement of diversity, intervention into personal sexual and relationship preferences were an open affront to all of my respondents. Evidently, in the confines of group conversations and discussions, I heard no indication of sexist or homophobic attitudes.

Despite this, numerous respondents were adamant that sexism and homophobia were prevalent within the Athenian anarchist and anti-authoritarian space. In Helena's words, 'people know what to say [to you]. They make what we call κοινοτοπία [platitudes]. But watch their behaviour', she warned, 'you'll see.' Similarly, in regard to sexism Yianni called the space 'at times unwelcoming, hostile and even putrid', using the Greek word 'σάπιος', which can also mean rotten. Indeed, it was outside of the intimate conversations held in squats or in a καφενείο (café) where I saw evidence of sexism and homophobia within the space.

Many instances of sexism and homophobia came through in the language directed at police in street-protest melees. Police were described variously as 'μουνια' (cunts), 'πουτανεσ' (whores) and 'πούστης' (faggots) (and I heard these words used repeatedly, and always by men). To be clear, these words were not used in a context where the word was to be reclaimed – such as in Inga Musico's work on the word 'cunt', in which she aims to 'seize a word that was kidnapped' (Musico, 2002). Rather, we have the use of highly charged, antagonistic and overtly sexist and homophobic words being deployed by some male anarchists and anti-authoritarians as weapons to attack and deride police. I also heard the phrase 'θα σας γαμήσουμε' (We are going to fuck you). This can be translated to mean 'We are going to fuck you over', as in to assault you physically, although literally it implies sexual and physical violence. Using the language of sexual assault – what Susan Brownmiller called 'man's basic weapon of force against woman, the principal agent of his will and her fear' – conveys a disregard for the impact of sexual violence as a political tool oppressing women (Brownmiller, 1975: 14).

When I raised the use of this language, the responses fell more or less into two camps. The majority of people I interacted with considered instances of sexist and homophobic language as a serious issue within the space. According to many respondents, they had heard these words used time and time again. Tina told me that, 'you hear it all the time – it is a product of the world we live in, but this is no excuse. In fact, this should be reason to challenge these traps.' Similarly, in a communiqué released by an Athens anti-sexist group, they saw this sexist use of language as undermining social liberation. Their response was to encourage the reader to, '[a]side from the cop ... [a]lso kill the sexist in your head' (Anonymous, 2010b: 247). Other interviewees saw it differently. Those in this camp, and they were all male, argued that the language was not sexist, as it was aimed at male police officers. Many of the responses here dismissed concerns because they themselves would not be offended if they were called these terms. As Kosta said in reference to the use of 'μουνια' (cunts), 'I am comfortable with my sexuality, and it doesn't concern me in the slightest if you want to call me a woman's sexual organ.'

Besides sexist and homophobic language directed at police, I also saw instances of what Janet Swim, Robyn Mallet and Charles Stagnor describe as 'subtl[y] sexist' (2004: 117) behaviour that was aimed towards other anarchists and anti-authoritarians. In a handful of incidences in assemblies and meetings, for example, I saw a lack of patience, which in turn indicated a lack of respect, from some males towards females while they were speaking. Sometimes it expressed a total disregard for what women were saying, to the point where an individual would turn their head and start talking to someone else, or walk in front of the speaker while they were talking. At other times, male antagonists would offer consistent commentary 'assisting' the female speaker whenever she would pause, as if she were unable to convey her thoughts independently. I only saw this behaviour directed at female speakers by males.

In response to my observations about these issues, some agreed that this sort of thing occurs and is demonstrative of sexist behaviour. Yet many repudiated this interpretation, and disputed the prevalence of these occurrences. Alternatively, Pari and Georgia offered different analyses, both of which referenced informal power structures. In so doing, they echoed some of the themes first raised in Jo Freeman's iconic essay, *The Tyranny of Structurelessness* (1970).

In her essay, Freeman argues that the women's liberation movement has inflated the value of informal, non-hierarchical structures and organising principles. In the absence of a formal structure, she says, a hidden power clique develops based on friendships, producing an elite circle that informally leads the group. Non-hierarchical organisational principles then 'become a way of masking power' for a small group within the collective (Freeman, 1970). Her solution involved recognising inequalities as inevitable, but at the same time formalising these (informal) power structures within a democratic system. This can include delegation of authority, allocation of tasks along 'rational criteria' and formalised task rotations (Freeman, 1970). As Gordon (2008: 56) and Anarcho (2008) observe, her solutions are similar to those of Murray Bookchin. On the issue of leadership, Bookchin wrote as follows:

[a] serious libertarian approach to leadership would indeed acknowledge the reality and crucial importance of leaders – all the more to establish the greatly needed formal structures and regulations that can effectively control and modify the activities of leaders and recall them when the membership decides their respect is being misused or when leadership becomes an exercise in the abusive exercise of power. (2003: 31–32, emphasis in original)

The major issue with Bookchin and Freeman's work is that their solutions are completely objectionable for collectives organising on anarchist and anti-authoritarian principles. Specifically in Freeman's work, her acceptance of inequalities as inevitable and her desire to formalise them seeks a return to hierarchical organising structures that are 'in no way anarchist in spirit' (Gordon, 2008: 63). Her solution dispenses with anarchist and anti-authoritarian problem-solving processes. She ignores the possibility of attempts to overcome the issues of informal power through negotiations, discussions and consensus. Rather, she assumes 'the consciousness-raising phase of the movement' is over (Freeman, 1970), resorting instead – at the first sign of trouble – to the formal structures of the old Left (Levine, 2002). Although Freeman's solutions may be applicable to organisations less concerned with anti-authoritarian principles, they seem contrary to the structures of the radical feminist collectives she was trying to help, and to anarchist and anti-authoritarian collectives more broadly.

Notwithstanding the critique of her solutions, Freeman raises a pertinent general concern regarding informal power within anti-authoritarian groups (Gordon, 2008: 65). Returning to Athens, Pari identified that rather than witnessing sexism in the meetings and assemblies, I had observed informal power networks exerting their authority. Pari suggested that some of the older anarchists and anti-authoritarians who had been around the movement for a long time would, on occasion, dispense with the 'formalities of horizontalising' in order to move forward or speed up organisational processes. Equally, these older anarchists have been known to offer advice and opinions without recourse to the guidelines of assemblies and meetings, by interjecting with 'additional information or to correct' a speaker [Pari]. Although he agreed that this could be problematic, Pari noted that there were times when he found interjections useful. Further, Pari was adamant that it was less of a gender issue and more of a power issue. He suggested that it was largely coincidental that my observations involved women, as he had seen the same sort of thing happen to young men.

In her work on power and domination, Starhawk referred to this kind of power as 'power-with', describing it as 'the power of a strong individual in a group of equals, the power not to command, but to suggest and be listened to', with its source being 'the willingness of others to listen' (1988: 9–10). In Max Weber's *The Theory of Social and Economic Organisation*, he describes a type of power where one commands and then one is obeyed (*herrschaft*) (1947: 131, 152). Starhawk's (1988) concept though is more about one suggesting and then being listened to. This is more in line with Michel Foucault's conception of how power operates, in the capillaries of social interactions (1980b: 99; see Gordon, 2008: 51). If, taking this into consideration, we assume for a moment that Pari is right and that it is a power issue separate from gender politics, then this raises another concern regarding hierarchies and the way in which power operates. While there is nothing inherently authoritarian about having a strong individual suggest things to a group, the ability of a select (male) few to bypass standard meeting practices expected of others can certainly compromise horizontal structures. Tony and Panayiotta agreed that there were certainly issues with the way assemblies and meetings operate, but they also pointed out that it was the obligation of fellow anarchists and anti-authoritarians to question this practice. Further, Tony insisted that these were rare occurrences, referring to them as 'anomalies'.

At the same time, however, participants Panayiotta, Vasilli, Tina and Yianni, all mentioned that informal power structures exist within the anarchist and anti-authoritarian space including outside of meetings and assemblies. The general acknowledgement was that older, nearly always male anarchists and anti-authoritarians, wield a degree of heightened influence, particularly over younger activists. Panayiotta described this as an 'excessive and often negative' influence. Yianni was more circumspect, suggesting that teaching new activists about the space required people of 'influence and knowledge'. At the same time, it was made clear that the newer activists were free and encouraged to 'challenge their teachers'. For Tina, challenging informal hierarchies and power-holders was a work in progress for the space, 'part of us all shedding the skin of our smothering hierarchies'.

While all of these respondents acknowledged the existence of informal power structures, another theme consistent throughout my interviews was that power holders were nearly always male. Boukalas (2011: 291) calls them the 'anarcho-father'. In his essay on the Marfin Bank arson (an incident discussed shortly), he argues that anarchy has failed in its 'protracted tolerance of its commanding "fathers"' (Boukalas, 2011: 291; see also Anonymous, 2010b). The presence of 'anarcho-fathers' is particularly interesting in the light of my initial concern regarding sexist behaviour at meetings. Of course, the mere presence of a male (informal) power holder does not imply that sexism exists. On the other hand, the presence of a number of male power holders does raise concerns about male dominance and sexism. My observations were supported by Georgia, who had witnessed the same sexist behaviour in meetings and assemblies. She insisted that the anarchist and anti-authoritarian space was riddled with sexism, and that some of her comrades treated women as second-class citizens.

Aside from sexist language and behaviour at meetings and in assemblies, whenever it was time for dinner in one of the squats, I saw a sexist division of tasks. Consistently, over the course of three evenings, I noted the three males in the squat did not offer to help cook or clean up. Two of the males had expressed some of the most forthright thoughts on the problems of sexism, but failed to challenge stereotypical task allocations when the occasion arose. When I told the males on the second night that I was going to help in the kitchen, one of the men turned to me and whispered, 'leave it, they don't mind'. I asked the two women in the kitchen whether this happened regularly and one of them replied, 'yeah, it's terrible. We are working on it.' I never had the chance to interview that woman because she left the squat the next day. I can only suspect that it was related to this issue. When I put my observations to Dino (he was not in this squat), he was furious with the actions of those who would call themselves anarchists, but who would choose to act in this way. It is also interesting to note that he pleaded with me not to include this anecdote in my work, for fear that it would misrepresent the Athenian anarchist and anti-authoritarian space. I told Dino that I was more than likely going to include my anecdote, and unfortunately Dino refused to talk to me after that.

A further tension within the anarchist and anti-authoritarian space relates to violence and gender politics (Thompson, 2010: 115). In the heat of a spiteful melee, as I watched anarchists and anti-authoritarians violently responding to police, Anna raised the idea that proliferation of violent tactics, such as Black Bloc, glorifies physical confrontations and machismo. Her argument was that these tactics elevate a particularly male way of confronting antagonisms through a show of physical strength and force. Similarly, Sian Sullivan argues that violent tactics appear to celebrate '"hegemonic masculinities" ... that valorise physical strength ... one which is akin to that also represented by the machismo of a male dominated body-armoured riot police' (2004: 29–30). This raises what Gordon refers to as 'serious feminist issues' for the anarchist and anti-authoritarian milieux (2008: 104). As we watched the conflict unfold, Anna said that this was 'how they prove their worth as anarchists, that they are men, that they are fighters'. Anna also made the point that while there were certainly women engaged in Black Bloc tactics, they were unconsciously replicating masculine actions, and that they were indoctrinated in a particular way of demonstrating their militancy. Kyriako, who was standing next to us, agreed with Anna's argument to some extent, adding, 'I don't like it, but it is what we do.'

Sullivan is also concerned that normalising machismo-informed political violence allows it to be reproduced in other aspects of life, such as the 'disempowering violence of everyday sexism' (2004: 29–30). Sullivan notes that the sexual harassment that occurred in an anarchist encampment in Thessaloniki during protests against the West Balkans summit may reflect a developing trend (2004: 29–30). On this issue though, none of my interviewees talked about reports of sexual harassment in Thessaloniki. I can only speculate, but perhaps this was not raised because of personal triggers and trauma, or it had something to do with me being a male interviewer.

When I put Anna's (and Kyriako's) analysis to some of my other interviewees, that proliferation of violent tactics, such as Black Bloc, glorifies physical confrontations and machismo, there were waves of rebuttal. Tina called it 'absurd', countering that saying that men act in certain violent ways while women are non-violent or passive was itself sexist. Anarchist-feminists deploy physically violent tactics, Tina claimed, not because they want to show masculine strength but as a tactical response to the failures of non-violence. A popular example retold by Tina, Acacia and Zizo was the story of the Mujeres Creando, an anarchist-feminist collective in Bolivia involved in anti-poverty campaigns. After some local indigenous farmers were unable to repay a debt, and with their families starving, the Mujeres Creando armed themselves with Molotov cocktails and dynamite and occupied the bank holding their loans – with some success (see Gelderloos, 2007: 72).

As someone who had very much embraced Black Bloc militancy, Acacia was upset by the implication that she was unconsciously replicating masculine tendencies. She felt that the suggestion she was an indoctrinated sheep disrespected the thought that had informed her choice to fight – violently: 'I don't understand the argument, what are women meant to do? Stand idly by while the pigs attack us? Assault us? It is madness.' Similarly, James's concern was that this argument delegitimises Black Bloc tactics, by tainting them with claims of sexism: 'I am not saying you have to be violent, but surely we can see the importance of some violent actions here [in Athens]. What about in December [2008]? Just ask for an apology from the police? Just because I don't want to engage in 'masculine' violence? This argument is based on a lack of solidarity.'

Laina Tanglewood expresses a related concern that rather than condemning Black Bloc militancy as sexist, and consequently non-inclusive of women (even though many women are involved in Black Bloc tactics), it should be the case that: '[B]oth women and men who want to fight should be welcome and encouraged to do so while those (male and female) who do not feel comfortable taking such risks can engage in a variety of other activities' (Tanglewood, quoted in Ruins, 2002). The reality is that amongst interviewees there is significant disagreement as to whether Black Bloc tactics are gendered.

I return to Doutsiou's observation presented at the start of my discussion on gender and sexuality, that we should not assume that the Athenian anarchist and anti-authoritarian space would be immune from sexist behaviour. While I agree that we should hardly be surprised when sexist behaviour is replicated within a space surrounded by patriarchal, capitalist, statist and other hierarchical institutions, it is nonetheless noteworthy that sexist (and homophobic) attitudes did not come through any of the more theoretical conversations on these issues. Instead, they were evident in behavioural interactions, as Helena suggested when she posited that people were making platitudes towards me. Furthermore, I observed a few individuals who had presented nuanced and engaging critiques of patriarchy then go on to display sexist and homophobic behaviour. Clearly, sexist and homophobic behaviour will cause conflict within a space that is premised on challenging these forms of discrimination. That some of my participants were blind to instances of the practical manifestation of sexism and homophobia is equally problematic and divisive.

Currents, tensions and tendencies

Another overt source of tension within the Athenian space stems from friction over different anarchist and anti-authoritarian practices. Each tendency has particular and often divergent approaches to ways of organising: what it means to be anarchist; how to interact with other groups; and what tactics are best suited for the space. The Athenian anarchist and anti-authoritarian space is a catalogue of tendencies, a scene described by Schwarz et al., in the following terms: '[a]narcho-junkies hanging out in that square, the nihilists hanging out in this corner, the libertarians hanging out in that bar, the hippies hanging out in that park, the Situationists hanging out in that squat, the classical anarcho-communists in that café and the insurrectionists in this one' (2010c: 368).

While anti-authoritarian and anarchic currents underscore all of these tendencies, differences can be pronounced. Take, for example, members from the Anti-Authoritarian Current (AK) and insurrectionist anarchists. Combined, individuals within these categories make up most of the Athenian anarchist and anti-authoritarian space. They share very similar attitudes on almost all of the general critiques coming from an anarchist and anti-authoritarian analysis, such as on the state, prisons, police and capitalism. Their anarchist praxis (by which I mean the practical implementation of their particular styles of anarchism), however, can differ widely. When broken down, tensions revolve around choices of tactics and the way in which best to create anarchism.

As mentioned, AK is a political network of anti-authoritarian assemblies diffused throughout Greece, based on direct democracy and horizontal organisational principles (see Bray et al., 2013). AK is an influential component of the anarchist space whose members are more inclined to create permanent spaces and organisational networks, forming solid foundations that incrementally build towards revolution. Their efforts are examples of prefigurative politics – behaviour and action that accords with anarchist and anti-authoritarian principles. AK examples of direct action include supporting the creation of social spaces that include large bartering networks, worker occupations of factories, and base unions, which are Greek grass-roots workers' unions organised on anarchist and anti-authoritarian principles of non-hierarchy and direct democracy. Advocates of AK, like Tony, described this approach as 'building tangible anarchism piece by piece'. All these examples occur alongside a rigorous commitment to participation in Athenian street-protests.

This particular approach to the implementation of anarchist and anti-authoritarian ideas is in contrast to the tactics preferred by the insurrectionist current in Athens. The more insurrectionist participants of my ethnography advocate informal, ephemeral networks of organisation and small affinity-group structures, rather than the overt, permanent organisational frameworks of AK. Insurrectionists also tend to support constant attacks on capitalist, state and consumerist institutions. These activities can include actions as diverse as raiding supermarkets and then distributing the food to the poor, to firebombing a luxury car dealership. In a lengthy conversation after Andreas and his comrades had performed an evening of private property attacks on wealthy corporate institutions, Andreas described their strategy as one of offence: 'We don't wait', he proudly told me, 'we attack.' In contrast to repertoires of direct actions more consistent with the insurrectionist current, some respondents like Andreas see AK's work as limiting. Andreas described the AK as 'mainstream anarchists, content with their petty organisations and social spaces and lethargic attacks on capitalism'. Alternatively, a response I heard a number of times from individuals associated with AK was that the insurrectionist tendency was full of 'wannabe vanguardists'. The suggestion here is that the insurrectionist current sees themselves at the forefront of the revolutionary movement and consider themselves the most 'pure' and 'radical' form of anarchist and revolutionary.

A consequence of these struggles over tactics and how best to implement anarchist and anti-authoritarian politics, is an increase in visible tensions within the space. My discussions about media usage and the operation of violent, covert cells, for example, would occasionally involve individuals from different currents. Conversations would at times become quite heated. One aspect of conducting research in Greece (and I accept that this is something of a cultural stereotype, but one that reflects the reality of my experiences) is that many Greeks communicate loudly, theatrically and with flailing arm movements. This can come across as aggressive and I was mindful of this cultural nuance. Be that as it may, on occasion, there was observable friction and belligerence during conversations around different tactics. Tensions are not limited to name calling. I observed a number of hostile disputes in assemblies, which left some respondents concerned that physical violence was never far from breaking out. These concerns stemmed from actual experience, as a number of physical confrontations have arisen directly from disputes between activists who subscribe to different currents.

Insofar as I have tried to catalogue some of the observable tactical differences between currents, neatly ascribing positions on praxis to these tendencies can be problematic. There is a degree of overlap between different currents. Some individuals within AK, for example, also support insurrectionist direct actions. Indeed, one of my participants who considered herself connected with AK (the Anti-Authoritarian Current) was one of Andreas's comrades, who was involved with wrecking the property of corporate institutions. Equally, I saw advocates of the insurrectionist current attending film screenings and music gigs at AK's social space, suggesting at least tacit support for the creation of more permanent venues for these events. At the same time, there are also divisions within the currents themselves. Some insurrectionists do not support more extreme actions like assassinations, and have mixed attitudes to the violent cells I discuss shortly. The Athenian anarchist and anti-authoritarian space is rife with disagreements about tactics and forms of direct action.

'The dogs of the mass media'

During the height of the Greek revolt in December 2008, a contentious proposal was advanced at an anarchist and anti-authoritarian assembly in Exarcheia. The proposal was to interrupt a major news broadcast by storming the studio, unfurling political banners and then escaping triumphantly back into the streets. The proposal was not generally supported. Some raised fears that this protest would ultimately serve the advertisers whose product appeared after the political action. Others, as if channelling Guy Debord, were concerned that such an action would contribute to the spectacle of the mass media, where, instead of living actual experiences, viewers watch representations of their life on TV and become politically neutralised spectators (Debord, 1967). At the same time, others were furious that comrades would want anything to do with what Dino called the 'dogs of the mass media'. They argued that any engagement with the mass media signalled nothing less than complicity with capitalism, the state and corporate media.

Despite these criticisms, the following week a different collective went ahead with the proposed action, targeting NET, one of Greece's largest TV stations. On 16 December 2008, after manoeuvres reminiscent of an Ian Fleming novel, the 3 pm live national news broadcast on NET was hijacked by activists storming the studio. For two or so minutes during a live broadcast, anarchists, anti-authoritarians and fellow non-defined activists unfurled political banners that read as follows: *Everyone Get Out in the Streets*, *Freedom to the Prisoners of the Insurrection* and *Freedom to Everyone* (Vortex, 2010).

In conversations, many of my respondents detested the notion of interacting with mainstream media, even in this militant form. Sam referred to it as 'putrid politics, selling out anarchism' because there were other more appropriate sources of communication such as Athens Indymedia, or alternative sources of do-it-yourself (DIY). For Sam, these alternative forms of communication and media were preferred as they offer a more sympathetic portrayal of the intended message. I was having this conversation with Sam as we waited for a night protest to start, when Aleko overheard the conversation. He chimed in, saying:

> yeah, it was just dumb politics. It plays the capitalist game. It uses their tools for our revolution. We have to construct an entirely new form of communication. It is lazy politics.

Linking this to a wider point about conducting interviews with international media, Aleko added:

> Occasionally you get a BBC journalist or Al Jazeera and they want an interview. I say no. I know others say yes, but it is the same thing as this trouble here [the NET raid]. As soon as you connect with this form of communication you are granting legitimacy. You are saying I accept you but I disagree with you. No. I do not accept you. No. I do not recognise you.

Plainly, this was not the attitude for all. The responses supporting this sort of action reflect an appreciation of a diversity of tactics. Aris, for example, saw a wide range of media tactics as, 'pragmatic, where we maximise our exposure, always of course mindful to assess the benefits and flaws in each action'. In a similar vein, Electra made a broader point about using different means to share the political message. She was standing next to Aleko and Sam at the time, and directly responding to them:

> Ok, so the only people that ever hear our message by your logic [Aleko and Sam] are the few who read our posters and the even fewer who are in our networks. It was an opportunity to extend the reach by pirating, by jumping on board this broadcast. They did not buy the station. They did not wear the station's logo. All they did was extend the message beyond our insular χώρος [space]. It is a false argument, a false claim you [Sam] make. It is false logic. You assume that these people only pursued this action. That they do not participate in other communication outlets. We need all the tools we have available to challenge this system. And sometimes, we need to extend this to a wider audience ... [Electra continued but I was not able to write quickly enough].

As I was frantically writing down her quote I missed the specifics of her postscript. But Electra finished by making sure Sam and Aleko knew she was critiquing their argument – and not personally attacking them. While critical of Aleko and Sam's position, Electra was reasonably amicable in the way she conveyed her point but her quote offended Sam despite her disclaimer. In response, Sam said, 'you are full of liberal pretentions', adding sarcastically, 'sorry, I am not attacking you. Your argument is full of liberal pretentions'.

Arson and manslaughter

Further internal tensions within the anarchist and anti-authoritarian space came to the fore shortly after the Marfin Bank fire on 5 May 2010. The day began with a general strike that brought upwards of 200,000 Athenians of various political stripes onto the streets (Indymedia Athens, 2011). According to media reports and my interviewees, it was a particularly antagonistic protest, with attacks on police more numerous than usual, as well as property damage and melees close to the doors of parliament (Brabant, 2010; *Guardian*, 2010; Indymedia Athens, 2011). During the march, a small group of anarchists and/or anti-authoritarians peeled off from the main protest column and threw Molotov cocktails at a Marfin Bank branch on Οδός Σταδίου (Stadiou Road) in central Athens. The building caught fire, killing three workers inside, Παρασκευή Ζούλια (Paraskevi Zoulia), Αγγελική Παπαθανασοπούλου (Angeliki Papathanasopoulou) and Επαμεινώνδας Τσάκαλης (Epaminondas Tsakalis).

In 2013, the chief executive officer of Marfin Bank, the bank's head of security and the manager of the Stadiou Road branch were found guilty of manslaughter and negligence causing bodily harm, for failing to have any safety measures in place despite previous warnings of an attack (ekathimerini.com, 2013a). While there was the occasional anecdotal suggestion that the anarchists or anti-authoritarians in question may not have been anarchists or anti-authoritarians at all, being instead undercover police, there was no concrete evidence brought forward in support of this contention.

Various anarchist and anti-authoritarian collectives and affinity groups debated the merits of this action – in general assemblies, statements, communiqués, pamphlets and blogs (see AK Athens, 2010; Anonymous, 2010b; Conspiracy of Fire Cells, 2010; Occupied London, 2010). The editors of *Revolt and Crisis in Greece* made space for Boukalas's entire chapter discussing the issues relating to the Marfin Bank manslaughters (Boukalas, 2011). While I have considered these arguments, I have mostly relied on my ethnographic data to convey the various attitudes to the deaths and solidarity within the space.

To begin with, some of the responses reflected the contemporary protest-mantra of 'respect for diversity of tactics', whereby you may disagree with a tactic but you acknowledge that it is part of the spectrum of tactical repertoires.[2] The idea is that individuals and collectives are free to choose their own tactics during collective actions, as violent or as non-violent as they may be, limited only by the implicit expectation that the safety of fellow activists are taken into consideration. Those engaging in deliberately violent confrontations with police, for example, could choose to locate this confrontation (if possible) away from non-violent protesters, so that more pacifist activists are not unnecessarily targeted by police. From my experiences in the larger demonstrations in Athens (and indeed elsewhere), however, police indiscriminately targeted protesters regardless of their individual behaviour.

This way of overcoming frictions created in pre-protest meetings seeking to produce an agreed-upon statement of action regarding violence is quite common when anarchists are involved in large protests (Gordon, 2008: 78). Such a mantra acknowledges the difficulties, indeed the impossibility, associated with establishing a consensus on violence and non-violence when there are various anarchist tendencies in the mix.

For my respondents Mary, Taki and Aris, this summed up their stance on the burning of a bank; namely, that although it is not a tactic they would choose, it is one that is part of the spectrum of anarchist and anti-authoritarian tactics. While the sentiment of these conversations conveyed sadness about the death of the three bank workers, there was no suggestion that activists should refrain from these actions; merely that they should take more care next time. Instead of chastising the militants involved in the bank burning, what came through from conversations with Mary, Taki and Aris were powerful displays of solidarity with the arsonists. While Mary expressed remorse at the loss of life and disagreed with the tactics, for example, she added that, 'they are fighters alongside us, we don't throw them to the dogs for their accidents, we hope they learn and we help them learn'. Taki conveyed a similar point when he said, 'loss is loss, you are cold if you don't recognise this, but I support their [the arsonists] intentions, just not their target. We are together in struggle.'

Kosta also expressed solidarity towards the militants involved in the Marfin Bank arson, but took a hard-line position concerning the loss of life. While he was not callous about the loss of life, for Kosta the dead bank workers should have been on strike with the rest of the working class and in support of the wider general strike. To that end, he supported targeting the bank on this particular day, regardless of whether there were workers inside. When I raised the counter-point that they may have had financial constraints or faced losing their job, Kosta was adamant that their profession as bank workers, with all its capitalist baggage, made it difficult for him to be overly sympathetic to the loss of life. In saying this, Kosta has extended the 'us and them' binary (Polletta and Jasper,

2001: 292), by charging the victims with complicity in the system against which he is fighting.

While Kosta was alone in his attitudes towards the dead workers, Dino, Sofia and Andreas echoed his attitude towards the general tactic of targeting a bank. For these three interviewees, those killed were part of the working class and were owed ethical consideration. Like some other respondents, they held the bank officials who were subsequently charged with manslaughter as equally responsible as the arsonists for the deaths of the workers. Dino, Sofia and Andreas expressed disregard for the outpouring of reflection and self-analysis amongst the anarchist and anti-authoritarian milieu regarding the consequences of the petrol bombing. As Sofia told me, 'I don't really care about how this looks, or how others feel about it, it is for the individuals, the protagonists in this drama [the arsonists] to consider their actions.' Sofia's words mirror Emile Armand's thoughts, an individualist anarchist active at the turn of the twentieth century. In his *Mini Manual of Individualistic Anarchism*, he argues that 'the individualist-anarchist is never accountable to anyone but himself [or herself] for his acts and gestures' (Armand, 2005 [1911]: 148). In a follow-up conversation, after brushing up on Armand's work in an Athenian internet café, I put this to Sofia and she agreed with Armand's sentiment. However, she was quick to stress that being accountable towards oneself was an immense burden. She said: 'If you live life with morals as an anarchist, with a compassionate heart, dreaming of a more satisfying existence for people then causing murder will fall heavily on their shoulders.'

As Sofia and I discussed her attitudes further, it became clear that at the heart of this disregard for reflection was a distinct lack of concern for 'how this looks' for anarchism as a social movement. Sofia said: 'I am not interested in [that]. I don't care about publicity, whatever we do, [someone] will inevitably pervert our message. I have no problem with the action. But I am sorry for the families [of those who died].'

Along the same lines, Dino insisted that: 'targeting a bank is obvious. It is in front of you, their church waiting to burn! Someone will always cry about a burning church ... fuck them.'

Underlying these arguments was a genuine lack of concern about how arson will play out in the broader Athenian leftist community or even to those sympathetic towards anarchist and anti-authoritarian politics. This comes from a lack of interest amongst many of my respondents in building a mass movement.

This is a prevalent theme within the Athenian anti-authoritarian and anarchist milieu, reflected in many conversations. Contemporary insurrectionist anarchists and anti-authoritarians, it seems, are estranged from the old anarchist mentality of building a mass movement (popular within the anarcho-syndicalist tradition). There is no call for recruitment, federations or memberships. There is immense cynicism towards the revolutionary potential of general strikes such as the one on the day of the Marfin Bank fire.

Greeks are no strangers to industrial action. In the period between 1980 and 2008, Greek mass industrial action accounted for 40 per cent of the entire general strikes in all of Western Europe (Kelly and Hamann, 2009: 14). The problem with industrial action, the argument goes, is that political elites and elites at economic centres of capital accumulation are acutely aware that, historically, strikes in Greece rarely last more than a day or two and 'achieve nothing of revolutionary value' [Dino]. Instead, this tendency within the anarchist and anti-authoritarian milieu chooses to violently attack institutions of power and capital. For some anarchists and anti-authoritarians, if people 'come with them', so be it, but this is not their primary objective.

In complete contrast, other respondents were scathing of these general attitudes towards the arson and manslaughter that occurred on 5 May, 2010. Vasilli was devastated by the attacks and subsequent deaths. He was not concerned with how this looked to the wider Greek community but how anarchists and anti-authoritarians should feel about this tragedy. Vasilli said:

'We should never have to use phrases like collateral damage. If someone died as a consequence of some kid's actions – regardless of whether a bank official was negligent – it is our fault [the fault of the anarchist and anti-authoritarian space]. There are no excuses; their death is a sad indictment of our failure.'

The failure mentioned by Vasilli is the constant fetishisation of a revolutionary identity, as discussed in Chapters 4 and 5, in which, as Tina said: 'kids get injected like addicts with heroic tales of violence, why are we surprised when they burn down a bank with people inside?'

It is interesting to note that both Tina and Vasilli used the word 'kids' to describe the assailants. They both genuinely had no idea who was involved in the attack but believed that those most likely to engage with this sort of militancy were younger anarchists and anti-authoritarians. Continuing, Tina called it a 'distinct element of the space, a nihilist-individualistic anarchy'. The problem for Tina was that it was antithetical to the nature of anarchism, which is a body of ideas that requires social interactions:

You can't create a space, a place for anarchism without other humans around you. You need to talk, to have dialogue, to discuss the merits of your thoughts. Sometimes your ideas are enjoyed by others. Other times you are wrong and you need to be told as such. And other times you disagree and so be it. But this idea that you can go and build anarchy, by yourself, with blood and fire, it is limiting.

Aside from these analytical statements, there was also general hostility towards the actions of the arsonists. Yianni, Christo and Panayiotta collectively denounced the actions as 'un-anarchist' and they were not alone in this. A number of respondents 'othered' the arsonists by excluding them from the metaphorical anarchist and anti-authoritarian space. In Boukalas's writings on the issue, he also identified this body of opinion noting that '[h]ere Anarchy proceeds to a rare and significant move: it identifies and ostracises its own heretics and misfits' (2011: 290). One of the most noticeable elements of the anarchist and anti-authoritarian space was that very rarely did I hear of a body of notionally anarchist ideas or actions completely shunned. Yet in this instance, that was most certainly the case.

Violence cells

Attitudes towards the collection of clandestine cells involved in arson, kidnapping, assassination and attacks on police stations are another source of tension. These include the likes of Επαναστατικός Αγώνας (Revolutionary Struggle), Σέχτα των Επαναστατών (The Sect of Revolutionaries), Αντικρατική Δικαιοσύνη (Anti-State Justice) and Συνωμοσία των Πυρήνων της Φωτιάς (Conspiracy of Fire) (The Children of the Gallery, 2011: 123). On the one hand, a few Athenian anarchists and anti-authoritarians were very supportive of these militants. Penelope described them as 'the front-line of attacks against our enemies' and Sam called them a 'necessary antagonism in our urban war'. Equally, Pari saw value in their tactics when he talked of the fear that these collectives bring to the police, industrialists and politicians, knowing that someone is willing to kidnap, injure and even murder them.

On the other hand, there was also significant hostility shown towards these militants. Electra refused to acknowledge that they were 'anarchists', calling them instead 'Leninists' and 'cop-provocateurs'. Her point was that they were either ideologically disconnected from anarchism, or they were simply police and paramilitary groups fanning chaos and confusion. Kyriako called them a 'hindrance' to the space, saying, 'we don't need lone wolves' because they brought unwanted attention. He was, however, quick to clarify that unwanted attention would still occur by the very nature of the fear held towards anarchist and anti-authoritarian politics. Yianni took a different approach. He was critical of their choice of action as an unwillingness 'to produce the day to day efforts' required in maintaining and building the anarchist and anti-authoritarian space. Mostly, attitudes are reflective of Helena's thoughts on the matter. Over the course of three interviews, we kept revisiting this issue until Helena settled on her perspective. During this last interview, she patiently composed her thoughts while I penned her words. Helena said:

Why do I not respect these groups? It is difficult, because I support their targets. Sure, fuck the industrialist. I have no care for a luxury car yard. Kill a riot-cop? Sure, they have murdered us. Spray a police station with a Kalashnikov? I don't care, actually good. Do it. A grenade? Sure, why not. It is not the target. Is it their politics? No. I read the statements. I read the communiques. I agree with almost everything. A bit Nihilist perhaps. But ok. If I break it down, if I think long and hard about it, it is that they are choosing, and I know this is controversial, to represent anarchy in a particular way. I support violence. I do. I support counter-attacks. I support militancy. I do. But I do not want what we are creating here to be defined by these very, very violent acts. I am not talking about how the media define them. I am talking about how other anarchists define them elsewhere. I don't want young anarchists and anti-authoritarians in other locations thinking that anarchy is killing a cop. I want us to export that as a tactic in certain situations. Ok. But I want the extraordinary amount of other actions exported too. I think when I think long and hard about this, it is this that hurts me. It is this that makes me hostile to their actions. That we are exporting insurrection not as a wonderfully creative thing, not even as a way to control the streets, but as violent and sadistic theatre.

Regardless of these opinions, it is worth noting that I had the distinct impression that no one would do anything to betray the militants. For all the hostility that some of my interviewees felt towards the cells and their 'antisocial, nihilistic bloodlust', a begrudging solidarity overwhelmed any enmity (The Children of the Gallery, 2011: 123).

Tensions and unity

It was evident from my time in Athens that the anarchist and anti-authoritarian space is full of a range of tensions, diverse opinions and disagreements. In the absence of a manifesto guiding praxis, this is hardly surprising. Fearful of the authoritarian consequences of defining 'anarchism' itself and locking down sets of beliefs and social interactions, most if not all anarchists and anti-authoritarians – as Gordon points out – have little time for detailed blueprints and designs for a free society (2008: 28). In fact, the embodiment of an authoritarian structure is a system in which beliefs are passed down and imposed involuntarily and without modification. In order to challenge this involuntary imposition, anarchist ideas and practices are saturated with encouragement to alter and radically redefine directions at will. In fact, its exponents demand it. For George Woodcock, this constant redirection presents:

the appearance, not of a swelling stream flowing on to its sea of destiny (an image that might well be appropriate to Marxism), but rather of water percolating through porous ground – here forming for a time a strong undercurrent, there gathering into a swirling pool, trickling through crevices, disappearing from sight, and then re-emerging where the cracks in the social structure may offer it a course to run. (2004 [1964]: 18)

In this absence of doctrine, the Athenian anarchist and anti-authoritarian space is rife with tensions and frictions that constitute the practical consequences of this freedom. Significant conflicts are apparent on issues of gender and sexual politics, and on suitable tactics and appropriate forms of direct action. There is no one Athenian anarchism or anti-authoritarian current that can be defined as the Athens's way. In the face of all these tensions, disagreements and catalysts for conflict, it is remarkable that the space is still such a prominent and prolific radical force.

As has been made clear throughout this book, when the time comes to participate in protests, marches and riots, these tensions are put on hold. The streets become full of anarchists and anti-authoritarians unified in a temporary solidarity, in which disparate individuals, collectives and affinity groups come together to protect the very existence of anarchist and anti-authoritarian praxis in Athens. These militant protests can be deeply emotional events. As these emotions are shared and negotiated within wider collectives and affinity groups, they shape and inform the space itself. It is the emotional consequences of collective action, and the ways in which these emotions inform anarchist and anti-authoritarian collective identity, that will be discussed in the next chapter.

Notes

1 Some interviewees also identified 'sex' (as in male, female and other) as a constructed category, in line with post-structural approaches to feminism (see also Shepherd, 2013).
2 For an interesting discussion on this tactic in terms of North American anarchism, see Graeber (2012).

7
Street-protests and emotions: a temporary unity

'When a debate ends we meet in the streets'

As we headed towards the march, I was warned, 'you'll be crying from the start'. True to form, the tear gas onslaught began in earnest. Instinctively, I wanted to run to escape from the fast-forming plumes, but as the tear gas canisters hit the pavement, a paradoxical calm breezed through the anarchists and anti-authoritarians around me. As veteran activists, they mechanically covered their faces for protection and lit small fires to counter the noxious gas. Betrayed by my expressions, Penelope discerned my uneasiness: 'It is important we don't panic', she instructed, '[t]his is our space and we are defending it, there is nothing to fear, we are together, united and we are strong!'

Although myriad tensions exist in the Athenian anarchist and anti-authoritarian space, temporary solidarity reigns during street-protests. As Penelope implied in her instructions, when it is time for action the tensions within the movement are largely suppressed, as activists come together for occupations, protests and riots. Similarly for Emma and many of her comrades, '[w]hen a debate ends we meet in the streets'. In the streets, the disagreements over the subtleties of anarchist and anti-authoritarian politics are peripheral in comparison to the violent threats confronting the space more broadly. As Stavro passionately explains: 'As they close our squats, as the fascists hit our migrant brothers and sisters, as they murder our kids, shove capitalism down our face, make slaves of us, beat us for our sexuality [and] our choices, well these are enemies we fight together. After all, they want nothing more than to paralyse us.'

In this chapter, I unravel some of the complexities within Athenian street-protests. I begin by looking at the characteristics of street-protests, performative violence and the role of Black Bloc tactics. I propose that militant street-protests are acts of political communication and examples of anarchist and anti-authoritarian prefigurative politics (as I wrote earlier, prefigurative politics means that the way in which activists conduct themselves today should convey an anarchist understanding of social relations). Following this, I explore some of the nuances of violence within street-protests and suggest that when it comes time to protest in the street, there is nothing at all pacifist about the space. Finally, I look at a range of emotions that are expressed, fermented and developed through acts of performative violence. Throughout the chapter, I show how experiences and elements of street-protest are shared and negotiated amongst actors (see Peterson, 2001; Yang, 2000), contributing to the ongoing construction of Athenian anarchist and anti-authoritarian collective identity.

Collective identity: street-protest rituals, performative violence and Black Bloc tactics

Street-protests are multifaceted forms of political and social communication that contain a high salience of performative violence, the latter referring to symbolic, antagonistic rituals of political, social and cultural communication. For the most part, street-protests are 'any temporary occupation by a number of people of an open place, public or private, which directly or indirectly includes the expression of political opinions' (Fillieule, 2012: 235). An integral component of the Athenian anarchist and anti-authoritarian space, street-protests represent 'the physical embodiment of a political vision based on anti-capitalism, physical confrontation, and a total rejection of the market and state' (Juris, 2005: 420–421). Even though repertoires of action in Athens vary, they often include large protest marches. This is usually followed by attacks on private property (nearly always symbols of wealth, capital and decadence, such as hotel chains, luxury car dealers, banks and other transnational corporations, rather than small business targets), as well as confrontations with police and far-right activists, and occupations of universities, government buildings or trade union offices.

Performative violence is an enduring presence within Athenian street-protests. It is, as Juris notes, a form of communication 'through which activists seek to produce social transformation by staging symbolic rituals of confrontation ... in order to generate radical identities while producing concrete messages challenging global capitalism and the state' (2005: 413). These violent collective actions serve as both politicised moments of modest rebellion, as well as communicative, symbolic protest-rituals (Juris, 2005: 415). I witnessed activists confronting a police line, for example, that was threatening to remove migrants who had claimed asylum within a university. The protesters' actions were a political attempt to challenge the authority of the state. At the same time, it was a symbolic form of communication expressing solidarity with subjugated communities outside of the space and, importantly, a nuanced form of internal communication regarding struggle within the space's submerged networks (Melucci, 1989: 56–57).

Acts of performative violence are examples of prefigurative anarchist and anti-authoritarian direct action. By creating regular political antagonisms and acts of revolt, as well as contributing to the communication and modification of anarchist politics within the milieu (see Graeber, 2002), Athenian activists are ensuring protest tactics reflect a commitment to direct action. This is a core anarchist and anti-authoritarian principle. An important aspect of this performative violence as prefigurative politics is the unmistakable presence of Black Bloc tactics, a major component of the Athenian street-protest.

A typical Athenian street-protest functions along these lines: a bunch of leftists will make their way from one location to another, often chanting and singing with banners in tow. Along the way, Black Bloc activists within the protest may branch out and engage in property damage. Other Black Bloc activists often march in side streets running parallel to the march in order to protect its flanks from riot police and fascist attacks. When the march reaches its destination, or a destination established by a police-line, Black Bloc protesters from the side, rear and middle of the march then filter to the front and wait for or begin confrontation. Alternatively, if an action begins at its destination, say outside a prison or at other solidarity demonstrations, Black Bloc'ers tend to wait until other leftists have said their piece, before commencing or retaliating to antagonism. I note that anarchists and anti-authoritarians who do not necessarily identify with Black Bloc tactics also engage in these militant rituals. Panagiotis Papadimitropoulos describes one of these rituals as:

> A riot takes place (and in Athens riots occur almost every week), anarchists (if they participate) decide to attack particular targets that represent the State and capitalism, they move first, the police respond, activists set up barricades, and a small scale street confrontation begins with anarchists throwing rocks or Molotov cocktails and the police responding with tear gas and, when possible, with arrests. (2010: 60)

It is worth interrogating Papadimitropoulos's use here of the word 'riot'. To be absolutely clear, Athenian street-protests are very often violent explosions of radical militancy performed by a crowd of anarchists and anti-authoritarians. If anything was to capture the essence of a riot – albeit with political sensibilities – then it would be these actions. The propensity for violence within Athenian street-protests is in stark contrast to the more carnivalised protest actions in parts of the anarchist and anti-authoritarian movements elsewhere, the likes of which Graham St John calls 'protestivals' (2008: 169). I saw no giant puppets or performers on stilts. There were people carrying chunks of wood, who appeared to be ready to smash things. When I spoke to my participants, they would often describe the event as a riot.

This regular use of the term 'riot' by many of my respondents is in complete contrast to Tilly's experiences. He writes that in

> cataloguing thousands of violent events – many of them called riots (or the local language equivalent) by authority and observers – from multiple countries and over several centuries, I have not once found an instance in which the participants called the event a riot or identified themselves as rioters. (2003: 18)

He raises a subsequent point that the term 'riot' embodies a negative political judgement (Tilly, 2003: 18).

In contrast to Tilly's work, della Porta and Gbikpi feel more comfortable in regularly deploying the term 'riot' in their study, even within the title of their book chapter 'The riots: a dynamic view' (2012: 87; see also Kotronaki and Seferiades, 2012; Simiti, 2012). Part of the reason that I believe my collaborators deployed the term was to convey the strength and the uncontrollable force of their resistance. A riot, after all, disturbs the calm and peace of public order and shakes the very foundations of safe, normative behaviour.

Ritualised forms of protest, such as the Athenian actions just discussed, inform the space's collective identity by acting as a dynamic 'network of active relationships between' actors (Melucci, 1995a: 44). As activists hit the streets, they share a space that requires social relationships and methods of communication. In Black Bloc's case, there is a collective unity expressed by virtue of the shared anonymity of masks and similar clothing. As Yianni noted in our discussions:

> In the protest, we are all together as a mass of black and hoods, but each equally autonomous, free to act as we deem suitable for our understanding of reality.

The shared stylistic codes and signifiers represented in black clothing, hoods, masks, batons and repertoires of actions, function as a dynamic form of communication within the movement (Juris, 2005: 420–421). They communicate exactly Yianni's sentiment; namely, that there is a cohesive unity and strength that comes from pooling tactics in this particular manner, but one that is premised on a commitment to anarchist-inspired individuality and autonomy. This is an aspect of Black Bloc tactics that is particularly appealing to anarchists and anti-authoritarians throughout the world (see Juris, 2005: 420–421; Katsiaficas, 2006: v). Consequently, the use of Black Bloc tactics also serves as a form of communication between local and visiting national and international activists. Indeed, the Athenian space has its fair share of anarcha-tourists. Black Bloc tactics, internationalised by global summit hopping, allow activists to travel from different parts of Greece, Europe and beyond, and instantly participate in street-protests. Of course, this is to some extent restricted by issues of finances, and trust and limited connections with local affinity groups.

Another component of the collective identity process relating to networks of active relationships is the organisational structure and form selected by protest participants (Melucci, 1995a: 44). Performative violence and associated Black Bloc tactics are inherently prefigurative in nature, a point cited regularly within field discussions. Not only is the street-protest and performative violence an act of anarchist and anti-authoritarian direct action, but the tactics also embody an ethos of prefigurative politics. When I asked my informants about their choices of tactics, many celebrated Black Bloc's flat and horizontal organisational structure, alongside its focus on solidarity. Tammy Kovich makes the same point in defence of Black Bloc tactics, arguing that a very important component of Black Bloc is its prefigurative characteristics, where '[c]rucial to the project of creating a new society is creating new ways of being, interacting and organizing with each other' (2011: 17). This helps produce a temporary solidarity within the space, as activists come together around these tactical repertoires (Polletta and Jasper, 2001: 293).

Collective identity: street-protest violence

A substantial component of Athenian street-protests involve violence. This is usually defined by respondents as either limited to physical violence against others, or widened to include both physical violence and attacks on property. As was noted in the Introduction, if pacifism is understood to mean opposition to violence then there is nothing pacifist about the Athenian anarchist and anti-authoritarian space. Violence is universally embraced and in diverse contexts. I am not arguing, however, that Black Bloc tactics, or anarchist and anti-authoritarian tactics more broadly, are necessarily predicated on smashing things up or violent acts (Graeber, 2012). Some respondents mentioned that physical and property violence are not their preferred method of implementing political and social change, but that their participation in violent acts reflects contemporary political circumstances. A case in point occurred during a night protest in support of migrants who had occupied the Athenian law school. Black Bloc protesters were there merely to express solidarity. Speaking to some of the participants before the action, they told me they had no desire to participate in a physical protest. But things did become violent, with that violence being originally sparked by a policeman using his shield as a baton to knock forcefully on a protester's head. I saw this happen a number of times. I also witnessed numerous counter-examples of violence from Black Bloc activists (as well as other anarchists and anti-authoritarians) that were instigated without immediate antagonism from police. I now move to explore these ideas of violence in detail, with an eye to how street-protest violence informs processes of collective identity construction in Athens.

Gordon's book chapter 'Peace, love and petrol bombs' looks at the attitudes and discussions around violence within the contemporary phase of anarchism (2008: 78–108). In this extensive analysis, he notes that after anarchism's dormancy during the middle of the twentieth century, this body of political ideas awoke to a wider culture of non-violence. Attitudes in the 1960s created an environment in stark contrast to anarchism's frequently violent past, which was marked by talk of armed insurrection and a taste for political assassinations (Gordon, 2008: 79). Instead, principles of non-violence largely guided activist tactics. Although there were, of course, notable exceptions, the US civil-rights movement, the anti-Vietnam war, the anti-nuclear and direct action environment movements, and even the May '68 events in Paris, were all, to a greater or lesser degree, characterised by non-violent forms of protest and civil disobedience (Gordon, 2008: 79; Kaufman, 2003: 289; King Jr, 1968: 59). Tactics within these movements were not exclusively non-violent, but it was non-violence that was popularised in public discourse (Gordon, 2008: 81). Peter Gelderloos rightly sees this celebration of non-violence as a 'falsified history of struggle', a phrase he uses to introduce his thesis that an exclusively non-violent ethos is ultimately racist, statist and patriarchal (2007: 2). He makes the point that the civil-rights movement was often more violent than it was made out to be. Gelderloos argues that '[p]acifist, middle-class black activists, including King, got much of their power from the specter of black resistance and the presence of armed black revolutionaries', noting the intense violent protests by blacks in Albany (1961) and Birmingham (1962) (2007: 13). Ward Churchill challenges similar assumptions regarding the US peace movement's role in ending the Vietnam War (Churchill, 2007).

Be that as it may, it was in this wider context of pacifist tactics dominating public discourse that anarchism awoke, with anarchists and anti-authoritarians sharing very different attitudes to violence. They were more inclined to advocate for urban confrontations that were violent when necessary (Gordon, 2008: 80). The arguments may have shifted from talk of political assassinations (perhaps with Greece as an exception), but for the most part anarchists and anti-authoritarians revived the historical anarchist trajectory supporting violence. Evidently, the Athenian milieu is testament to this propensity for violent performative protests.

But what does violence mean in the context of an Athenian street-protest? In February 2009, a police station in Κορυδαλλός (Korydallos), Athens, was sprayed with bullets and attacked with a hand grenade (Al Jazeera, 2009).

There is something notably different between lobbing back a tear gas canister at police during protests and throwing a grenade at a police station. Juris's attempts at clarification are helpful in establishing a distinction. He suggests that the difference between anarchist performative violence and what he calls 'direct political violence' is that the latter causes 'death or injury to human beings' (2005: 415). Juris adds that the difference 'is often one of degree' (2005: 415). I am sympathetic to this distinction because although some of my informants went to protests with a *willingness* to inflict harm on police or fascists (if it came to that), these same activists did not usually attend actions with the *intention* of inflicting harm on others. The difference here between willingness and intention is important even though, as Juris anticipates, respondents were aware that Athenian street-protests regularly involved physically violent confrontations, leading to at least injury. Alternatively, a number of respondents told me that they were there to, in Kosta's words, 'smash faces', although the idea of killing someone was never mentioned. In this context, there is a substantive difference between being involved in probable political violence that may result in the injury of antagonists, and a targeted assassination. As such, I see performative violence in Athenian street-protests as including all forms of physical violence, but in most instances excluding the intention to cause death.

This brings us to a consideration of whether property damage in a street-protest is a violent act. On the one hand, a minority of informants contend that attacks on property are not acts of violence. One informant, Panayiotta, likens any implication that they are to a 'colonisation of humanity by capitalist property talk'. Her argument is that private property should not be anthropomorphised and granted the same status as an individual's right to exist, free of harm. Equally, Aris argues that property damage is merely symbolic destruction of 'an inanimate object' and therefore is not a violent act. The ACME[1] collective, an anarchist/anti-authoritarian affinity group involved in property attacks during the World Trade Organization (WTO) protests in Seattle in 1999, expresses a similar sentiment. The ACME collective had this to say on the issue of property damage:

> We contend that property destruction is not a violent activity unless it destroys lives or causes pain in the process. By this definition, private property – especially corporate private property – is itself infinitely more violent than any action taken against it ... When we smash a window, we aim to destroy the thin veneer of legitimacy that surrounds private property rights. (2000, cited in Gordon, 2008: 81)

In contrast, most of my respondents saw it differently. Property damage was an act of violence both because its intention was to inflict harm upon others (usually the owners of the property) and because of the internal emotions conveyed through the act itself; that is, the intention of the protagonist was to be violent. On the latter point, Acacia said that as she launched a projectile at a bank window, she was venting her frustrations. The feelings she had 'can only be described as a bit bloodthirsty' [Acacia]. Taki had just smashed an ATM when I asked him if he thought it was a violent act. Taki responded:

> Of course ρε [mate], did you see me go at the machine? I know it's not real – I know it is just an ATM. But I am sending a warning that capitalism is not welcome here. Is this a violent message? What do you say? Of course. It is a physical concoction designed to say fuck off! Or I'll break you too!

In his writing about anarchism, a similar theme is taken up by Ashen Ruins who sees property damage as a violent act:

> Instead of claiming that smashing a window isn't violent – a point that average people reject out of common sense (and therefore makes me wonder about the common sense of some anarchists) – why don't we drop the semantics and admit that, yes, it's very clearly violent and then make a case for it? Do we consider the Israeli bulldozing of Palestinian homes non-violent? If, on the other hand, smashing a window is merely a symbolic act, but not violent, what message are we trying to send? (2002, para. 7)

Evidently, a definition of political violence is fraught with complexities even within the narrow confines of anarchist political violence. Some have drawn from this the conclusion that violence cannot be defined clearly (Gelderloos, 2007: 3). It seems to me that the absence of a definition is completely unsatisfactory, as it makes any analysis of 'violence' even more confusing than it otherwise would be, because we are not clear about precisely what it is that we are talking about. For this reason, I begin with Gordon's definition as a starting point for my own definition, though one that requires modifying.

Gordon, writing with contemporary anarchist and anti-authoritarian violence in mind, defines an act as violent, '*if its recipient experiences it as an attack or as deliberate endangerment*' (Gordon, 2008: 93, emphasis in original). Here, he includes attacks on humans as well as property, although he attaches a disclaimer to the latter. He says that property damage is only violent if a person or persons with a stake in the property (owners or employees, for example) witness and experience the attack as violent, or if a passer-by sees the act and, as a result, fears for his or her own life (Gordon, 2008: 94). Thus, in the context of the wrecking of ATMs in an Athenian riot where no bank employees or associated officials witness the act, then it is not a violent act, regardless of the harm it causes. For Gordon, then, the victim's experience of the attack as violent largely defines violence.

While I agree with the sentiment that violence needs to be witnessed and experienced as such if it is to count as violence, Gordon's definition misses an additional consideration. Definitions of violence also need to consider the intentions of the perpetrator of the acts in question. Gordon's definition largely ignores the agency of the perpetrators of violence. This passes over an important political point. If the perpetrator witnesses and intends an act to cause harm, then it is violent. Here, I am referring to the individual or group that commits the violent act because they believe themselves to be oppressed or subjugated and respond by choosing violence. After all, agency and autonomy are important elements of anti-authoritarian and anarchist politics and should inform a definition of violence that is describing their actions. I am deliberately politicising the definition so that perpetrators' concerns also inform a description of what is a violent act. In the examples I presented earlier with Taki and the ATM, as well as Acacia and the bank window, both of them wanted it known that when they participate in property damage, they consider it a violent act. For that reason, alongside parts of Gordon's definition, Charles Tilly's definition of collective violence is also useful.

Tilly is also concerned with political violence and the nuances of property damage, but unconcerned about whether the victim of the harm experienced it directly. Tilly defines collective violence as an 'episodic social interaction that immediately inflicts physical damage on persons and/or objects [involving] at least two perpetrators of damage [resulting] at least in part from coordination among persons who perform the damaging acts' (2003: 3).

Tilly's use of the phrase 'social interaction' – whereby collective violence 'amounts to a kind of conversation, however brutal or one-sided that conversation may be' – is very apt for the performative symbolic aspect of violent street-protest that has been discussed (2003: 6). I would only add that collective violence need not involve 'at least two perpetrators of the damage', but may also entail individual acts of violence that are part of a broader collective movement. Consequently, I define violence as an 'episodic social interaction that inflicts physical damage on persons and/or objects', as defined by the perpetrator and the aggrieved party. This more aptly conveys Athenian anarchist and anti-authoritarian sentiments on street-protest violence.

As I have already pointed out, there is nothing pacifist about the Athenian anarchist and anti-authoritarian movement's attitudes to street-protests. No one I interviewed supports an exclusive ethos of non-violent street-protests. Even those who advocate non-violent action (on occasion) felt it necessary to justify violence as a legitimate tactic under certain conditions. Take the Marfin Bank example discussed in the previous chapter, which began as part of a street-protest. Some activists were hostile to the

Marfin Bank arson but only because the arson was not deemed appropriate violence. Zizo encapsulated this position when he said, 'I don't think we want to be pro-violence every time we leave the squat, sure. But I am not going to stand there and watch my brothers and sisters get hurt. That is unconscionable.'[2] Although their threshold for violence varies, all respondents saw violence as appropriate in certain instances. No one said that violence was never justified. Polletta and Jasper suggest that inasmuch as protest participation reflects the will of the individual, the 'forms of protest' deployed are informed by a space's collective identities (2001: 284). In the case of Athenian anarchists and anti-authoritarians, processes of collective identity are influenced by an ethos of what I call *appropriate* violence. That is, it is perfectly acceptable to use violence if it can be justified.

Not surprisingly, there is a range of reasons for why Athenian anarchists and anti-authoritarians participate in violent, militant activity within a street-protest. Along with the historical influences that were mentioned in previous chapters (and the work on emotions to be discussed), contemporary political circumstances were also tendered as justifications. Stavro and Aleko cited the behaviour of the Athenian police, particularly the MAT (Μονάδες Αποκατάστασης Τάξης, the riot police) and ΔΕΛΤΑ squads (Δύναμη Ελέγχου Ταχείας Αντιμετώπισης, the rapid response force) as being important justifications for violence. Here, Stavro and Aleko refer to allegations against the Athenian police that include claims of torture, deprivation of liberties and complicity with fascist pogroms (Amnesty International, 2013; Dalakoglou, 2013; Margaronis, 2012; Occupied London, 2013). This has echoes of Franz Fanon's justification and support for counter-violence against colonialist forces by colonised masses (1965: 249). Fanon argues that violence is appropriate counter-action because of the relentlessly dehumanising attacks from the colonialist state (1965: 249). Taking a slightly different but related approach, Tina, Christo, Helena and Yianni spoke of their desire to defend their liberated spaces, such as squats, parks and even a neighbourhood (Exarcheia). Tina described the scene as 'constantly under barrage', whether from the police trying to evict them from squats or the government trying to commercialise a public space. In this context, violence is viewed as a necessary tactic for defending the anarchist and anti-authoritarian space.

Others spoke more broadly about participating in antagonisms against the state and its forces, which is part of the struggle against all forms of domination in society. Whereas Tina justifies violence when it is a response to physical attacks on the space, Andreas calls for violence against general 'aggressions against anarchism', like the presence of capitalist institutions in Athens. Kosta extends Andreas's wider conceptualisation of what constitutes an attack – and therefore a justified counter-attack – calling anarchist and anti-authoritarian manoeuvres an 'act of war' against hostile enemies. He argues that it is completely acceptable to attack banks, government offices and the police, because of the 'battle' against all forms of domination [Kosta].

Linking all these justifications is the notion that street-protest violence is acceptable because it 'is precisely prefigurative of anarchist social relations' (Gordon, 2008: 99). There is a general acceptance that violent, physical struggle is almost inevitable in Greece, in the light of the historical attacks against radical leftists, be they Marxists, communists or anarchists (and for that matter even social democrats, at least during the Junta years). In company with individual justifications, like defence of the space against external attacks, the propensity to engage in violent street-protests is justified by general anarchist and anti-authoritarian principles. All of my respondents agreed that in an anarchist and anti-authoritarian society, violence might be required to defend the space against attempts to reimpose hierarchical social orders; hence violence is an accepted component of anarchist and anti-authoritarian praxis.

Shared and negotiated attitudes on violent street-protests give shape to the Athenian anarchist and anti-authoritarian space. Conversations and interactions around these perspectives produce 'cognitive definitions concerning the ends, means, and field of action' (Melucci, 1995a: 44). These conversations are encoded within a set of rituals and practices. These rituals and practices are perpetually constructed through negotiation, conflict and compromise. Take, for example, the rituals associated with militant street-protests. Since 1984, when Black Bloc tactics appeared in Athens at a conference of Europe's Far Right, violent militancy has often been the preferred suite of street-protest styles for anarchists and anti-authoritarians. This is a product of constant and relentless negotiations between activists. As the nature of these rituals are negotiated and discussed by contemporary activists, they continue to inform the processes of collective identity. In Athens, therefore, militant protesting is an informative influence on the anarchist and anti-authoritarian space, as opposed to the more carnivalised protest actions in other parts of the world (St John, 2008).

The combative intensity of Athenian street-protest builds solidarity amongst anarchists and anti-authoritarians. As activists engage in street-protests, negotiations and conversations unfold about violence, actions and unity. For Dino, a street-protest means, 'you have to engage with your comrades [in the protest]. Help them. Work together. Otherwise you'll get fucked over by the pigs.' Along the same lines, Pari talked of the strong relationships developed during protests. 'We might disagree on many things', Pari said, 'but there, together we fight as brothers and sisters.' Confrontation with the enemy or an antagonist, even if it comes from a ritualised and expected process, can produce a positive emotional output. Borrowing from Émile Durkheim, Randall Collins refers to this as 'effervescence', where collective action produces bursts of shared euphoric emotion, which binds participants through the experience (Barker, 2001: 188; Collins, 2001: 30–31).

This, in turn, has the potential to replenish and boost the confidence of collectives involved, enhancing cohesion within the movement (Collins, 2004: 47–49; Polletta and Jasper, 2001: 290).[3]

Collective identity: emotions in street-protests

Athenian street-protests are like a 'dramatic dance between multiple social actors' (Seferiades and Johnston, 2012b: 18), as anarchists and anti-authoritarians come together to fight for their space, confront police and fascists and to damage banks, hotels and government buildings. This ritualised protest form is far more than a 'hollow ritual' (Peterson et al., 2012: 282). Rather, these events have significant emotional meaning for participants, its potency enhanced by the use of one's body as radical resistance (Juris, 2008: 126). Emotions are the glue that binds people together, allowing forms of interactions that produce social movements. At the same time, they can 'drive people apart and push them to tear down social structures and to challenge cultural traditions' (Turner and Stets, 2005: 1). Emotions forged before, during and after the melees of street-protests play a central role in the reflexive processes of collective identity construction (Yang, 2000).

In Chapter 2, I noted that my approach to emotions in social movements is guided by Jasper's social-constructivist typology of protest-related emotions in his article 'Emotions and social movements: twenty years of theory and research' (2011). Here, it is important to repeat that I am not referring to emotions that come from what Jasper calls urges, like the 'urgent bodily needs that crowd out other feelings and attention until they are satisfied: lust, hunger, substance addictions, the need to urinate or defecate, exhaustion or pain' (2011: 286). Instead, I am interested in three types of emotions, namely reflex emotions, long-term emotions and moral emotions (Jasper, 2011: 287). Reflex emotions are those that come from 'reactions to our immediate physical and social environment, usually quick to appear and to subside, and accompanied by a package of facial expressions and bodily changes' (Jasper, 2011: 287). These emotions include reactions to moral shocks and injustices that occur before our eyes and produce feelings like hatred and anger. I lost count of the number of times I would be mid-way through a conversation during a protest, for example, when my interviewee would catch something out of the corner of their eye – some perceived villainy usually on the part of the police – causing them to bolt from our conversation to the site of the offence or launch abuse at the offending parties.

The second type of emotions I consider in this chapter are long-term emotions, which include feelings of affinity and revenge as well as affective loyalties such as 'love, liking, respect, trust, admiration' (Jasper, 2011: 287). These emotions can occur before and after the street-protest. After one incident at an occupation where a young protester was bleeding heavily, a fellow anti-authoritarian, whom she did not know, attended to her injuries, bandaged and patched her up. Over the course of the next month, a strong emotional bond matured between them, as they kept bumping into each other in Exarcheia. Before I left Athens, I interviewed them both and they talked of a project they were developing together based on sharing first-aid skills with protesters.

The third type of emotions is what Jasper calls moral emotions, which is the 'feelings of approval and disapproval based on moral intuitions and principles ... such as compassion for the unfortunate or indignation over injustice' (2011: 287). These emotions do not necessarily play out immediately and can include feelings of pride, liberation and empowerment. A notable sentiment within the Athenian milieu, for example, is that Athens is a significant part of the front-line of international anarchism. With this comes a vigorous commitment to the anarchist and anti-authoritarian project, mindful of an obligation to anarchists in other regions active in much smaller and less advanced milieux. Over a coffee after a protest, Tina mentioned the following:

> From time-to-time I think about how what we do in the streets inspires other comrades elsewhere – especially – comrades living under worse conditions and oppression. With this burden and obligation comes an immense satisfaction and feeling of privilege, and yes, my [direct action] intensity is educated by this.

Tina's feelings of satisfaction and pride in fighting for her beliefs are examples of moral emotions. I now move on to specific emotions, starting with trust.

Emotional politics: anger is a gift

I consider trust an emotion for the following reason. One aspect of trust is that it stems from a calculated assumption about a particular event or person. In part, it is based on a rational belief constructed from experiences and knowledge. At the same time, Bernd Lahno (2001) identifies that it is also based on something else that transcends this rational calculation. The trust we feel for another individual is ultimately a relationship based on building up a database of their interactions with ourselves but also includes our feelings towards them. In that sense, 'trust is beyond the direct control of reason' and therefore is an emotion (Calhoun, 1984; de Sousa, 1987; Lahno, 2001: 185).

Earlier in this chapter, I quoted Dino stating that an expectation within street-protests is that 'you have to engage with your comrades [in the protest]. Help them. Work together. Otherwise you'll get fucked over by the pigs.' An important aspect to his comment is the emotion of trust. Trust encourages activists to act in particular ways that help to unify the space. It provides confidence in the forms of relationships and organising networks prevalent throughout anarchist and anti-authoritarian milieux (for a discussion on trust as it relates to Hardt and Negri's notion of the commons, see Arvanitakis 2007). In Athens and elsewhere, unity within affinity groups, which is a critical element of anarchist networks, is forged by emotional connections around anarchist politics. As Nathan Clough argues, '[w]ithout trust, comradely connection, and a non-hierarchic organization, anarchist politics cannot be practiced' (2012: 1674). In street-protests, tightly knit affinity groups provide a measure of safety and security, whereby if an activist is targeted by antagonists, there is nearly always committed help nearby.

Beyond affinity groups, there is also trust among activists who only know each other slightly. Vasili and Pari separately spoke of their faith and trust that they would not be betrayed to the police, regardless of the acts they chose to pursue in street-protests. Vasili referred to this as an 'anonymity bond'. This extends beyond their immediate circle of activists, taking in fellow anarchists and anti-authoritarians that they may only know by name or face, or even not at all. In her article on the role of emotions in social movements, Marina Sitrin observed persistent talk of trust amongst the Occupy participants in New York as well as leftist activists in Greece and Spain (2013). It is a highly political understanding of trust, based less on love and affection for one another and more on a way of communicating political messages. She writes that it is not a '"love thy neighbour" sort of politics, but an affirmation of one another in the new relationships we are creating grounded in trust and affect' (Sitrin, 2013: para. 5). The political messages conveyed in Athens promote freedom of action and praxis, actions that may be dissected and critiqued but will not result in betrayal leading to incarceration. Verta Taylor and Nancy Whittier saw trust in a similar fashion as a pivotal component of community building in the radical feminist movement in the 1960s (1995).

Observations about the significance of trust are not limited to anarchist theorists, academics or activists. They also include the police and security agencies. Clough (2012) writes that state enforcement agencies are very much aware of the importance of trust in anarchist organising structures, to the extent that they actively target and aim to disrupt trust networks. A number of methods are used, including 'infiltration, surveillance, and spreading paranoia and dissent among such groups' (Clough, 2012: 1678). Amory Starr and her colleagues (2008) advise that the end result of police infiltration is the creation of a culture of fear and a heightened concern regarding the cost of participating in social movement activity for actors. Based on my own observations and those of my respondents, I would suggest that the possibility of police infiltration has not had the same demobilising effect discussed by Clough (2012) and Starr et al. (2008). Attempts by police to disrupt trust networks have been largely unsuccessful and have instead acted to strengthen the reliance on personal interactions and connections. It definitely produces paranoia and mistrust within the movement, but this is overcome by strong interpersonal connections, and – in my experience – time. The integrity of networks is on show during conflicts, manifesting itself in a unified force.

Emboldened by emotional bonds of trust and the relative safety they bring, Athenian activists feel themselves free to pursue rebellious actions within street-protests. In turn, rebellious acts of revolt have the potential to produce shared moments of joy and euphoria, further binding the anarchist and anti-authoritarian space. Alongside the political benefits of participation in militant direct action (like occupying a government building, or throwing a Molotov cocktail at a luxury car dealership), and the personal satisfaction the central protagonist in this event might receive, actions also help bind the anarchist and anti-authoritarian space. These actions produce shared moments of joy or euphoria. Elias Canetti (1962: 20) alludes to this in his description of the crowd, where an 'individual feels that he [sic] is transcending the limits of his own person'. I noticed this most evidently after the fact, when 'shared moments of euphoria and joy' occurred and these were often reiterated after the protest, on our return to the square or a squat, where stories of the day's protest were exchanged. Reliving heroic events is part of the process of communication that binds participants of collective actions; a socialising process leading to adhesion, solidarity and pleasure. Fillieule (2012: 237) sees this behaviour as yielding 'the sense that "we" are together in word and deed'. Jasper (2011: 294) also suggests that collectives are strengthened when they share emotional responses to particular events.

Linked with this is Gavin Grindon's representation of the importance of 'joy, desire and mythic moments of potent affect' in acts of protest (2007: 94; see also Routledge and Simons, 1995). Referring specifically to the global justice movement, Grindon retells the story of an activist evading police arrest by jumping off a pole and over the heads of the police into the raised hands of waiting activists, who then whisked him away (2007: 94–95). Such events serve as part of the festival of protest, whereby performative acts contribute to protest narratives (Grindon, 2007: 95). This is equally the case in Athens, where particular protest actions, such as a protester escaping the grasps of the police or a well-volleyed return of a tear gas canister, have a heightened degree of potency because they produce almost mythical moments. From them come euphoric emotions, like joy, jubilation or a sense of ecstatic empowerment (see Yang, 2000). Graeber (2002: 65) also wrote of his own 'exhilarating experience' when he participated in bringing down a security barrier in the Quebec City Summit of the Americas protest.

Athenian anarchists and anti-authoritarians are mindful of the emotional importance of exhilarating protest moments. Amongst respondents, there was a fair degree of hostility towards pacifist, liberal-democratic protest tactics. Paraphrasing part of the argument, traditional tactics fail to challenge normative, liberal-pluralist political interactions and are merely subservient to a repertoire deemed appropriate by the state and entrenched political organisations, including trade unions. The shared understanding was that as well as being ineffective politically, they fail to produce equivalent moments of pleasure (see Handelman, 1990). Apart from structural hostility towards liberal-democratic repertoires, I heard accusations that these tactics were tedious. Insofar as liberal-democratic repertoires of action, like marching, singing and then going home, are purposeful protest actions that '"stimulate the will" of *actors* engaging in action' (Roth, 1995: 319, emphasis in original), Pari felt that these were rather mundane. Traditional protest-march repertoires 'are boring' he said, as they are unable to produce moments of rebellious pleasure. In contrast, smashing a symbol of capitalism or a fiery interaction with the state's armed forces can produce solidarity and connectivity amongst participants, because of its radicalism. As Clough observes, there is something ultimately unifying about a group of individuals taking a 'flying leap ... from the precipice of sanctioned behavior' (Clough, 2012: 1677). I noticed after Dino had put the final pieces of a barricade together with some other black-clad men and women, he came towards me with a huge smile on his face. Dino had experienced a form of shared pleasure derived from rebellious anarchistic action and urban insurrection.

In Elisabeth Jean Wood's study on insurrectionist activity against state forces in El Salvador (1987–96), her participants 'took profound pride and pleasure in their insurrectionary activities' (2001: 273). I saw an equivalent example of emotional pleasure and joy when Mary talked about her pride in maintaining and rejuvenating the anarchist and anti-authoritarian space. Mary who receives immense satisfaction from being part of a vibrant milieu, said 'it doesn't bother me that I have to riot, [because] living in a squat and living Anarchy with others makes it worth it'. Pride in the space also plays out with respect to developing the international reputation of Athenian anarchism and anti-authoritarian politics. I mentioned earlier that pride contributes to some of the violent street-action justifications, whereby there is pride in Athens's place as one of the more significant anarchist and anti-authoritarian milieux. From pride comes concern over reputation – not of individual reputation – but the reputation of the anarchist and anti-authoritarian space. In a conversation with Electra, she talked about the obligations that come from Athens being one of the world's foremost anarchist and anti-authoritarian locations and what it meant to her: 'We have tourist-activists, and now academics coming to study us' she said as she nodded her head to me; 'that is not why we come out here, but I know that we have to keep up the fight because we are leading the way'. With this, comes a sense of belonging and connection with other activists, whereby pride produces what Thomas Scheff calls a 'secure bond' between participants (1994: 3).

Associated with pride is the feeling of self-liberation and empowerment. In a street-protest, Aris and Bill felt empowered because they have a physical and emotional outlet for their radical critique of the system. Aris explained: 'Fundamentally, I am against fascism. When I have the chance to prevent fascism from operating, even for a moment, it is immensely satisfying. I feel powerful. Our goals are possible.'

Aris experiences empowerment as part of a collective that is disrupting demonstrations organised by the Far Right. With Bill, his story ran deeper. Up until his early twenties, Bill identified with the democratic Left and aspects of Greek national identity, to the point where he was more than happy to register for compulsory military service; my understanding is that this is extremely uncommon for anyone who is now either an anarchist or an anti-authoritarian, or both. His service coincided with his personal journey of anarchist radicalisation, apparently 'a horrible environment to be in when you realise you are fond of anarchist politics'. Bill describes the maturation of his anarchist identity as a difficult process as he started to challenge the institutions that he had once held dear. It was only during the emotionally potent riots of December 2008, when he saw his comrades torching a police car, that he finally began 'to feel liberated' [Bill]. Helena Flam talks about the 'long process of emotional liberation', in which individuals abandoned bonds, loyalties and 'other positive emotions from institutions and organizations they were' attached to (2005: 31–32). Flam sees this as a gradual process of emotional transformation, involving the severance of old emotional bonds and the formation of new bonds. As Bill watched other anarchists and anti-authoritarians engaging in militant direct action during a street-protest, he was forming new emotional bonds with the milieu that he is part of today.

Whereas Bill experienced a sense of liberation, an event like December 2008 – sparked by the murder of Grigoropoulos – also acts as a moral shock, drawing people to the space. In the discussion of December 2008, Zizo talked of a swelling in the ranks of the movement and the sense of unity that ensued. Indeed, we should hardly be surprised that there is a direct link between particularly offensive police acts and a counter-desire to join a movement and be part of a response (see Nepstad and Smith, 2001: 164; Risley, 2011; Wettergren, 2005).

Besides potential spikes in recruitment, moral shocks also play an important role within collectives, by strengthening and further radicalising movement actors (Polletta and Jasper, 2001: 292). During the uprising, Aris observed the 'power in the streets', while Kyriako also spoke of his amazement at having '20,000 people alongside you' and how this felt 'immense'. Aris and Kyriako's descriptions convey a heightened energy within the space, bolstering unity in the face of a moral shock. In her work on the

1986 *Bowers* v. *Hardwick* case involving the US gay and lesbian movement, where the court upheld the US state of Georgia's sodomy laws criminalising consensual homosexual acts, Gould contends that moral shocks can entrench radicalism and help to maintain allegiances and commitment (2009: 134; see also Brockett, 2005: 295). Along with the emotional and physical responses to the moral shock of December 2008 came a greater fortitude and tenacity amongst movement actors in Athens.

An additional consequence of moral shock is a desire for revenge. In the Athenian context, I saw it materialise as a fusion of revenge and rage. I witnessed violent street actions fuelled by a desire to right perceived injustices, punctuated by a fervent desire to inflict harm. Kosta was its most ardent proponent. In every street-protest he participated in, his goal was to inflict harm on police. He felt that he owed it to his fallen comrades to pursue this goal relentlessly. His insistence upon revenge was part of his ambition to prevent the state dehumanising anarchists and anti-authoritarians. In his words, 'I want them [police and elites] to be constantly suffering, so they always know we are there and that we are alive.' Kosta is revolting against dehumanising attempts by forces conspiring against the anarchist and anti-authoritarian space. I heard this attitude repeated many times. As Paulo Freire notes, 'dehumanization, although a concrete historical fact, is *not* a given destiny but the result of an unjust order that engenders violence in the oppressors, which in turn dehumanizes the oppressed' (2000 [1970]: 21, emphasis in original). When Kosta and those like him come together in a street-protest, they are able to share their desires for revenge and reclaim agency they believe has been stripped from their community.

Andreas echoes Kosta's attitude. I saw him propelling a chunk of marble at a security barrier protecting some bank windows, when three policemen charged at him and tried to pin him down. He fought them with such ferocity and aggression that he was able to escape relatively unharmed while also having landed some punches of his own. I spoke to him very shortly after and he calmly said that 'nothing gives me more satisfaction than inflicting pain on them, for their relentless abuses'. Wood's (2001: 268) research on El Salvador reinforces this notion that a political response inspired by rage can be as much emotional as it is cognitive. In the early days of resistance to state oppression, Wood's respondents recognised that expression of their rage 'at the arbitrary and brutal violence of authorities' was intertwined with a desire to reclaim agency (2001: 268). Andreas, Kosta and others are acting and feeling much the same way as Wood's respondents. Through the actions of rebelling aggressively and in anger, they are attempting to restore dignity in the face of the injustices of security forces. Linking the reclamation of agency to an 'emotional' response like rage blurs the dichotomous distinction of rational and irrational action. Examples like Wood's indicate that rage can be both a cognitive and physical response to particular circumstances – as much rational as it is irrational (Calhoun, 2001a: 47; Jasper,

2003: 155). Kosta and Andreas's behaviour was calculated, in that before every street-protest they had the stated intention of injuring police. They would talk to their comrades about these exact desires and share their plans. Nonetheless, they are also driven by rage, which is triggered when they are confronted with the lines of riot police. I was able to view this same rage amongst other activists as the 'enemy' was sighted.

I now turn to examples of hatred that although predicated on an ongoing sense of injustice, were fuelled and escalated during the protest itself, rather than being premeditated as with than Kosta and Andreas' actions. Writing broadly about social movements, Seferiades and Johnston note that 'hatred can be activated quickly by precipitating events that reveal intolerable levels of injustice, by suddenly imposed grievances and/or by excessively coercive conduct on the part of the police' (2012b: 12). Hostile and immediate reactions to perceived injustices are part of the street-protest landscape in Athens. During an action where a huge police line had charged a small group of protesters, encircling them and then punishing them with their shields, I could see people around me begin to get angrier and louder and start looking for things to hurl. The chants and the taunts directed at the police became more vitriolic, where police were described as γουρούνια [pigs] and δολοφονοι [killers]. Indeed, The chant I heard most commonly was 'μπατσοι, γουρουνια, δολοφονοι', which, as mentioned earlier, translates as cops (slang), pigs, killers. It was often in these instances that I saw respondents who had not given any indication of a propensity for violence, unleash projectiles in anger. In a different action, Electra, who had earlier that day talked to me about the machismo element of violent interaction, was one such protagonist launching rocks at police with a group of her comrades. When we made eye contact, I smiled and raised my eyebrows as if to say 'what's going on?' She came over to me and said, 'I am not a fan of violence, but please, did you see what they did? They were aiming the tear gas flat, at our bodies. Enough! Everyone has a limit.' Electra was referring to the fact that rather than shooting the tear gas canister with a lobbing motion, the police were shooting with a flat trajectory. Electra was suggesting this was a deliberate attempt to hurt protesters with the impact of the tear gas canister. She and her fellow activists collectively responded to this sense of injustice by militantly engaging with the police.

Activists also shared other instances of anger and hatred. It was often the case that events would be calm, but for some chanting and taunting, only for a policeman (they were always men) to push, grab or rough up an activist. This was often the catalyst for anarchists and anti-authoritarians to react angrily. In her comparative analysis of political violence in Germany and Italy, della Porta observes that, '[s]tronger solidarity within radical groups fuelled hatred for opponents – members of right-wing groups, and also the police – who, in the militants' eyes, became progressively dehumanized' (1995: 204). For spaces like Athens, with an acute embrace of solidarity, there was overt hatred directed at the police and, on occasion, fascists. This was always accompanied by the dehumanising that was mentioned by della Porta, in which, as in my earlier example, they equate the police with pigs and killers.

Hatred can also lead to a greater propensity for violence. In Chapter 5, I presented Aleko's thoughts on gaining protest experience, whereby his heart still pumped quickly in the heat of the protest, but that experience gave him composure. Despite his claims, Aleko was actually one of the more emotional activists I engaged with, in that he was deeply moved by the physical injustices he saw. He would get so angry at police agitation that I saw him – more than any – run into melees with the police. He would do this with the help of his comrades. In her work, della Porta notes that '[t]he activists' acceptance of violence grew along with their emotional investment in politics, and their emotional investment intensified with their experience of violence' (1995: 204). Aggravated by events within actions, hatred leads to more intense violence against a common threat. As a result, the street-protest acts as a site both for the physical manifestation of common struggle and as a place where emotional investment that comes from this struggle is shared and negotiated.

Athenian street-protests can be deeply emotional events. Emotional investment is a core component of the processes of collective identity construction, enabling 'individuals to feel like part of a common unity' (Melucci, 1995a: 44; see also Yang 2000: 596). As these emotions are shared and negotiated within the protest they shape and inform the movement itself (see Denzin 1984: 93). The most common outcome is the production of solidarity. This can take the form of a temporary solidarity limited by the life of the street-protest (see Denzin, 1984: 79), like sharing an immediate reaction and response to a perceived injustice. It can also take the form of more long-term emotional connections, such as solidarity that transcends the collective action, in the form of trust relationships forged in the heat of the protest, yet transferable to other interactions within the space. For the purpose of a coherent discussion, I have neatly catalogued emotions but in reality, emotions overlap and coalesce – being repeatedly negotiated and discussed (Jasper, 2011: 299). The negotiation and sharing of emotions give shape to the anarchist and anti-authoritarian space. Here we learn of the pride in the Athenian space, the concern about reputation, the desire for empowerment and the want of revenge. These emotional interactions shape the Athenian anarchist and anti-authoritarian processes of collective identity.

Conclusion: unity in action

In social movement research, studies of demonstrations and protests traditionally focus on aspects that inform the political processes of a movement, like protest goals, recruitment, successes and failures (McAdam, 1982; Tarrow, 1994; Tilly, 1986). While offering beneficial insights into social movements more generally, they tend to exclude a range of perspectives, meanings and relationships produced within social movements. Instead, I have focused on the complex and reflexive interactions that occur as movement actors interact with each other, be it in the squat, in assemblies or in the protest's furnace. I have looked at the influence of rituals, symbols, affinities, bonds and emotions. In the last decade since 2002, there has been an increase in the body of research collecting data on individual and group participation, in a range of protests against neo-liberalism (Blocq et al., 2012; Fominaya, 2007; Juris, 2005). With a focus on often-neglected emotional dynamics, this chapter has offered a further contribution to this growing body of research.

Melucci (1995a, 1996) presents collective identity, not as a fixed conglomeration of individual identities, but a process, whereby political actors themselves produce meanings and negotiate decisions on action. In Athens, actors are consciously reflecting, alone and in groups, on the effects of street-protests on the space. One aspect is the way in which performative violence and emotions give meaning to the social and political interactions that occur during street-protests and occupations as well as assemblies and meetings. Looking at armed political collectives, Bosi and Giugni (2012) found a number of positive outcomes for groups engaged in political violence. They identify a range of emotional consequences, such as the reclamation of dignity, group affirmation and achievement and the improvement of morale as contributing to a collective's internal solidarity (Bosi and Giugni, 2012: 32). In my study of Athenian anarchists and anti-authoritarians, I found that militant street-protests help to produce a distinct – albeit potentially temporary – solidarity amongst actors within the space. As activists defend their political existence, they are unified in the face of destructive forces.

Despite tensions within the anarchist and anti-authoritarian milieu, militant street-protests offer a glue to bind activists. Street-protest rituals like performative violence act as forms of communication between activists, strengthening the bonds that link networks within the space. The combative ferocity of street-protests also builds solidarity as activists engage in negotiations about 'appropriate' violence and direct action, all the while confronting antagonistic enemies. Furthermore, the street-protest acts as a focus for the expression of a confluence of emotions, where anarchists and anti-authoritarians share intense feelings such as hatred, trust, empowerment, revenge and rage. The effect of this interplay allows people to be part of a common unity, again contributing to solidarity within the space. Even though there are significant tensions and sources of disagreement in the Athenian anarchist and anti-authoritarian space, the ritualised street-protest form produces solidarity. In turn, this tangibly informs the movement's collective identity.

By sharing emotions and experiences in street-protests and direct actions, the multitude of currents, tendencies and frictions are temporarily overcome in the face of common antagonists. Anarchists and anti-authoritarians of all stripes and colours are under such a constant barrage of attacks from the police and from the Far Right, that it is noteworthy that the movement has survived and flourished over the past three decades. Their moments of unity and shared experiences in conflict arguably account for a component of this longevity. I revisit this and other central themes in my concluding remarks.

Notes

1 This is not an acronym.
2 The Greek word Zizo used was παράλογος. It can also mean preposterous.
3 On the other hand, in her work on altruistic social movement groups, Erika Summers Effler shows how poorly implemented rituals can have the opposite effect by discouraging participation (Effler, 2010: 42; Jasper, 2011; 294).

Conclusion: imagining and fighting for alternative realities

I began this book by locating Athenian anarchists and anti-authoritarians within Greece's contemporary economic, social and political crisis. I noted that neo-liberal economic policies have led to mass unemployment and declines in health and educational services, which in turn produced a climate of deep political volatility. As a result of imposed austerity and unemployment, more than a fifth of the Greek population live below the poverty line. The nation's small birth rate has fallen by 15 per cent in the last three years, and the incidences of stillbirths are up by 21.5 per cent, because many pregnant women cannot afford prenatal screening (Smith, 2013b).

At the start of 2015, Tsipras's SYRIZA and their coalition allies came to power riding a wave of nationalistic revolt over Troika-imposed austerity measures, buoyed by heady, if unrealistic, popular expectations for change. By July of the same year, battered into submission by a brutal negotiation process and unwilling to resist further, they were instead legislating in favour of continued austerity. This new Troika package is depressingly bleak and likely to trigger fresh, incendiary domestic political stresses. In this context, SYRIZA's successful September 2015 election result may seem surprising. After all, SYRIZA won the governmental election in the January 2015 election on an explicitly anti-austerity platform. They then proposed a referendum in July, which again overwhelmingly supported this policy direction. Despite these clear directives from a large number of Greek voters, the majority within SYRIZA succeeded in legislating to extend the austerity programme. Yet, the abandonment of such a treasured platform was barely punished by the electorate – the September 2015 election saw SYRIZA's representation in parliament only marginally reduced. Alexis Tsipras continued as prime minister.

On the one hand, it appears a significant proportion of Greek voters are still hostile to the old parties of PASOK and ND – the negligent captains that steered Greece into an economic maelstrom. For them, arguably, SYRIZA offers a glimmer of hope, or more simply they are not yet tarnished by ineptitude. On the other hand, although the September 2015 result reflects the voters' will, electoral turnout was remarkably low. It is significant that only 55 per cent of registered voters had their say, suggesting that voters have electoral fatigue or have little faith in any of the parties competing for power.

As for the anarchists and the anti-authoritarians, the focus of direct action has momentarily shifted. Insofar as further engaged fieldwork is necessary to apprehend the reality on the ground, 2015 did see a marked decline in the visible mass street-protests of the recent past. While weekend rituals of political melees continue, they appear as scuffles rather than explosive battles. Indeed, an occupation of SYRIZA's headquarters in March 2015 was poignant in that anarchists and anti-authoritarians stormed the building with calls of 'this is a symbolic protest' implying that no property damage would occur (Perseus999, 2015). This was previously unheard of. If, as I have argued, cohesiveness is significantly enhanced through these types of collective actions, then this abeyance may be concerning.

At the same time, there appears to be a concerted focus on other forms of direct action, like workers' self-management of factories and other workplaces, and actions geared towards the refugee crisis in Greece. Regarding the latter, and against the backdrop of declining living standards and acute uncertainty about the future, Greece is facing relentless waves of refugee arrivals by sea with more than 820,000 arriving in 2015 (IMO, 2015), an average of 2,250 per day. Around 500 Syrian refugees spent August 2015 living in Πεδίον του Άρεως (Areos Park) in Athens. Assistance to refugee communities and local victims of austerity measures is a continual concern for the Athenian anarchist and anti-authoritarian space.

Such manifestations of human misery, combined with Greece's long history of radical politics and regime change, has inspired both resistance and a belief in the real possibility of alternative political realities. The Athenian anarchist and anti-authoritarian movement has been at the forefront in imagining and fighting for these alternative realities.

This Conclusion revisits and summarises what I have learned about the movement, its internal constitution, dynamics and identity.

Retracing steps

The primary aim of my book was to unravel some of the internal complexities within the Athenian anarchist and anti-authoritarian milieu, and to provide a better understanding of the forces that give the movement its shape. To this end, I began by identifying the broader significance of this research agenda, and the contribution that the book makes. I emphasised two key aspects. On the one hand, understanding the form and substance of Athenian anarchist and anti-authoritarian politics is significant because of its geographical location. Greece, and more specifically Athens, has become the epicentre of capitalist economic crisis and radical resistance to that crisis. The people of Greece have borne the full brunt of the austerity measures demanded by the institutions of neo-liberal orthodoxy and executed by a servile Greek Parliament. This, coupled with Greece's fluctuating political dynamics, has produced fertile soil from which diverse movements for radical political change, both of the left and right, have grown and flourished. As such, Greece's fate may be telling for the future of the Eurozone project, parliamentary democracy and the current phase of capitalism. It may indeed present an image of the future for other indebted Western states.

On the other hand, the book is significant in that it contributes to our understanding of a subset of a much broader global movement – anarchists and anti-authoritarians who are at the forefront of resistance to the current phase of capitalism in multiple locations. Insofar as participants in this movement are linked by a commitment to challenge all forms of domination, they are not at all homogenous in the way that a unitary term such as 'movement' might seem to imply. Internationally, and in Athens, there is much diversity within this space, with individuals and different affinity groups producing their own interpretations of what are broadly anarchist politics. I have been at pains to both describe and explain this diversity, while also being mindful of that which holds it together – a shared commitment to a particular form of militant street resistance, which is central in the process of anarchist and anti-authoritarian identity formation.

With Melucci's process of collective identity as a theoretical frame through which to filter the bewildering array of experiences that I encountered in my fieldwork, I argued that despite internal tensions, the ritualised performative violence of the street-protest forges a sense of unity and thus temporarily binds the space. I presented the process of collective identity as a set of tools facilitating a more penetrative understanding of the factors informing collective action (Melucci, 1985: 793). I looked at the subtle and sometimes hidden aspects of the Athenian anarchist and anti-authoritarian space, as well as the more obvious and confronting images. With this came a heightened appreciation of phenomena like rituals, encoded language, symbols and emotional interactions between movement actors. It also helped to understand attitudes to history and the production and negotiation of activist folklore. This recalibration of the research agenda, away from the arguably more limited analysis of collective action within the political process theories, is evident throughout the book.

Another important component of my theoretical approach is the emphasis on agency and listening to and reproducing the voices of Athenian anarchists and anti-authoritarians themselves. As I noted, researchers tend to overlook the heterogeneity, diversity and complexity that exists within collectives. Whether lost in 'irrational' characterisations within collective behaviour models, or hidden in the 'rationality' of resource mobilisation and political process theory, important voices and narratives were either ignored or only addressed in passing. Related to this, activists' emotions and the way individuals react to different circumstances have also been ignored, which is tantamount to ignoring an essential part of what makes us human.

The result of such an approach led to a denial or at least an avoidance of movement actors' agency. This is even more acute for studies on anarchist and anti-authoritarian movements, which struggle for autonomy in a world of domination and subjugation. My work contributes to the countering of this trend both by its choice of theory and fieldwork framework.

To capture the data and insights necessary to comment on the internalities within the anarchist and anti-authoritarian space, I selected a militant ethnographic fieldwork approach. This meant that I was deliberately blurring the line between researcher and political activist by participating, as much as I felt able to, in Athenian direct actions. Apart from establishing significant bonds of trust that led to immensely productive conversations for this book, my personal involvement helped make the logic used by activists fluid and accessible (Juris, 2007: 165). Equally, militant ethnography mirrors the way anarchists and anti-authoritarians are producing their own analyses and commentary on their space – as insiders producing politically applicable work. It would be remiss and even disrespectful to engage with militants at the front line against the excesses of neo-liberalism and fascism, both of which have produced devastating consequences and negatively impacted the lives of millions, to subsequently produce research that is only relevant to an elite few. I admit that this is a difficult balancing act and it is for others to comment on the success of this tightrope walk.

With this in mind, in Chapter 3 I also noted that I shared my conclusions with a number of activist forums in Australia, as well as with many of the Athenian activists who helped form the arguments within the book. While militant ethnographic methods should produce politically applicable knowledge, the most beneficial forum for those insights is not necessarily restricted to the location of the study. I believe my work is far more relevant to activists outside of the Athenian space than to those within the milieu. In my experience, it has been far more insightful for those outside of the Athenian space to learn more about anarchism in action and the nuances of violent street-protests. I suggest this because I found the movement already highly aware and critical of itself and, at least in conversations, generally alert to the significance of street-protests. Furthermore, many of my observations came from the insights of actors themselves and were replicated in written work (Schwarz et al., 2010; Vradis and Dalakoglou, 2011; Occupied London, 2014).

Supported by this politically engaged and emotionally committed fieldwork method, as well as the process of collective identity toolbox, Chapters 4 and 5 presented and analysed conversations regarding activists' interpretation of their region's anarchist history. In line with my preferred theoretical framework, I explored these narratives with the purpose of presenting forces informing today's anarchist and anti-authoritarian movement's collective identity. In Chapter 4, I showed that contemporary activists consider themselves unconnected to the region's rich anarchist history prior to World War

II. In the few times when there was mention or acknowledgement of historical events, they reflected an insurrectionist and violent theme. This theme was more fully detailed in Chapter 5. Here, historical narratives conveyed a space inspired and informed by insurrectionist and anti-authoritarian events that are often consumed with violent and militant direct actions. For a variety of reasons, my respondents consistently chose to celebrate these forms of direct action. Yet as useful as these historical narratives are in capturing the dominance of violent repertoires within activist folklore, they do not tell the whole story. While contemporary activity is certainly informed by these trends, the propensity towards street-protest and violent acts are not premised on replicating history. I argued that attitudes to history inform contemporary processes of collective identity, but they do not govern them. There are many other factors informing participation in collective action, which fuels and is a symptom of difference and tension within the space.

The internal tensions within the Athenian anarchist and anti-authoritarian space belie any simplistic idea of unitary and homogenous collective actors. Tensions included but were not limited to divergent opinions on appropriate forms of direct action and how best to implement anarchist and anti-authoritarian ideas, alongside varying attitudes to violence, the mainstream media and gender and sexuality politics. That this is the case is not particularly surprising; anarchist and anti-authoritarian collectives and movements are, after all, premised on heterogeneity and the ability to dissent and challenge prevailing norms. In that regard, I have shown how Melucci's focus on collective identity as an ongoing and reflexive process makes it particularly suited to the study of heterogeneous and autonomous movements that celebrate and encourage internal diversity.

This focus on internal dimensions and tensions does not diminish the significance of collective action. On the contrary, collective action informs and gives shape to the space. I elaborated this further in Chapter 7. I argued that collective action, often in the form of violent street-protests, plays a central role. Performative violence and street-protest rituals serve a variety of purposes. Prima facie, they serve as a venue for the expression of collective grievances, the desire for retaliation against police injustice, and as a manifestation of anarchist praxis in the form of direct action. More subtly, they act as a form of communication between activists, produce an encoded language shared within activist networks, and act as a location for a menagerie of emotional interactions. On this latter point, I detailed how intense emotions such as hatred, trust, empowerment, revenge and rage are expressed and then shared amongst movement actors in the heat of street-protests.

My central finding was that despite significant tensions, often stemming from diverse perceptions on the applicability of anarchist and anti-authoritarian politics, when actors came together in the streets they produced a temporary unity. To that end, the performative violence of street-protests informs the collective identity of the movement by providing it with a process that acts as a glue binding the space. In her similar study on collective identity formation within the heterogeneous global justice movement, Fominaya identified assemblies as a forum for the construction of collective cohesiveness (Fominaya, 2010). She argues that as individuals interact, they form relationships that strengthen the movement. From my Athenian experiences, while the assemblies are an important location for actor interaction and the development of political ideas, I saw them more as a site of conflict rather than a source of unity. I explored this in Chapter 6 when I looked at gender politics within assemblies. Instead, in Athens I saw the streets as the forum for the construction of collective cohesiveness.

Throughout this book, I have also documented numerous examples of the unending attacks against the anarchist and anti-authoritarian space. Whether by police, paramilitary or fascists, repression of the radical left is conspicuous. These attacks can take the form of violence and harassment, and even torture and murder. This makes the movement's longevity and its ability to carve out a degree of autonomy within the Athenian neighbourhood of Exarcheia all the more noteworthy. As I have mentioned, the movement is arguably the world's most visible and militant anarchist and anti-authoritarian milieu, to the point where it attracts anarcha-tourists. The relative unity produced in street-protests helps account for the resilience of the movement in the face of these persistent attacks. And these attacks may soon intensify. The confluence of refugees and the economic crisis adds up to a textbook scenario for the rise of political extremism. Waiting in the wings is the Greek neo-Nazi movement, a dark and pernicious beast concealed by a façade of concern for the well-being of Greek citizens and various charity fronts. It uses violence to advance its aims and actively promotes racism, anti-Semitism, anti-Islamic sentiment, homophobia and social division, particularly by assaulting and demonising immigrants as scapegoats for the nation's woes.

Historically, a show of force and a unified front against external forces renews and rejuvenates the strength of the anarchist and anti-authoritarian space against hostilities. There is immense personal satisfaction and motivation that is gained from this collective action, forging bonds of solidarity, unity and affinity (Barr and Drury, 2009; Fantasia, 1989). Importantly for Athenian anarchists and anti-authoritarians, they are bonds created during acts of prefigurative politics and direct action, in accordance with broader anarchist principles: bonds that may prove critical in their very real and bitter struggle against fascism, capitalism and the state.

GLOSSARY

Affinity groups — Affinity groups first came to prominence as a mode of anarchist organising during the Spanish Civil War. They are small, sometimes ephemeral collectives that are autonomous and based on high degrees of trust, camaraderie and emotional connections. It is a translation of the Spanish phrase *grupo de afinidad*.

Black Bloc (tactics) — Originating in Germany amongst the *Autonomen* and squatter movement, Black Bloc is a set of tactics used by affinity networks, with targeted property destruction against state and capitalist pillars. In Greece, the state and corporate media refer to practitioners of these tactics as Κουκουλοφόροι (the hooded ones).

Golden Dawn (Χρυσή Αυγή) — A far-right political party in Greece, regularly described as fascist or neo-Nazi in practice. Led by a holocaust denier, the party's symbolism is awash with Nazi imagery, vocalised in vehemently anti-migrant, homophobic, anti-Semitic and anti-Muslim rhetoric. It is Greece's third largest political party. In the September 2015 Greek legislative election, it won 18 of 300 seats.

Greek Αντιεξουσιαστικη Κινηση (Anti-Authoritarian Current or AK) — A political network of anarchists and anti-authoritarians diffused throughout Greece, basing themselves on direct democracy and horizontal organisational principles. They tend to advocate permanent forms of resistance and anarchist praxis.

Insurrectionist anarchists or anti-authoritarians	Anarchists who are more inclined to advocate ephemeral networks of organisations and small affinity-group structures, rather than overt, permanent organisational frameworks. They tend to be hostile to pathways of anarchist revolution that involve the building of a mass movement, which are actions synonymous with the anarcho-syndicalist current. Insurrectionists nearly always support constant attacks on capitalist, state and consumerist institutions and are synonymous with illegalism, propaganda by the deed and, often (although not exclusively), Black Bloc tactics. In Greece, they are referred to as anti-authoritarians (αντιεξουσιαστικοί).

BIBLIOGRAPHY

23.10 (2010). "I Began to Get Involved When I Was 16". In A. G. Schwarz, Tasos Sagris and Void Network (eds.), *We Are an Image from the Future: The Greek Revolt of December 2008*, pp. 17–19. Oakland, CA: AK Press.

ACME collective (2000). "N30 Black Bloc Communique". Available at: www.zmag.org/acme.htm. [Accessed 20 May 2016].

Adams, Tony E. (2008). "A Review of Narrative Ethics". *Qualitative Inquiry*, 14(2), pp. 175–194.

Addelson, Kathryn (1991). "The Man of Professional Wisdom". In Mary M. Fonow and Judith Cook (eds.), *Beyond Methodology: Feminist Scholarship As Lived Research*, pp. 16–34. Bloomington, IN: Indiana University Press.

Adler, Patricia and Adler, Peter (2002). "The Reluctant Respondent". In Jaber F. Gubrium and James A. Holstein (eds.), *Handbook of Interview Research: Context and Method*, pp. 515–536. Thousand Oaks, CA: SAGE Publications.

Administrator Anarchy.GR (2009). "Περι πραξης η οι παρενεργειες του ακτιβισμου" [The side effects of activism], *Anarchy.Gr*. Available at: http://anarchy.gr/index.php?option=com_content&view=article&id=264&catid=36&Itemid=50&lang=en [Accessed 20 May 2016].

AK Athens (2010). *Ανακοίνωση της Αντιεξουσιαστικής Κίνησης για τα Γεγονότα της Πορείας* [Antiauthoritarian Motion's Announcement on the Events of the 5 May March].

Al Jazeera (2009). "Gunmen Attack Athens Police Station". *Al Jazeera Online News*. Available at: www.aljazeera.com/news/europe/2009/02/200923145610454958.html [Accessed 20 May 2016].

Alexander, Yonah and Pluchinsky, Dennis A. (1992). *Europe's Red Terrorists: The Fighting Communist Organizations*. New York: Taylor and Francis.

Alkis (2010). "December is a Result of Social and Political Processes Going Back Many Years, Part 1". In A. G. Schwarz, Tasos Sagris and Void Network (eds.), *We Are an Image from the Future: The Greek Revolt of December 2008*, pp. 8–13. Oakland, CA: AK Press.

Alvarez, Sonia E., Dagnino, Evelina and Escobar, Arturo (Eds.) (1998). *Cultures of Politics, Politics of Cultures: Re-Visioning Latin American Social Movements*. Boulder, CO: Westview Press.

Amin, Samir (2013). *The Implosion of Contemporary Capitalism*. New York: Monthly Review Press.

Aminzade, Ron and McAdam, Doug (2002). "Authority in Contention". *Mobilization*, 7(2), pp. 107–109.

Amnesty International (2013). "Greek Police 'Photoshop Away' Signs of Brutality from Mugshots". *Amnesty International Online*. Available at: http://amnesty.org/en/news/greek-police-photoshop-away-signs-brutality-mugshots-2013-02-04 [Accessed 20 May 2016].

Amster, Randall, DeLeon, Abraham, Fernandez, Luis A., Nocella II, Anthony J. and Shannon, Deric (eds.) (2009). *Contemporary Anarchist Studies: An Introductory Anthology of Anarchy in the Academy*. London: Routledge.
Anarcho (2008). "Review of Social Ecology and Communalism". *Anarchist Writers*. Available at: http://anarchism.pageabode.com/anarcho/review-social-ecology-communalism [Accessed 20 May 2016].
Anonymous (2008). "Katalipsi sti NET tin ora ton eidiseon apo neous gia ti dolofonia tou Grigoropoulou" [Καταληψη στη NET την ωρα τον ειδισεον απο νεους για τη δολοφονια του Γρηγορόπουλος, The occupation of NET by youths during the news report about the murder of Grigoropoulos], *YouTube*, Available at: www.youtube.com/watch?v=PK9lpMk7fiY&feature=youtube_gdata_player [Accessed 20 May 2016].
Anonymous (2009). *The Potentiality of Storming Heaven*. Available at: http://void-mirror.blogspot.com.au/2009/08/potentiality-of-storming-heaven-film.html. [Accessed 20 May 2016].
Anonymous (2010a). "Kill the Sexist in Your Head – the Menses Flow: A communique released by an Athens anti-sexist group". In A. G. Schwarz, Tasos Sagris and Void Network (eds.), *We Are an Image from the Future: The Greek Revolt of December 2008*, p. 247. Oakland, CA: AK Press.
Anonymous (2010b). *Κάποιοι Αναρχικοί από τη Θεσσαλονίκη Παραμύθια και Εφιάλτες* [Some Anarchists in Thessaloniki, Fables and Nightmares]. Pamphlet.
Anonymous (2012a). "Greece on the Brink of Social Insurrection". *Anarchist News*. Available at: www.anarchistnews.org/?q=node/10820 [Accessed 6 July 2013, inactive as at 20 May 2016].
Anonymous (2012b). *Revolutionary Struggle Case*. Available at: http://revolutionarystrugglecase.blogspot.com.au/ [Accessed 20 May 2016].
Apoifis, Nicholas (2008). *"Eco-Spirituality"*. Unpublished Master's thesis. University of New South Wales.
Armand, Emile (2005 [1911]). "Mini-Manual of the Anarchist Individualist". In Robert Graham (ed.), *Anarchism: A Documentary History of Libertarian Ideas, vol. I: From Anarchy to Anarchism (300CE to 1939)*, pp. 145–150. Montreal: Black Rose Books.
Arvanitakis, James (2007). "The Commodification and Re-Claiming of Trust: 'Does Anyone Care About Anything but the Price of Oil?'", *The International Journal of Interdisciplinary Social Sciences*, 2(3): pp. 41–50.
Arvanitakis, James (2013). "Golden Dawn: Greek Fascists Come Down Under". *The Conversation*. Available at: http://theconversation.com/golden-dawn-greek-fascists-come-down-under-13212 [Accessed 20 May 2016].
Ashen Ruins (2002). *Beyond the Corpse Machine: Defining a Post-leftist Critique of Violence*. Available at: http://theanarchistlibrary.org/library/ashen-ruins-against-the-corpse-machine-defining-a-post-leftist-anarchist-critique-of-violence. [Accessed 20 May 2016].
Associated Press (2010). "Greek Police Officer Guilty of Shooting Teenager". *Guardian*. Available at: www.guardian.co.uk/world/2010/oct/11/gree-police-officer-guilty-shooting-teenager [Accessed 20 May 2016].
Atkinson, Rowland and Flint, John (2001). *Accessing Hidden and Hard-to-Reach Populations: Snowball Research Strategies*. Available at: www.soc.surrey.ac.uk/sru/SRU33.pdf#search=%22sociology%20at%20surrey%20snowball%22. [Accessed 20 May 2016].

Autonomedia (2003). "Invitation to Thessaloniki, Against the European Union Summit, June, 2003". *Autonomedia*. Available at: http://dev.autonomedia.org/node/1963 [Accessed 20 May 2016].

Avramidis, Konstantinos (2012). "'Live Your Greece in Myths': Reading the Crisis on Athens' walls". *Professional Dreamers*. Available at: www.professionaldreamers.net/_prowp/wp-content/uploads/Avramides-Reading-the-Crisis-on-Athens-walls-fld.pdf [Accessed 20 May 2016].

Avruch, Kevin (2001). "Notes Toward Ethnographies of Conflict and Violence". *Journal of Contemporary Ethnography*, 30(5), pp. 637–648.

Axtell, James (1979). "Ethnohistory: A Historian's Viewpoint". *Ethnohistory*, 26(1), pp. 1–13.

B, Mike (2005). "The Massacre of the Internationalist Communists in Greece". *Marxists.org*. Available at: www.marxists.org/subject/greek-civil-war/revolutionary-history/stinas/memoirs.htm [Accessed 20 May 2016].

Βαγγέλης, Σακκάτος (2003). *Ανδρέας Λασκαράτος και Μικέλης Άβλιχος. Δύο μεγάλοι Κεφαλλονίτες Σατιρικοί* [Andreas Laskaratos and Mixalis Avlichos. Two Notable Kefallonian Satirists], Αθήνα: ENTOS.

Bakunin, Mikhail (1920). *God and the State*, New York: Mother Earth Publishing Association.

Bakunin, Mikhail (1971 [1842]). "The Reaction in Germany". In Sam Dolgoff (ed.), *Bakunin on Anarchy*, pp. 55–57. New York: Vintage Books.

Bakunin, Mikhail (2010). *Selected Writings from Mikhail Bakunin*, Florida: Red and Black.

Barker, Colin (2001). "Fear, Laughter, and Collective Power: The Making of Solidarity at the Lenin Shipyard in Gdansk, Poland, August 1980". In Jeff Goodwin, James Jasper and Francesca Polletta (eds.), *Passionate Politics. Emotions and Social Movements*, pp. 175–194. Chicago, IL: University of Chicago Press.

Barker, Colin (2003). "Review of Dynamics of Contention and Silence and Voice in the Study of Contentious Politics". *Sociology*, (37), pp. 605–607.

Barr, Dermot and Drury, John (2009). "Activist' Identity as a Motivational Resource: Dynamics of (Dis) Empowerment at the G8 Direct Actions, Gleneagles, 2005", *Social Movement Studies*, 8, pp. 243–60.

BBC News (2004). "Greece Admits Fudging Euro Entry". *BBC News*. Available at: http://news.bbc.co.uk/2/hi/business/4012869.stm [Accessed 20 May 2016].

BBC News (2008). "Top Greek Industrialist Kidnapped". *BBC News*. Available at: http://news.bbc.co.uk/2/hi/europe/7445971.stm [Accessed 20 May 2016].

BBC News (2010a). "Murder Verdict in Greek Riot Case". *BBC News*. Available at: www.bbc.co.uk/news/world-europe-11513309 [Accessed 20 May 2016].

BBC News (2010b). "Officer Given Life for Boy's Murder in Greek Riot Case". *BBC News*. Available at: www.bbc.co.uk/news/world-europe-11513309 [Accessed 20 May 2016].

Beatty, Andrew (2010). "How Did It Feel for You? Emotion, Narrative, and the Limits of Ethnography". *American Anthropologist*, 112(3), pp. 430–443.

Behrakis, Yannis and Maltezou, Renee (2012). "Greek Tourism Battered by Political Crisis, Fear". *Reuters*. Available at: www.reuters.com/article/2012/06/07/us-greece-tourism-idUSBRE8560D320120607 [Accessed 20 May 2016].

Benford, Robert (1993). "You Could Be the Hundredth Monkey: Collective Action Frames and Vocabularies of Motive within the Nuclear Disarmament Movement". *Sociological Quarterly*, 34, pp. 195–216.

Benford, Robert (1997). "An Insider's Critique of the Social Movement Framing Perspective". *Sociological Inquiry*, 67(4), pp. 409–430.
Benford, Robert and Snow, David A (2000). "Framing Processes and Social Movements: An Overview and Assessment". *Annual Review of Sociology*, 26, pp. 611–639.
Berezin, Mabel (2001). "Emotions and Political Identity: Mobilizing Affection for the Polity". In Jeff Goodwin, James Jasper and Francesca Polletta (eds.), *Passionate Politics. Emotions and Social Movements*, pp. 83–98. Chicago, IL: University of Chicago Press.
Bergen, Raquel K. (1996). *Wife Rape: Understanding the Response of Survivors and Service Providers*. Thousand Oaks, CA: SAGE Publications.
Bevington, Douglas and Dixon, Chris (2005). "Movement-relevant Theory: Rethinking Social Movement Scholarship and Activism". *Social Movement Studies*, 4(3), pp. 185–208.
Bey, Hakim (2003). *T.A.Z.: The Temporary Autonomous Zone, Ontological Anarchy, Poetic Terrorism*, Brooklyn, NY: Autonomedia.
B-Fest (2013). *B-Fest Antiauthoritarian Festival*. Available at: www.bfest.gr/ [Accessed 3 October 3 2013, inactive as at 20 May 2016].
Bickman, Leonard and Rog, Debra J. (eds.) (1998). *Handbook of Applied Social Research Methods*, Thousand Oaks, CA: SAGE Publications.
Birnbaum (1971). *Towards a Critical Sociology*. Oxford: Oxford University Press.
Bistis, George (2013). "Golden Dawn or Democratic Sunset: The Rise of the Far Right in Greece". *Mediterranean Quarterly*, 24(3), pp. 35–55.
Black, Bob (1986). *The Abolition of Work and Other Essays*, Port Townsend: Loompanics Unlimited.
Blee, Kath and Taylor, Verta (2002). "Semi-structured Interviewing in Social Movement Research". In Bert Klandermans and Suzanne Staggenborg (eds.), *Methods of Social Movement Research*, pp. 92–117. Minneapolis: The University of Minnesota Press.
Blee, Kathleen M. (2007). "Ethnographies of the Far Right". *Journal of Contemporary Ethnography*, 36(2), pp. 119–128.
Blocq, Daniel, Klandermans, Bert and van Stekelenburg, Jacquelien (2012). "Political Embeddedness and The Management Of Emotions". *Mobilization*, 17(3), pp. 319–334.
Blumer, Herbert (1969a). *Symbolic Interactionism: Perspective and Method*, Berkeley, CA: University of California Press.
Blumer, Herbert (1969b). "The Field of Collective Behavior". In Alfred McClung Lee (ed.), *Principles of Sociology*, pp. 67–121. New York: Barnes and Noble.
Blumer, Herbert (1997 [1969]). "Elementary Collective Groupings". In Steven Buechler and F. Kurt Cylke (eds.), *Social Movements: Perspectives and Issues*, pp. 72–90. Mountain View, NY: Mayfield.
Bonanno, Alfredo (1977). "Armed Joy". *The Anarchist Library*. Available at: http://theanarchistlibrary.org/library/alfredo-m-bonanno-armed-joy [Accessed 20 May 2016].
Bookchin, Murray (2003). "The Communalist Project". *Harbinger: A Journal of Social Ecology*, 3(1). pp. 20–37. Available at: www.social-ecology.org/2002/09/harbinger-vol-3-no-1-the-communalist-project/. [Accessed 20 May 2016].
Borda O. F. (2001). "Participatory (Action) Research in Social Theory: Origins and Challenges". In P. Reason and H. Bradbury (eds.), *Handbook of Action Research*, pp. 27–37. London: SAGE Publications.

Bornstein, Kate (2013). *Gender Outlaw: On Men, Women and the Rest of Us.* London: Routledge.

Bosi, Lorenzo and Giugni, Marco (2012). "The Outcomes of Political Violence: Ethical, Theoretical and Methodological Challenges". In Seraphim Seferiades and Hank Johnston (eds.), *Violent Protest, Contentious Politics, and the Neoliberal State*, pp. 29–38. Surrey: Ashgate.

Boukalas, Christos (2011). "No One Is Revolutionary until the Revolution! A long, hard reflection on Athenian anarchy through the prism of a burning bank". In Antonis Vradis and Dimitris Dalakoglou (eds.), *Revolt and Crisis in Greece: Between a Present Yet to Pass and a Future Still to Come*, pp. 279–297. Edinburgh: AK Press.

Bourdieu, Pierre (2003). "Participant Objectivation". *The Journal of the Royal Anthropological Institute*, 9(2), pp. 281–294.

Bourdieu, Pierre and Wacquant, Loïc J. D. (eds.) (1992). *An Invitation to Reflexive Sociology*, Chicago, IL: University of Chicago Press.

Bowers v. Hardwick (1986). *US Supreme Court 478 U.S 186.*

Brabant, Malcolm (2010). "Three Killed in Greece Protests". *BBC News.* Available at: http://news.bbc.co.uk/2/hi/8661385.stm [Accessed 20 May 2016].

Braidotti, Rosi (2004). "New European Identities and Mediated Cultures: Revisiting the Politics of Location", paper presented at the *Advanced European Summer School in Women's Studies from Multicultural and Interdisciplinary Perspectives.* Ljubljana, Slovenia: Humanities and Social Sciences : Net Online. Available at: http://h-net.msu.edu/cgi-bin/logbrowse.pl?trx. [Accessed 20 May 2016].

Bray, Mark, Spannos, Chris and Kaur, Preeti (2013). "The Future of Greece: A Society of Barbarism or of Social Spaces for Freedom". *The New Significance.* Available at: www.thenewsignificance.com/2013/02/13/the-future-of-greece-a-society-of-barbarism-or-of-social-spaces-for-freedom/ [Accessed 5 May 2013, inactive as at 20 May 2016].

Brockett, Charles D. (2005). *Political Movements and Violence in Central America*, Cambridge: Cambridge University Press.

Brown, Elsa Barkley (1992). "'What Has Happened Here': The Politics of Difference in Women's History and Feminist Politics". *Feminist Studies*, 18(2), pp. 295–312.

Brownmiller, Susan (1975). *Against Our Will: Men, Women And Rape*, New York: Simon and Schuster.

Bruce, Katherine McFarland (2013). "LGBT Pride as a Cultural Protest Tactic in a Southern City". *Journal of Contemporary Ethnography.* 42(5), pp. 608–635.

Brumley, Krista M. (2013). "From Responsible Debtors to Citizens Collective Identity in the Debtors' Movement in Monterrey, Mexico". *Journal of Contemporary Ethnography*, 42(2), pp. 135–168.

Bryman, Alan (2012). *Social Research Methods*, 4th edn. Oxford: Oxford University Press.

Buechler, Steven (1993). "Beyond Resource Mobilization? Emerging Trends in Social Movement Theory". *Sociological Quarterly*, 34(3), pp. 217–235.

Buechler, Steven (2000). *Social Movements in Advanced Capitalism*, New York: Oxford University Press.

Buechler, Steven (2004). "The Strange Career of Strain and Breakdown Theories of Collective Action". In David A Snow, Hanspeter Kriesi and Sarah A Soule (eds.), *The Blackwell Companion To Social Movements*, pp. 47–67. Oxford: Blackwell.

Burdick, John (1995). "Uniting Theory and Practice in the Ethnography of Social Movements: Notes Toward a Hopeful Realism." *Dialectical Anthropology*, 20(3/4), pp. 361–385.
Burgess, Ernest and Park, Robert (1969 [1921]). *Introduction to the Science of Sociology*, Chicago, IL: University of Chicago Press.
Burgmann, Verity (2003). *Power, Profit and Protest. Australian Social Movements and Globalisation*, Crows Nest: Allen and Unwin.
Butler, Judith (1990). *Gender Trouble: Feminism and the Subversion of Identity*, New York: Routledge.
Cadena-Roa, Jorge (2005). "Strategic Framing, Emotions, and Superbarrio – Mexico City's Masked Crusader". In Johnston Hank and John A. Noakes (eds.), *Frames Of Protest: Social Movements And The Framing Perspective*, pp. 69–88. Lanham, MD: Rowman & Littlefield.
Calhoun, Cheshire (1984). "Cognitive Emotions?" In Cheshire Calhoun and Robert Solomon (eds.), *What Is an Emotion? Classical Readings in Philosophical Psychology*, pp. 327–342. New York: Oxford University Press.
Calhoun, Cheshire and Solomon, Robert (eds.) (1984). *What is an Emotion? Classical Readings in Philosophical Psychology*, New York: Oxford University Press.
Calhoun, Craig (2001). "Putting Emotions in Their Place". In Jeff Goodwin, James Jasper and Francesca Polletta (eds.), *Passionate Politics. Emotions and Social Movements*, pp. 45–57. Chicago: University of Chicago Press.
Campbell, Howard and Heyman, Josiah (2007). "Slantwise Beyond Domination and Resistance on the Border". *Journal of Contemporary Ethnography*, 36(1), pp. 3–30.
Canetti, Elias (1962). *Crowds and Power*. London: Orion.
Carroll, William (1997). "Social Movements and Counterhegemony: Canadian Contexts and Social Theories". In William Carroll (ed.), *Organizing Dissent: Contemporary Social Movements in Theory and Practice*, pp. 3–38. Toronto: Garamond Press.
Casas-Cortés, Maribel and Cobarrubias, Sebastián (2007). "Drifting Through the Knowledge Machine". In Stevphen Shukaitis, David Graeber and Erika Biddle (eds.), *Constituent Imagination: Militant Investigations. Collective Theorization*, pp. 112–126. Oakland, CA: AK Press.
Casas-Cortés, Maribel, Osterweil, Michal and Powell, Dana E. (2013). "Transformations in Engaged Ethnography: Knowledge, Networks, and Social Movements", In Jeffrey Juris and Alex Khasnabish (eds.), *Insurgency Encounters: Transnational Activism, Ethnography, and the Political*. pp. 199–228, Durham, NC: Duke University Press.
Castells, Manuel (1983). *The City and the Grassroots*, Berkeley, CA: University of California Press.
Chaves, Kelly (2008). "Ethnohistory: From Inception to Postmodernism and Beyond". *The Historian*, 70(3), pp. 486–513.
Chomsky, Noam (1995). "Red and Black Revolution". *Noam Chomsky on Anarchism, Marxism & Hope for the Future*. Available at: http://flag.blackened.net/revolt/rbr/noamrbr2.html [Accessed 20 May 2016].
Choupis, Michail (2011). "The Crisis in the Greek Economy and Its National Implications". *Mediterranean Quarterly*, 22(2), pp. 76–83.
Churchill, Ward (2007). *Pacifism as Pathology*. Oakland, CA: AK Press.

Ciancabilla, Giuseppe (n.d.). "Against Organisation". *The Anarchist Library*. Available at: http://theanarchistlibrary.org/library/giuseppe-ciancabilla-against-organisation [Accessed 20 May 2016].

Clark, Jon and Diani, Marco (eds.) (1996). *Alain Touraine*. London: Falmer Press.

Clifford, James (1986a). "Introduction: Partial Truths". In James Clifford and George E. Marcus (eds.), *Writing Culture: The Poetics and Politics of Ethnography*, pp. 1–26. Berkeley, CA: University of California Press.

Clifford, James (1986b). "On Ethnographic Allegory". In James Clifford and George E. Marcus (eds.), *Writing Culture: The Poetics and Politics of Ethnography*, pp. 98–121. Berkeley, CA: University of California Press.

Clifford, James and Marcus, George E. (eds.) (1986). *Writing Culture: The Poetics and Politics of Ethnography*. Berkeley, CA: University of California Press.

Clogg, Richard (1986). *A Short History of Modern Greece*. Cambridge: Cambridge University Press.

Clogg, Richard (2002). *A Concise History of Greece*. Cambridge: Cambridge University Press.

Clough, Nathan L. (2012). "Emotion at the Center of Radical Politics: On the Affective Structures of Rebellion and Control". *Antipode*, 44(5), pp. 1667–1686.

cnbc.com (2011). "The 10 Toughest Greek Austerity Measures". *cnbc.com*. Available at: www.cnbc.com/id/43577791/page/1 [Accessed 20 May 2016].

Cohen, David (1989). "The Undefining of Oral Tradition". *Ethnohistory*, 36(1), pp. 9–18.

Colectivo Situaciones (2007). "Something More on Research Militancy: Footnotes on Procedures and (In)Decisions", trans. Sebastian Touza and Nate Holdren. In Stevphen Shukaitis, David Graeber and Erika Biddle (eds.), *Constituent Imagination: Militant Investigations. Collective Theorization*, pp. 73–93. Oakland, CA: AK Press.

Colectivo Situaciones (2011), *Colectivo Situaciones On Militant Research [Genocide in the Neighborhood]*. Available at http://occupyeverything.org/2011/on-militant-research-with-colectivo-situaciones-on-the-researcher-militant-politics-cultural-memory-imposible-justice-and-reading-from-genocide-in-the-neighborhood/ [Accessed 20 May 2016].

Collins, Randall (2001). "Social Movements and the Focus of Emotional Attention". In Jeff Goodwin, James Jasper and Francesca Polletta (eds.), *Passionate Politics. Emotions and Social Movements*, pp. 27–44. Chicago, IL: University of Chicago Press.

Collins, Randall (2004). *Interaction Ritual Chains*. Princeton, NJ: Princeton University Press.

Connolly, Kate (2000). "World Bank and IMF cut short Prague meeting". *Guardian*. Available at: www.theguardian.com/business/2000/sep/28/imf.economics [Accessed 20 May 2016].

Conspiracy of Fire Cells (2010). "Conspiracy of Fire Cells 'Announcement Regarding the Recent Events of 5/5'" [Συνομωσία Πυρήνων της Φωτιάς 'Ανακοίνωση Σχετικά με τα Πρόσφατα Γεγονότα της 5/5']. Pamphlet.

Constitution of Greece (2013 [1975]). *The Constitution of Greece*. Available at: www.hri.org/docs/syntagma/ [Accessed 20 May 2016].

Cordner, Alissa, Ciplet, David, Brown, Phil and Morello-Frosch, Rachel (2012). "Reflexive Research Ethics for Environmental Health and Justice: Academics and Movement Building". *Social Movement Studies*, 11(2), pp. 161–176.

Cox, Laurence (2003). "Eppur si muove: Thinking 'the Social Movement'". Available at: http://eprints.nuim.ie/427/1/Eppur_si_muove.pdf [Accessed 6 May 2013, inactive as at 20 May 2016].
Cox, Laurence and Barker, Colin (2002). "'What Have the Romans Ever Done for Us?' Academic and Activist Forms of Movement Theorizing", paper presented at the *8th Annual Conference on Alternative Futures and Popular Protest*. Metropolitan University, Manchester. Available at: http://eprints.nuim.ie/428/1/AFPPVIII.pdf [Accessed 20 May 2016].
Cox, Laurence and Nilsen, Alf Gunvald (2007). "Social Movements Research and the 'Movement of Movements': Studying Resistance to Neoliberal Globalisation". *Sociology Compass*, 1(2), pp. 424–442.
Coy, Peter, Malkoutzis, Nick, Matlack, Carol and Thesing, Gabi (2012). "What a Return to the Drachma Really Looks Like". *BusinessWeek: Global Economics*. Available at: www.businessweek.com/articles/2012-05-24/what-a-return-to-the-drachma-really-looks-like [Accessed 20 May 2016].
Crapanzano, Vincent (2010). "At the Heart of the Discipline: Critical Reflections on Fieldwork". In James Davies and Dimitrina Spencer (eds.), *Emotions in the Field: The Psychology and Anthropology of Fieldwork Experience*, pp. 55–78. Stanford, CA: Stanford University Press.
Creasap, Kimberly (2012). "Social Movement Scenes: Place-Based Politics and Everyday Resistance". *Sociology Compass*, 6(2), pp. 182–191.
Creswell, John W (1998). *Qualitative Inquiry and Research Design. Choosing Among Five Traditions*. London: SAGE Publications.
CrimethInc (2010). "Say You Want an Insurrection". *CrimethInc. Ex-Worker's Collective*. Available at: www.crimethinc.com/texts/recentfeatures/insurrection.php [Accessed 20 May 2016].
Crossley, Nick (2003). *Making Sense of Social Movements*. Buckingham: Open University Press.
Dakin, Douglas (1993). *The Greek Struggle in Macedonia 1897–1913*, Thessaloniki: Institute for Balkan Studies.
Dalakoglou, Dimitris (2013). "Hello, Dr. Strangelove: The Neo-Nazi Golden Dawn and State Apparatuses in Greece". *Occupied London: From the Greek Streets*. Available at: http://blog.occupiedlondon.org/2013/11/03/hello-dr-strangelove-the-neo-nazi-golden-dawn-and-state-apparatuses-in-greece/ [Accessed 12 November 2013, inactive as at 20 May 2016].
Dalakoglou, Dimitris and Vradis, Antonios (2011a). "Introduction". In Antonios Vradis and Dimitris Dalakoglou (eds.), *Revolt and Crisis in Greece: Between a Present Yet to Pass and a Future Still to Come*, pp. 13–28. Edinburgh: AK Press.
Dalakoglou, Dimitris and Vradis, Antonios (2011b). "Spatial Legacies of December and the Rights to the City". In Antonios Vradis and Dimitris Dalakoglou (eds.), *Revolt and Crisis in Greece: Between a Present Yet to Pass and a Future Still to Come*, pp. 77–88. Edinburgh: AK Press.
Dalton, Russel J and Kuechler, Manfred (eds.) (1990). *Challenging the Political Order: New Social and Political Movements in Western Democracies*. Cambridge: Cambridge Polity Press.
Dark Star Collective (ed.) (2002). *Quiet Rumours: An Anarcha-Feminist Reader*. Edinburgh: AK Press.

Davies, Charlotte Aull (1998). *Reflexive Ethnography: A Guide to Researching Selves and Others*. Oxon: Routledge.
Davies, James (2010). "Introduction: Emotions in the Field". In James Davies and Dimitrina Spencer (eds.), *Emotions in the Field: The Psychology and Anthropology of Fieldwork Experience*, pp. 1–35. Stanford, CA: Stanford University Press.
Davies, James and Spencer, Dimitrina (eds.) (2010). *Emotions in the Field: The Psychology and Anthropology of Fieldwork Experience*, Stanford, CA: Stanford University Press.
Davies, Nick (2008). "The Bloody Battle of Genoa". *The Guardian*. Available at: www.theguardian.com/world/2008/jul/17/italy.g8 [Accessed 20 May 2016].
Day, Richard (2005). *Gramsci Is Dead; Anarchist Currents in the Newest Social Movements*. Toronto: Pluto Press.
Debord, Guy (1967). *The Society of the Spectacle*, Zone Books [online]. Available at: www.antiworld.se/project/references/texts/The_Society%20_Of%20_The%20_Spectacle.pdf [Accessed 20 May 2016].
Della Porta, Donatella (1995). *Social Movements, Political Violence, and the State: A Comparative Analysis of Italy and Germany*. Cambridge: Cambridge University Press.
Della Porta, Donatella and Diani, Mario (1999). *Social Movements: An Introduction*. Oxford: Blackwell.
Della Porta, Donatella and Gbikpi, Bernard (2012). "The Riots: A Dynamic View". In Seraphim Seferiades and Hank Johnston (eds.), *Violent Protest, Contentious Politics, and the Neoliberal State*, pp. 87–100. Surrey: Ashgate.
Demotix (n.d.). "Polytechnic Occupation for the Murder of Michalis Kaltezas". *Demotix*. Available at: www.demotix.com/news/518314/polytechnic-occupation-murder-michalis-kaltezas [Accessed 9 August, inactive as at 20 May 2016].
Denzin, Norman K (1997). *Interpretive Ethnography: Ethnographic Practices for the 21st Century*. London: SAGE Publications.
Denzin, Norman K (1984), *On Understanding Emotion*. San Francisco, CA: Jossey-Bass.
Denzin, Norman K. (1970). *The Research Act: A Theoretical Introduction to Sociological Methods*. ChicagoIL: Aldine Publishing.
Denzin, Norman K. and Lincoln, Yvonna S. (1994). *Handbook of Qualitative Research*, Thousand Oaks, CA: SAGE Publications.
Denzin, Norman K. and Lincoln, Yvonna S. (1998). "Introduction: Entering the Field of Qualitative Research". In Norman K. Denzin and Yvonna S Lincoln (eds.), *The Landscape of Qualitative Research: Theories and Issues*, pp. 1–17. Thousand Oaks, CA: Sage Publications.
Diani, Mario (2004). "Networks and Participation". In David A. Snow, Sarah A. Soule and Hanspeter Kriesi (eds.), *The Blackwell Companion to Social Movements*, pp. 340–359. Oxford: Blackwell.
Diphoorn, Tessa (2013). "The Emotionality of Participation Various Modes of Participation in Ethnographic Fieldwork on Private Policing in Durban, South Africa". *Journal of Contemporary Ethnography*, 42(2), pp. 201–225.
Dixon, Chris (2012). "Building 'Another Politics': The Contemporary Anti-Authoritarian Current in the US and Canada". *Anarchist Studies*, 20(1), pp. 32–60.

Domoney, Ross (2012). "From the Greek Streets › Antifascist motorbike patrol – video by Ross Domoney". *Occupied London*. Available at: http://blog.occupiedlondon.org/2012/11/17/antifascist-motorbike-patrol-video-by-ross-domoney/ [Accessed 28 August 2013, inactive as at May 20, 2016].
Doutsiou, Sissy (2010). "The Limitations of Anti Sexism". In A. G. Schwarz, Tasos Sagris and Void Network (eds.), *We Are an Image from the Future: The Greek Revolt of December 2008*, pp. 248–260. Oakland, CA: AK Press.
Downton, James V. and Wehr, Paul Ernest (1997). *The Persistent Activist: How Peace Commitment Develops and Survives*. Boulder, CO: Westview Press.
Dreier, Peter (2011). "Glenn Beck's Attack on Frances Fox Piven". *Dissent. A Quarterly of Politics and Culture*. Available at: www.dissentmagazine.org/online_articles/glenn-becks-attack-on-frances-fox-piven [Accessed 20 May 2016].
Drakonakis, Antonis (2014). "Space and society of Greek anarchism: a socio-spatial anatomy of the Greek anarchist movement within the 21st century", *European Social Science History Conference Vienna*, April 23–26.
Durkheim, Émile (1951 [1897]). *Suicide*, translated by John A. Spaulding. New York: Free Press.
Durkheim, Émile (1964 [1893]). *The Division of Labor in Society*. New York: Free Press.
Durkheim, Émile (2001 [1912]). *The Elementary Forms of Religious Life*. Oxford: Oxford University Press.
Eagainst.com (2012). "The Greek antifascist volunteers in the Spanish Civil War". *Eagainst.com*. Available at: http://eagainst.com/articles/the-greek-antifascist-volunteers-in-the-spanish-civil-war/ [Accessed 20 May 2016].
Ed (2010). *'Epi ta Proso' ('Forward'): A Greek Anarchist Newspaper*. Libcom.org. Available from: https://libcom.org/history/epi-ta-proso-forward-1890s-greek-anarchist-collective-newspaper [Accessed 20 May 2016].
Edwards, Stewart (1971). *The Paris Commune 1871*. London: Eyre and Spottiswoode.
Effler, Erika Summers (2010). *Laughing Saints and Righteous Heroes: Emotional Rhythms in Social Movement Groups*. Chicago, IL and London: The University of Chicago Press.
Ehrlich, Howard J. (ed.) (1979). *Reinventing Anarchy: What Are Anarchists Thinking These Days?* London: Routledge.
ekathimerini.com (2012). "Greece Completes Anti-migrant Fence at Turkish Border". *ekathimerini.com*. Available at: www.ekathimerini.com/4dcgi/_w_articles_wsite1_1_17/12/2012_474782 [Accessed 20 May 2016].
ekathimerini.com (2013a). "Greek Unemployment Rate Hits 27.6 Percent in July". *ekathimerini.com*. Available at: www.ekathimerini.com/4dcgi/_w_articles_wsite2_1_10/10/2013_522451 [Accessed 20 May 2016].
ekathimerini.com (2013b). "Three Bank Executives Convicted of Manslaughter for Fatal 2010 Marfin Fire". *ekathimerini.com*. Available at: www.ekathimerini.com/4dcgi/_w_articles_wsite1_1_22/07/2013_510621 [Accessed 20 May 2016].
Eley, Geoff (2002). *Forging Democracy: The History of the Left in Europe, 1850–2000: The History of the Left in Europe, 1850–2000*. Oxford: Oxford University Press.
Ellinas, Antonis A. (2013). "The Rise of Golden Dawn: The New Face of the Far Right in Greece". *South European Society and Politics*. [online]. Available at: http://works.bepress.com/antonis_ellinas/12 [Accessed 20 May 2016].

Elliott, Larry, Inman, Phillip and Smith, Helena (2013). "IMF admits: we failed to realise the damage austerity would do to Greece". *Guardian*. Available at: www.theguardian.com/business/2013/jun/05/imf-underestimated-damage-austerity-would-do-to-greece [Accessed 20 May 2016].

Ellis, Carolyn (2004). *The Ethnographic I: A Methodological Novel About Autoethnography*, Walnut creek: Rowman Altamira.

Ellis, Carolyn, Adams, Tony E. and Bochner, Arthur P. (2011). "Autoethnography: An Overview". *Forum: Qualitative Social Research*, 12(1), [online] Available at: www.qualitative-research.net/index.php/fqs/article/view/1589/3095 [Accessed 20 May 2016].

European Commission (2010). "European Commission – The Bologna Process – Towards the European Higher Education Area". *European Commission*. Available at: http://ec.europa.eu/education/higher-education/bologna_en.htm [Accessed 20 May 2016].

Eyerman, Ron (2005). "How Social Movements Move. Emotions and Social Movements". In Helena Flam and Debra King (eds.), *Emotions and Social Movements*, pp. 41–56. New York: Routledge.

EZLN (1995). *Documentos Y Comunicados 2*. Mexico City: Era.

Fanon, Frantz (1965). *The Wretched of the Earth*. New York: Grove Press.

Fantasia, Rick (1989). *Cultures of Solidarity: Consciousness, Action, and Contemporary American Workers*. Berkeley, CA: University of California Press.

Feixa, Carles, Pereira, Inés and Juris, Jeffrey S. (2009). "Global Citizenship and the 'New, New' Social Movements: Iberian Connections". *Young: Nordic Journal of Youth Research*, 17(4), pp. 421–442.

Fernandez, Luis A. (2008). *Policing Dissent: Social Control and the Anti-Globalization Movement*. New Brunswick, NJ: Rutgers University Press.

Fernandez, Luis A. (2009). "Being There: Thoughts on Anarchism and Participatory Observation". In Randall Amster, Abraham DeLeon, Luis A. Fernandez, Anthony J. Nocella II and Deric Shannon (eds.), *Contemporary Anarchist Studies: An Introductory Anthology of Anarchy in the Academy*, pp. 93–102. London: Routledge.

Ferree, Myra Marx (1992). "The Political Context of Rationality: Rational Choice Theory and Resource Mobilization". In Aldon D. Morris and Carol McClurg Mueller (eds.), *Frontiers in Social Movement Theory*, pp. 29–53. New Haven, CT: Yale University Press.

Ferree, Myra Marx and Merrill, David A. (2004). "Hot Movements, Cold Cognition: Thinking about Social Movements in Gendered Frames". In Jeff Goodwin and James Jasper (eds.), *Rethinking Social Movements: Structure, Meaning, and Emotion*, pp. 247–262. Lanham, MD: Rowman and Littlefield.

Ferrell, Jeff (2009). "Against Method, Against Authority ... For Anarchy". In Randall Amster, Abraham DeLeon, Luis A. Fernandez, Anthony J. Nocella II and Deric Shannon (eds.), *Contemporary Anarchist Studies: An Introductory Anthology of Anarchy in the Academy*, pp. 73–81. London: Routledge.

Feyerabend, Paul (1970). *Against Method*. Minneapolis: University of Minnesota Press.

Fillieule, Olivier (2012). "The Independent Psychological Effects of Participation in Demonstrations". *Mobilization*, 17(3), pp. 235–248.

Flacks, Richard (2004). "Knowledge for What? Thoughts on the State of Social Movement Studies". In Jeff Goodwin and James Jasper (eds.), *Rethinking Social Movements: Structure, Meaning, and Emotion*, pp. 135–154. Lanham, MD: Rowman and Littlefield.
Flam, Helena (2005). "Emotions' Map: A Research Agenda". In Helena Flam and Debra King (eds.), *Emotions and Social Movements*, pp. 19–40. New York: Routledge.
Flam, Helena and King, Debra (eds.) (2005). *Emotions and Social Movements*, New York: Routledge.
Fo, Dario (1992). *Accidental Death of an Anarchist*. London: Methuen Books.
Fominaya, Cristina Flesher (2007). "Autonomous Movements and the Institutional Left: Two Approaches in Tension in Madrid's Anti-globalization Network". *South European Society and Politics*, 12(3), pp. 335–358.
Fominaya, Cristina Flesher (2010a). "Collective Identity in Social Movements: Central Concepts and Debates". *Sociology Compass*, 4(6), pp. 393–404.
Fominaya, Cristina Flesher (2010b). "Creating Cohesion from Diversity: The Challenge of Collective Identity Formation in the Global Justice Movement". *Sociological Inquiry*, 80(3), pp. 377–404.
Fonow, Mary M. and Cook, Judith (eds.) (1991). *Beyond Methodology: Feminist Scholarship As Lived Research*. Bloomington, IN: Indiana University Press.
Foucault, Michel (1980a). *Power/Knowledge: Selected Interviews and Other Writings 1972–1977*, ed. Colin Gordon. New York: Pantheon.
Foucault, Michel (1980b). "Two Lectures". In Michal Foucalt, *Power/Knowledge: Selected Interviews and Other Writings 1972–1977*, ed. Colin Gordon, pp. 78–108. New York: Pantheon.
Fragos, Spyros and Sotros, James (2005). "The General Social, Political and Economical Situation in Greece and the Anarchist Organisation". *Anarkismo*. Available at: www.anarkismo.net/article/299 [Accessed 20 May 2016].
Freeman, Jo (1970). *The Tyranny of Structurelessness*. Available at: http:// flag.blackened.net/revolt/hist_texts/structurelessness.html: Black Rose 1.[Accessed 20 May 2016].
Freire, Paulo (2000 [1970]). *Pedagogy of the Oppressed*. London: Continuum.
Freud, Sigmund (1959). *Group Psychology and the Analysis of the Ego*. New York: Norton.
Gallant, Thomas W. (2001). *Modern Greece*. London: Arnold.
Gamson, Joshua (1995). "Must Identity Movements Self-Destruct? A Queer Dilemma", *Social Problems*, 42(3), 390–407.
Gamson, William (1992). "The Social Psychology of Collective Action". In Aldon D. Morris and Carol McClurg Mueller (eds.), *Frontiers in Social Movement Theory*, pp. 53–76. New Haven, CT: Yale University Press.
Gamson, William and Meyer, David (1996). "Framing Political Opportunity". In Doug McAdam, John D. McCarthy and Mayer N. Zald (eds.), *Comparative Perspectives on Social Movements: Political Opportunities, Mobilizing Structures, and Cultural Framings*, pp. 275–290. Cambridge: Cambridge University Press.
Gelderloos, Peter (2007). *How Nonviolence Protects the State*. Cambridge: South End Press.
Gerlach, Luther P. and Hine, Virginìa H. (1970). *People, Power, Change: Movements of Social Transformation*. Indianapolis, IN: Bobbs-Merrill.

Ghaziani, Amin (2008). *The Dividends of Dissent: How Conflict and Culture Work in Lesbian and Gay Marches on Washington*. Chicago, IL: University of Chicago Press.

Giddens, Anthony (1991). *Modernity and Self-identity: Self and Society in the Late Modern Age*. Stanford, CA: Stanford University Press.

Gillan, Kevin and Pickerill, Jenny (2012). "The Difficult and Hopeful Ethics of Research on, and with, Social Movements". *Social Movement Studies*, 11(2), pp. 133–143.

Gimenez, Martha E. (2001). "Marxism, and Class, Gender, and Race: Rethinking the Trilogy", *Race, Gender and Class*, 8 (2), pp. 23–33.

Giovanopoulos, Christos and Dalakoglou, Dimitris (2011). "From Ruptures To Eruption: A Genealogy of the December 2008 Revolt in Greece". In Antonios Vradis and Dimitris Dalakoglou (eds.), *Revolt and Crisis in Greece: Between a Present Yet to Pass and a Future Still to Come*, pp. 91–114. Edinburgh: AK Press.

Glass, Pepper G. (2012). "Doing Scene Identity, Space, and the Interactional Accomplishment of Youth Culture". *Journal of Contemporary Ethnography*, 41(6), pp. 695–716.

Glass, Pepper G. (2009). "Unmaking a Movement: Identity Work and the Outcomes of Zapatista Community Centers in Los Angeles". *Journal of Contemporary Ethnography*, 38(5), pp. 523–546.

Goetz, Judith Preissie and LeCompte, Margaret D. (1984). *Ethnography and Qualitative Design in Educational Research*. Orlando, FL: Academic Press.

Goffman, Erving (1974). *Frame Analysis: An Essay on the Organization of Experience*. Boston, MA: Northeastern University Press.

Goldman, Emma (2004 [1917]). *The Psychology of Political Violence*. Montana: Kessinger Publishing.

Goldman, Emma (2008). *Emma Goldman: A Documentary History of the American Years Made for America, 1890–1901*, ed. Candace Falk, Barry Pateman and Jessica Morgan. Chicago: University of Illinois Press.

Goldstone, Jack (2012). "Protest and Repression in Democracies and Autocracies: Europe, Iran, Thailand and the Middle East 2010–11". In Seraphim Seferiades and Hank Johnston (eds.), *Violent Protest, Contentious Politics, and the Neoliberal State*, pp. 103–117. Surrey: Ashgate.

Gongaware, Timothy B (2011). "Keying the Past to the Present: Collective Memories and Continuity in Collective Identity Change". *Social Movement Studies: Journal of Social, Cultural and Political Protest*, 10(1), pp. 39–54.

Goode, Erich and Ben-Yehuda, Nachman (1994). *Moral Panics: The Social Construction of Deviance*. Cambridge: Blackwell.

Goodwin, Jeff (2012). "Introduction to a Special Issue on Political Violence and Terrorism: Political Violence as Contentious Politics". *Mobilization*, 17(1), pp. 1–5.

Goodwin, Jeff and Jasper, James (1999). "Caught in a Winding Snarling Vine. The Structural Bias of Political Process Theory". *Sociological Forum*, 14, pp. 27–54.

Goodwin, Jeff and Jasper, James (eds.) (2003). *The Social Movements Reader: Cases and Concepts*. Oxford: Blackwell.

Goodwin, Jeff and Jasper, James (2004a). "Caught in a Winding Snarling Vine. The Structural Bias of Political Process Theory". In Jeff Goodwin and James Jasper

(eds.), *Rethinking Social Movements: Structure, Meaning, and Emotion*, pp. 3–30. Lanham, MD: Rowan and Littlefield Publishers.
Goodwin, Jeff and Jasper, James (2004b). "Trouble in Paradigms". In Jeff Goodwin and James Jasper (eds.), *Rethinking Social Movements: Structure, Meaning, and Emotion*, pp. 75–96. Lanham, MD: Rowman and Littlefield.
Goodwin, Jeff and Jasper, James (eds.) (2004c). *Rethinking Social Movements: Structure, Meaning, and Emotion*, Lanham, MD: Rowman and Littlefield.
Goodwin, Jeff and Jasper, James (eds.) (2011). *Contention in Context: Political Opportunities and the Emergence of Protest*, Stanford, CA: Stanford University Press.
Goodwin, Jeff, Jasper, James and Polletta, Francesca (2000). "The Return of the Repressed: The Fall and Rise of Emotions in Social Movement Theory". *Mobilization*, 5(1), pp. 65–83.
Goodwin, Jeff, Jasper, James and Polletta, Francesca (eds.) (2001a). *Passionate Politics. Emotions and Social Movements*. Chicago, IL: University of Chicago Press.
Goodwin, Jeff, Jasper, James and Polletta, Francesca (2001b). "Introduction: Why Emotions Matter". In Jeff Goodwin, James Jasper and Francesca Polletta (eds.), *Passionate Politics. Emotions and Social Movements*, pp. 1–26. Chicago, IL: University of Chicago Press.
Gordon, Hava Rachel (2007). "Allies Within and Without How Adolescent Activists Conceptualize Ageism and Navigate Adult Power in Youth Social Movements". *Journal of Contemporary Ethnography*, 36(6), pp. 631–668.
Gordon, Uri (2007). "Practising Anarchist Theory: Towards a Participatory Political Philosophy". In Stevphen Shukaitis, David Graeber and Erika Biddle (eds.), *Constituent Imagination: Militant Investigations. Collective Theorization*, pp. 276–287. Oakland, CA: AK Press.
Gordon, Uri (2008). *Anarchy Alive! Anti-authoritarian Politics from Practice to Theory*, London: Pluto Press
Gordon, Uri (2009). "Dark tidings. Anarchist Politics in the Age of Collapse". In Randall Amster, Abraham DeLeon, Luis A. Fernandez, Anthony J. Nocella II and Deric Shannon (eds.), *Contemporary Anarchist Studies: An Introductory Anthology of Anarchy in the Academy*, pp. 249–258. London: Routledge.
Gordon, Uri (2010). "Power and Anarchy: In/equality + In/visibility in Autonomous Politics". In Nathan J. Jun and Shane Wahl (eds.), *New Perspectives on Anarchism*, pp. 39–66. Lanham, MD: Lexington.
Gordon, Uri (2011). "Anarchism: the A word". *New Internationalist*. Available at: http://newint.org/features/2011/06/01/anarchism-explained/ [Accessed 20 May 2016].
Gould, Deborah (2001). "Passionate Political Processes: Bringing Emotions Back into the Study of Social Movements". In Jeff Goodwin and James M. Jasper (eds.), *Rethinking Social Movements: Structure, Meaning, and Emotion*, pp. 155–176. Lanham, MD: Rowman and Littlefield.
Gould, Deborah (2009). *Moving Politics: Emotion and Act Up's Fight Against AIDS*, Chicago: The University of Chicago Press.
Graeber, David (2002). "The New Anarchists". *New Left Review*, (13), pp. 61–73.
Graeber, David (2004). *Fragments of Anarchist Anthropology*, Chicago, IL: Prickly Paradigm Press.

Graeber, David (2009). *Direct Action: An Ethnography*. Oakland, CA: AK Press.
Graeber, David (2011a). "Occupy Wall Street's Anarchist Roots". *Al Jazeera Online News: Opinion*. Available at: www.aljazeera.com/indepth/opinion/2011/11/2011112872835904508.html [Accessed 20 May 2016].
Graeber, David (2011b). *Debt: The First 5,000 Years*. Brooklyn: Melville House Publishing.
Graeber, David (2012). "Concerning the Violent Peace-Police". *nplusonemag.com*. Available at: http://nplusonemag.com/concerning-the-violent-peace-police [Accessed 20 May 2016].
Graham, Robert (ed.) (2005). *Anarchism. A Documentary History of Libertarian Ideas*, vol. I: *From Anarchy to Anarchism (300CE to1939)*. Montreal: Black Rose Books.
Gramsci, Antonio (1992). *Prison Notebooks*, vol. 1. New York: Columbia University Press.
Gramsci, Antonio (2001). *Selections from the Prison Notebooks of Antonio Gramsci*, edited by Quintin Hoare and Geoffrey Nowell-Smith, London: Electric Book.
Grancharoff, Jack (2013). "My Experience of Anarchism in Bulgaria". Available at: www.wsm.ie/c/anarchism-bulgaria-history-jack-grancharoff-audio [Accessed 20 May 2016].
Green, Anna and Troup, Kathleen (eds.) (1999). *The Houses of History: A Critical Reader in Twentieth-Century History and Theory*. Manchester: Manchester University Press.
Green, Bryan S. (2002). "Learning from Henry Mayhew: The Role of the Impartial Spectator in Mayhew's London Labour and the London Poor". *Journal of Contemporary Ethnography*, 31(2), pp. 99–134.
Grindon, Gavin (2007). "The Breath of the Possible". In Stevphen Shukaitis, David Graeber and Erika Biddle (eds.), *Constituent Imagination: Militant Investigations. Collective Theorization*, pp. 94–107. Oakland, CA: AK Press.
Groves, Julian (2001). "Animal Rights and the Politics of Emotion: Folk Constructions of Emotion in the Animal Rights Movement". In Jeff Goodwin, James Jasper and Francesca Polletta (eds.), *Passionate Politics: Emotions and Social Movements*, pp. 212–232. Chicago, IL: University of Chicago Press.
Guardian (2010). "Greek Crisis Protests: Three Killed after Bank Set on Fire". *Guardian*. Available at: www.theguardian.com/world/gallery/2010/may/06/greece-crisis-protest-killed [Accessed 20 May 2016].
Gubrium, Jaber F. and Holstein, James A. (eds.) (2002). *Handbook of Interview Research: Context and Method*. Thousand Oaks, CA: SAGE Publications.
Gubrium, Jaber F. and Holstein, James A. (2002). "From the Individual Interview to the Interview Society". In Jaber F. Gubrium and James A. Holstein (eds.), *Handbook of Interview Research: Context and Method*, pp. 3–32. Thousand Oaks, CA: SAGE Publications.
Guenther, Katja M. (2012). "A Movement Without Memory: Feminism and Collective Memory in Post-Socialist Germany". *Mobilization*, 17(2), pp. 157–714.
Le Guin, Ursula K. (1974). *The Dispossessed*. New York: HarperCollins.
Gurr, Ted Robert (1970). *Why Men Rebel*. Princeton, NJ: Princeton University Press.
Habermas, Jürgen (1975). *Legitimation Crisis*. Boston, MA: Beacon Press.
Habermas, Jürgen (1981). "New Social Movements". *Telos*, 49, pp. 33–37.

Hale, Charles R. (2006). "Activist Research v. Cultural Critique: Indigenous Land Rights and the Contradictions of Politically Engaged Anthropology". *Cultural Anthropology*, 21(1): 96–120.
Hall, Stuart (1997). "The Centrality of Culture". In Kenneth Thompson (ed.), *Media and Cultural Regulation*, pp. 207–238. London: SAGE Publications.
Hallett, Tim and Fine, Gary Alan (2000). "Ethnography 1900 Learning from the Field Research of an Old Century". *Journal of Contemporary Ethnography*, 29(5), pp. 593–617.
Handelman, Don (1990), *Models and Mirrors: Towards an Anthropology of Public Events*. Cambridge: Cambridge University Press.
Hank, Johnston and Noakes, John A. (eds.) (2005). *Frames of Protest: Social Movements and the Framing Perspective*. Lanham, MD: Rowman and Littlefield.
Haraway, Donna (1988). "Situated Knowledges": The Science Question in Feminism and the Privilege of Partial Perspective. *Feminist Studies*, 14(3), pp. 575–599.
Hardt, Michael and Negri, Antonio (2000). *Empire*. Cambridge, MA: Harvard University Press.
Hardt, Michael and Negri, Antonio (2004). *Multitude: War and Democracy in the Age of Empire*. New York: Penguin Books.
Harkin, Michael E. (2010). "Ethnohistory's Ethnohistory: Creating a Discipline from the Ground Up". *Social Science History*, 34(2), pp. 113–128.
Hartwig, Pautz and Kominou, Margarita (2013). "Reacting to 'Austerity Politics': The Tactic of Collective Expropriation in Greece". *Social Movement Studies*, 12(1), pp. 103–10.
Harvey, David (2005). *A Brief History of Neoliberalism*. Oxford: Oxford University Press.
Harvey, David (2006). *Spaces of Global Capitalism. Towards a Theory of Uneven Geographical Development*. London: Verso
Hedican, Edward (2006). "Understanding Emotional Experience in Fieldwork: Responding to Grief in a Northern Aboriginal Village". *International Journal of Qualitative Methods*, 5(1), pp. 17–24.
Helman, Sara and Rapoport, Tamar (1997). "Women in Black: Challenging Israel's Gender and Socio-political Orders". *British Journal of Sociology*, 48(4), pp. 681–700.
Henley, Jon and Davies, Lizzy (2012). "Greece's Far-right Golden Dawn Party Maintains Share of Vote". *Guardian*. Available at: www.theguardian.com/world/2012/jun/18/greece-far-right-golden-dawn [Accessed 20 May 2016].
Herzfeld, Michael (2011). "Crisis Attack: Impromptu Ethnography in the Greek Maelstrom". *Anthropology Today*, 27(5), pp. 22–26.
Hesse-Biber, Sharlene Nagy and Leavy, Patricia (2010). *The Practice of Qualitative Research*. London: SAGE Publications.
Hirsch, Eric (1990). "Sacrifice for the Cause: Group Processes, Recruitment, and Commitment in a Student Social Movement". *American Sociological Review*, 55(2), pp. 243–254.
Hirschauer, Stefan (2006). "Putting Things into Words. Ethnographic Description and the Silence of the Social". *Human Studies*, 29(4): 413–441.
Hoffmann, Elizabeth A. (2007). "Open-Ended Interviews, Power, and Emotional Labor". *Journal of Contemporary Ethnography*, 36(3), pp. 318–346.

hooks, bell (2004). *The Will to Change: Men, Masculinity, and Love*. New York: Atria Books.
Hooper, John (2003). "Genoa officer in 'suspicious' car crash". *Guardian*. Available at: www.theguardian.com/world/2003/aug/06/globalisation.italy [Accessed 20 May 2016].
Horgan, John (2009). *Walking Away From Terrorism: Accounts of Disengagement From Radical and Extremist Movements*. New York: Routledge.
Hourigan, Niamh (2004). *Escaping the Global Village: Media, Language, and Protest*. Oxford: Lexington Books.
ieconomics (2015). "Trading Economics: Greece". *Trading Economics*. Available at: http://ieconomics.com/greece [Accessed 20 May 2016].
IMO (2015). "Irregular Migrant, Refugee Arrivals in Europe Top One Million in 2015: IOM". *International Organization For Migration*. Available at: https://www.iom.int/news/irregular-migrant-refugee-arrivals-europe-top-one-million-2015-iom [Accessed 20 May 2016].
Ince, Anthony (2012). "In the Shell of the Old: Anarchist Geographies of Territorialisation", *Antipode*, 44(5), pp. 1645–1666.
Indymedia Athens (2008). "Solidarity to Konstantina Kuneva". *Indymedia Athens*. Available at: https://athens.indymedia.org/front.php3?lang=elandarticle_id=957227 [Accessed 20 May 2016].
Indymedia Athens (2011). "Live Updates on the General Strike in English". *Indymedia Athens*. Available at: https://athens.indymedia.org/front.php3?lang=elandarticle_id=1265013 [Accessed 20 May 2016].
Indymedia Athens (2012). "State Attacks Villa Amalia's Squat in Athens". *Indymedia Athens*. Available at: https://athens.indymedia.org/front.php3?lang=enandarticle_id=1444373 [Accessed 20 May 2016].
Indymedia Athens (2014). *Indymedia Athens*. Available at: https://athens.indymedia.org [Accessed 20 May 2016].
Indymedia UK (2013). "Athens Indymedia under the Suppression of the Government". *Indymedia UK*. Available at: www.indymedia.org.uk/en/2013/04/508404.html?c=on [Accessed 20 May 2016].
Inglehart, Ronald (1990). *Culture Shift in Advanced Industrial Society*, Princeton, NJ: Princeton University Press.
Inglehart, Ronald (1997). *Modernization and Postmodernization: Cultural, Economic, and Political Change in 43 Societies*. Princeton, NJ: Princeton University Press.
International Monetary Fund (2010). *International Monetary Fund, Country Report No. 10/372. Greece*.
Itano, Nicole (2007). "Why Is Greece on Fire?" *Christian Science Monitor*. Available at: www.csmonitor.com/2007/0827/p01s03-woeu.html [Accessed 20 May 2016].
James, Bob (2009). "Anarchism, Australia". In Immanuel Ness (ed.), *The International Encyclopedia of Revolution and Protest. 1500 to the Present*, pp. 105–108. Malden: Blackwell.
Jasper, James (1997). *The Art of Moral Protest: Culture, Biography, and Creativity in Social Movements*. Chicago, IL: Chicago University Press.
Jasper, James (1998). "The Emotions of Protest: Affective and Reactive Emotions in and around Social". *Sociological Forum*, 13(3), pp. 397–424.

Jasper, James (2003). "Emotions of Protest". In Jeff Goodwin and James Jasper (eds.), *The Social Movements Reader: Cases and Concepts*, pp. 175–184. Oxford: Blackwell.
Jasper, James (2010). "Social Movement Theory Today: Toward a Theory of Action?" *Sociology Compass*, 4(11), pp. 965–976.
Jasper, James (2011). "Emotions and Social Movements: Twenty Years of Theory and Research". *Annual Review of Sociology*, 37, pp. 285–303.
Jasper, James M. and Poulsen, Jane D. (1995). "Recruiting Strangers and Friends: Moral Shocks and Social Networks in Animal Rights and Anti-Nuclear Protests". *Social Problems*, 42(4), pp. 493–512.
Jenkins, Craig and Perrow, Charles (1977). "Insurgency of the Powerless: Farm Worker Movements (1946–1972)". *American Sociological Review*, 42(2), pp. 249–268.
Johnston, Hank (ed.) (2009a). *Culture, Social Movements, and Protest*. Surrey: Ashgate.
Johnston, Hank (2009b). "Protest Cultures: Performance, Artifacts, and Ideations". In Hank Johnston (ed.), *Culture, Social Movements, and Protest*, pp. 3–32. Surrey: Ashgate.
Johnston, Hank (2012). "Age Cohorts, Cognition and Collective Violence". In Seraphim Seferiades and Hank Johnston (eds.), *Violent Protest, Contentious Politics, and the Neoliberal State*, pp. 39–54. Surrey: Ashgate.
Johnston, Hank and Klandermans, Bert (eds.) (1995). *Social Movements and Culture*. Minneapolis: University of Minnesota Press.
Johnston, Hank and Seferiades, Seraphim (2012). "The Greek December, 2008". In Seraphim Seferiades and Hank Johnston (eds.), *Violent Protest, Contentious Politics, and the Neoliberal State*, pp. 149–56. Surrey: Ashgate Publishing.
Jun, Nathan J. and Wahl, Shane (eds.) (2010). *New Perspectives on Anarchism*, Lanham, MD: Rowman and Littlefield.
Jung, Patricia Beattie (1993). *Heterosexism: An Ethical Challenge*, Albany, NY: State University of New York Press.
Juris, Jeffrey S. (2005). "Violence Performed and Imagined. Militant Action, the Black Bloc and the Mass Media in Genoa". *Critique of Anthropology*, 25(4), pp. 413–32.
Juris, Jeffrey S. (2007). "Practicing Militant Ethnography with the Movement for Global Resistance in Barcelona". In Stevphen Shukaitis, David Graeber and Erika Biddle (eds.), *Constituent Imagination: Militant Investigations. Collective Theorization*, pp. 164–176. Oakland: AK Press.
Juris, Jeffrey S. (2008). *Networking Futures: The Movement Against Corporate Globalization*. Durham: Duke University Press.
Juris, Jeffrey S. (2009). "Anarchism, or the Cultural Logic of Networking". In Randall Amster, Abraham DeLeon, Luis A. Fernandez, Anthony J. Nocella II and Deric Shannon (eds.), *Contemporary Anarchist Studies: An Introductory Anthology of Anarchy in the Academy*, pp. 213–223. London: Routledge
Juris, Jeffrey S. and Khasnabish, Alex (eds.) (2013a). *Insurgency Encounters: Transnational Activism, Ethnography, and the Political*. Durham, NC: Duke University Press.
Juris, Jeffrey S. and Khasnabish, Alex (2013b). "Introduction: Ethnography and Activism within Networked Spaces of Transnational Encounter". In Jeffrey S,

Juris and Alex Khasnabish (eds.), *Insurgency Encounters: Transnational Activism, Ethnography, and the Political*, pp. 1–36. Durham, NC: Duke University Press.

Kalamaris, Panagiotis (2010). "There Were Many People Who Felt We Had an Unfinished Revolution". In A.G Schwarz, Tasos Sagris and Void Network (eds.), *We Are an Image from the Future: The Greek Revolt of December 2008*, pp. 14–16. Oakland, CA: AK Press.

Kallergis, Kostas (2012). *The Wake Up Call*. Available at: http://thewakeupcall.gr/ [Accessed 20 May 2016].

Kallianos, Yannis (2011). "December as an Event in Greek Radical Politics". In Antonios Vradis and Dimitris Dalakoglou (eds.), *Revolt and Crisis in Greece: Between a Present Yet to Pass and a Future Still to Come*. pp. 151–166. Edinburgh: AK Press.

Kallivretakis, Leonidas (2004). "Πολυτεχνείο '73: Το ζήτημα των θυμάτων: Νεκροί και τραυματίες [Polytechnic School '73: The question of the victims: dead and injured]". In Γιώργος Κ. Γάτος (ed.), *Πολυτεχνείο '73* [Polytechnic School '73], pp. 38–55. Athens: Εκδόσεις Φιλιππότη. Available at: http://helios-eie.ekt.gr/EIE/handle/10442/8782 [Accessed 20 May 2016].

Kanellopoulos, Kostas (2012). "The Accidental Eruption of an Anarchist Protest". In Seraphim Seferiades and Hank Johnston (eds.), *Violent Protest, Contentious Politics, and the Neoliberal State*, pp. 171–81. Surrey: Ashgate.

Karamichas, John (2009). "The December 2008 Riots in Greece". *Social Movement Studies*, 8(3), pp. 289–93.

Kassimeris, George (2001). *Europe's Last Red Terrorists: The Revolutionary Organization 17 November*, New York: New York University Press.

Kathimerini (2006). "Η Θεσσαλονίκη των πολιτικών δολοφονιών, [The Political Assassination in Thessaloniki]". *Kathimerini*. Available at: http://news.kathimerini.gr/4dcgi/_w_articles_ell_1_17/12/2006_209092 [Accessed 20 May 2016].

Katsiaficas, George N. (2006). *The Subversion of Politics: European Autonomous Social Movements and the Decolonization of Everyday Life*, Edinburgh: AK Press.

Kaufman, Cynthia (2003). *Ideas for Action: Relevant Theory for Radical Change*, Cambridge: South End Press.

Keane, John (2009). *The Life and Death of Democracy*. London: Simon and Schuster.

Kelly, John and Hamann, Kerstin (2009). "General Strikes in Western Europe 1980–2008". Paper presented at *The European Regional Congress of the International Industrial Relations Association*, Copenhagen, 28 June – 1 July.

Kinna, Ruth (ed.) (2012). *The Continuum Companion to Anarchism*, London: Continuum.

King, Debra (2002). "Operationalizing Melucci: Metamorphosis And Passion In The Negotiation Of Activists' Multiple Identities". *Mobilization*, 9(1), pp. 73–92.

King Jr, Martin Luther (1968). *Where Do We Go from Here: Chaos Or Community?*, Boston, MA: Beacon Press.

Kirilov (2011). "Paper Rifles". In Antonis Vradis and Dimitris Dalakoglou (eds.), *Revolt and Crisis in Greece: Between a Present Yet to Pass and a Future Still to Come*. Edinburgh: AK Press.

Kitsantonis, Niki (2009). "Debate Rages in Greece About Right of Police to Enter University Campuses". *New York Times*. Available at: www.nytimes.com/2009/12/10/world/europe/10iht-greece.html [Accessed 20 May 2016].

Kitschelt, Herbert (1986). "Political Opportunity Structures and Political Protest: Anti-Nuclear Movements in Four Democracies". *British Journal of Political Science*, 16, pp. 57–85.
Klandermans, Bert (1992). "The Social Construction of Protest and Multiorganizational Fields". In Aldon Morris and Carol Mueller (Eds.), *Frontiers in social movement theory*. pp. 77–103, New Haven, CT: Yale University Press.
Klandermans, Bert and Staggenborg, Suzanne (eds.) (2002a). *Methods of Social Movement Research*, Minneapolis: University of Minnesota Press.
Klandermans, Bert and Staggenborg, Suzanne (2002b). "Introduction". In Bert Klandermans and Suzanne Staggenborg (eds.), *Methods of Social Movement Research*, pp. ix-xix. Minneapolis: University of Minnesota Press.
Klandermans, Bert, Staggenborg, Suzanne and Tarrow, Sidney (2002c). "Conclusion: Blending Methods and Building Theories in Social Movement Research". In Bert Klanderman and Suzanne Staggenborg (eds.), *Methods of Social Movement Research*, pp. 314–350. Minneapolis: University of Minnesota Press.
Kolesidis, John and Papadimas, Lefteris (2011). "Clashes in Athens Over Anti-migrant Fence". *Reuters*. Available at: www.reuters.com/article/2011/01/15/us-greece-immigration-clashes-idUSTRE70E1LP20110115 [Accessed 20 May 2016].
Koliopoulos, John (1987). *Brigands with a Cause – Brigandage and Irredentism in Modern Greece 1821–1912*, Oxford: Clarendon Press.
Koliopoulos, John S. and Veremis, Thanos M. (2010). *Modern Greece: A History since 1821*. West Sussex: John Wiley and Sons.
Koliopoulos, John and Veremis, Thanos (2002). *Greece. The Modern Sequel. From 1821 to the Present*. London: C. Hurst and Co.
Koopmans, Ruud (2003). "A Failed Revolution – but a Worthy Cause". *Mobilization*, 8, pp. 116–119.
Koopmans, Ruud and Rucht, Dieter (2002). "Protest Event Analysis". In Bert Klandermans and Suzanne Staggenborg (eds.), *Methods of Social Movement Research*, pp. 231–259. Minneapolis: University of Minnesota Press.
Kornegger, Penny (2002). "Anarchism: The Feminist Connection". In Dark Star Collective (ed.), *Quiet Rumours: An Anarcha-Feminist Reader*, pp. 21–32. Edinburgh: AK Press.
Koro-Ljungberg, Mirka and Greckhamer, Thomas (2005). "Strategic Turns Labeled 'Ethnography': From Description to Openly Ideological Production of Cultures". *Qualitative Research*, 5(3): 285–306.
Kornetis, Kostis (2010). "No More Heroes? Rejection and Reverberation of the Past in the 2008 Events in Greece". *Journal of Modern Greek Studies*, 28(2), pp. 173–197.
Kornhauser, William (1959). *Politics of Mass Society*. Glencoe, IL: Free Press.
Kotronaki, Loukia and Seferiades, Seraphim (2012). "Along the Pathways of Rage: The Space-Time of an Uprising". In Seraphim Seferiades and Hank Johnston (eds.), *Violent Protest, Contentious Politics, and the Neoliberal State*, pp. 157–170. Surrey: Ashgate Publishing.
Kouki, Hara (2011). "Short Voyage to The Land of Ourselves". In Antonios Vradis and Dimitris Dalakoglou (eds.), *Revolt and Crisis in Greece: Between a Present Yet to Pass and a Future Still to Come*, pp. 167–80. Edinburgh: AK Press.
Kovich, Tammy (2011). "The Black Bloc and the New Society". *Upping the Anti*, (12), pp. 17–18.

Kremmyda, Stamatia (2013). "Educational Conflicts concerning Private Universities in Greece". *Educate~*, 13(1), pp. 18–33.

Kriesberg, Louis (ed.) *Research in Social Movements, Conflicts and Change*. Greenwich: JAI Press.

Kropotkin, Peter (1993 [1896]). *Anarchism: Its Philosophy and Ideal*, Montreal: Black Rose Books.

Kropotkin, Peter (2009a [1904]). *Mutual Aid: A Factor of Evolution*. New York: Cosimo.

Kropotkin, Peter (2009b [1926]). *The Conquest of Bread*. New York: Cosimo.

Kulick, Don (1995). "Introduction: The Sexual Life of Anthropologists: Erotic Subjectivity and Ethnographic Work". In Don Kulick and Margaret Wilson (eds.), *Taboo: Sex, Identity, and Erotic Subjectivity in Anthropological Fieldwork*, pp. 1–28. London: Routledge.

Kulick, Don and Wilson, Margaret (eds.) (1995). *Taboo: Sex, Identity, and Erotic Subjectivity in Anthropological Fieldwork*. London: Routledge.

Kuhn, Gabriel (2009). "Anarchism, Postmodernity, and Poststructuralism". In Randall Amster, Abraham DeLeon, Luis A. Fernandez, Anthony J. Nocella II and Deric Shannon (eds.), *Contemporary Anarchist Studies: An Introductory Anthology of Anarchy in the Academy*, pp. 18–25. London: Routledge.

Kyriakidou, Dina (2009). "Gunmen Kill Greek Anti-terrorist Policeman". *Reuters*. Available at: www.reuters.com/article/2009/06/17/us-greece-shooting-idUSTRE55G0RS20090617 [Accessed 20 May 2016].

Lahno, Bernd (2001). "On the Emotional Character of Trust". *Ethical Theory and Moral Practice*, 4, pp. 171–189.

Laclau, Ernesto and Mouffe, Chantal (1985). *Hegemony and Socialist Strategy: Towards a Radical Democratic Politics*. London: Verso.

Laraña, Enrique, Johnston, Hank and Gusfield, Joseph R. (eds.) (1994a). *New Social Movements: from Ideology to Identity*. Philadelphia, PA: Temple University.

Laraña, Enrique, Johnston, Hank and Gusfield, Joseph R. (1994b). "Identities, Grievances, and New Social Movements". In Enrique Laraña, Hank Johnston and Joseph R Gusfield (eds.), *New Social Movements: from Ideology to Identity*, pp. 3–35. Philadelphia, PA: Temple University

Laure (2005). "No Border Bulgaria/Greece". *Anarkismo.net*. Available at: www.anarkismo.net/article/1271 [Accessed 20 May 2016].

Le Bon, Gustave (1969 [1895]). *The Crowd: A Study of the Popular Mind*. New York: Ballantine Books.

Lefebre, Henri (1973). *La Production de l'Espace* [The Production of Space]. Paris: Gallimard.

Legge, James (2013). "Two Golden Dawn supporters shot dead in drive-by in Greece". *Independent*. Available at: www.independent.co.uk/news/world/europe/two-golden-dawn-supporters-shot-dead-in-driveby-in-greece-8918723.html [Accessed 20 May 2016].

Leonardos, Kottis (2006). *Konstantinos Speras: The Life and Activities of a Greek Anarcho-Syndicalist*. Berkeley, CA: Kate Sharpley Library.

Lerner, Gerda (1986). *The Creation of Patriarchy*. Oxford: Oxford University Press.

Levine, Cathy (2002). "The Tyranny of Tyranny". In Dark Star Collective (ed.), *Quiet Rumours: An Anarcha-Feminist Reader*, pp. 63–68. Edinburgh: AK Press.

Lichterman, Paul (2002). "Seeing Structure Happen: Theory-Driven Participant Observation". In Bert Klandermans and Suzanne Staggenborg (eds.), *Methods of Social Movement Research*, pp. 118–145. Minneapolis: University of Minnesota Press.
Lofland, John, Snow, David A., Anderson, Leon and Lofland, Lyn (2006). *Analyzing Social Settings: A Guide to Qualitative Observation and Analysis*. Belmont: Wadsworth.
Lountos, Nikos (2012). "Radical Minorities, a Decade of Contention and the Greek December 2008". In Seraphim Seferiades and Hank Johnston (eds.), *Violent Protest, Contentious Politics, and the Neoliberal State*, pp. 183–191. Surrey: Ashgate.
Lukes, Steven (1973). *Émile Durkheim: His Life and Work : A Historical and Critical Study*. Harmondsworth: Penguin Books.
Luxemburg, Rosa (1986 [1906]). *The Mass Strike*. London: Bookmarks.
Lynteris, Christos (2011). "The Greek Economic Crisis as Evental Substitution". In Antonios Vradis and Dimitris Dalakoglou (eds.), *Revolt and Crisis in Greece: Between a Present Yet to Pass and a Future Still to Come*, pp. 207–213. Edinburgh: AK Press.
Maddison, Sarah (2003). *'Collective Identity and Australian Feminist Activism: Conceptualising a Third Wave'*. Unpublished PhD thesis. University of Sydney.
Makrygianni, Vaso and Tsavdaroglou, Haris (2011). "Urban Planning and Revolt: A Spatial Analysis of the December 2008 Uprising in Athens". In Antonis Vradis and Dimitrios Dalakoglou, D. (eds.), *Revolt and Crisis in Greece: Between a Present Yet to Pass and a Future Still to Come*. pp. 29–57. London: AK Press.
Malatesta, Errico (2001 [1892]). *Anarchy*. London: Freedom Press.
Malatesta, Errico (2009 [1927]). "A Project of Anarchist Organisation". *The Anarchist Library*. Available at: http://theanarchistlibrary.org/HTML/Errico_Malatesta_and_Nestor_Makhno__About_the_Platform.html [Accessed 20 May 2016].
Malkoutzis, Nick (2012). "The Greek Election May Yet Prove a Victory for Syriza". *Guardian*. Available at: www.theguardian.com/commentisfree/2012/jun/18/greek-election-victory-syriza [Accessed 20 May 2016].
Marcus, George E. (1995). "Ethnography In/Of The World System". *Annual Review of Anthropology*, 24, pp. 95–117.
Marcus, George E. (1998). *Ethnography Through Thick and Thin* Princeton, NJ: Princeton University Press.
Margaritis, George (2009). "Greece, Socialism, Communism, and the Left, 1850–1974". In Immanuel Ness (ed.), *The International Encyclopedia of Revolution and Protest. 1500 to the Present*, pp. 1439–1447. Malden: Blackwell.
Margaronis, Maria (2012). "Greek Anti-fascist Protesters 'Tortured by Police' after Golden Dawn Clash". *Guardian*. Available at: www.guardian.co.uk/world/2012/oct/09/greek-antifascist-protesters-torture-police [Accessed 20 May 2016].
Margaronis, Maria (2013). "It's Absurd that Golden Dawn Is Being Allowed to Hound My Friend into Court". *Guardian*. Available at: www.theguardian.com/commentisfree/2013/sep/01/absurd-golden-dawn-hound-friend-court/print [Accessed 20 May 2016].

Marshall, Peter (2010). *Demanding the Impossible: A History of Anarchism*, Oakland: PM Press.
Marx, K. (1880) "A Workers' Inquiry". *Marxists.org*. Available from: www.marxists.org/archive/marx/works/1880/04/20.htm [Accessed 18 May 2016].
Marx, Karl and Engels, Friedrich (1972 [1848]). *The Communist Manifesto*, Middlesex: Penguin Books.
Mayer, Margit (1995). "Social Movement Research in the United States: A European Perspective". In Stanford M. Lyman (ed.), *Social Movements: Critiques, Concepts, Case-Studies*, pp. 168–195. London: Macmillan.
Mazower, Mark (2011). "Democracy's Cradle, Rocking the World". *New York Times*. Available at: www.nytimes.com/2011/06/30/opinion/30mazower.html [Accessed 20 May 2016].
McAdam, Doug (1982). *Political Process and the Development of Black Insurgency, 1930–1970*. Chicago, IL: University of Chicago Press.
McAdam, Doug (1986). "Recruitment to High-Risk Activism: The Case of Freedom Summer". *American Journal of Sociology*, 92, pp. 64–90.
McAdam, Doug, McCarthy, John D. and Zald, Mayer N. (eds.) (1996a). *Comparative Perspectives on Social Movements: Political Opportunities, Mobilizing Structures, and Cultural Framings*. Cambridge: Cambridge University Press.
McAdam, Doug, McCarthy, John D. and Zald, Mayer N. (1996b). "Introduction: Opportunities, Mobilizing Structures, and Framing Processes-Toward a Synthetic, Comparative Perspective on Social Movements". In Doug McAdam, John D McCarthy and Mayer N Zald (eds.), *Comparative Perspectives on Social Movements: Political Opportunities, Mobilizing Structures, and Cultural Framings*, pp. 1–21. Cambridge: Cambridge University Press.
McAdam, Doug, Sampson, Robert, Weffer-Elizond, Simón and Macindoe, Heather (2005). "'There Will be Fighting in the Streets': The Distorting Lens of Social Movement Theory". *Mobilization*, 10(1), pp. 102–113.
McAdam, Doug and Tarrow, Sidney (2011). "Introduction: Dynamics of Contention Ten Years on". *Mobilization*, 16(1), pp. 1–10.
McAdam, Doug, Tarrow, Sidney and Tilly, Charles (2001). *Dynamics of Contention*. York: Cambridge University Press.
McCarthy, John D. and Zald, Mayer N. (1973). *The Trend in Social Movements in America; Professionalization and Resource Mobilization*, Morristown: General Learning Press.
McCarthy, John D. and Zald, Mayer N. (1977). "Resource Mobilization and Social Movements: A Partial Theory". *American Journal of Sociology*, 82, pp. 1212–1241.
McDonald, Kevin (2002). "From Solidarity to Fluidity: Social Movements Beyond 'Collective identity' – the Case of Globalization Conflicts". *Social Movement Studies*, 1(2), pp. 109–128.
McKay, Iain (2009). "An Anarchist FAQ". *The Anarchist Library*. Available at: http://theanarchistlibrary.org/HTML/The_Anarchist_FAQ_Editorial_Collective__An_Anarchist_FAQ__13_17_.html [Accessed 20 May 2016].
McPhail, Clark (2006). "The Crowd and Collective Behavior: Bringing Symbolic Interaction Back In". *Symbolic Interaction*, 29(4), pp. 433–464.
Mead, Margaret (1977). *Letters from the Field, 1925–1975*. New York: HarperCollins.

Megas, Yianni (1994). *Οι "βαρκάρηδες" της Θεσσαλονίκης: η Αναρχική Βουλγάρικη Ομάδα και οι Βομβιστικές Ενέργειες του 1903* [The "Boatmen" of Thessaloniki: the Anarchist Bulgarian Group and the Bombing Actions of 1903]. Athens: Trochalia.
Melucci, Alberto (1985). "The Symbolic Challenge of Contemporary Movements". *Social Research*, 52(4), pp. 789–815.
Melucci, Alberto (1989). *Nomads of the Present: Social Movements and Individual Needs in Contemporary Society*, Philadelphia, PA: Temple University.
Melucci, Alberto (1994). "A Strange Kind of Newness: What's 'New' in New Social Movements?" In Enrique Laraña, Hank Johnston and Joseph R. Gusfield (eds.), *New Social Movements: from Ideology to Identity*, pp. 101–130. Philadelphia, PA: Temple University.
Melucci, Alberto (1995a). "The Process of Collective Identity". In Hank Johnston and Bert Klandermans (eds.), *Social Movements and Culture*, pp. 41–63. Minneapolis: University of Minnesota Press.
Melucci, Alberto (1995b). "The New Social Movements Revisited: Reflections on a Sociological Misunderstanding". In Louis Maheu (ed.), *Social Movements and Social Classes. The Future of Collective Action*, pp. 107–119. London: SAGE Publications.
Melucci, Alberto (1996). *Challenging Codes: Collective Action in the Information Age*. Cambridge: Cambridge University Press.
Melucci, Alberto, Yamanouchi, Yasushi and Yazawa, Shujiro (1994). *An Interview with Alberto Melucci*. Available at: www.thefreelibrary.com/An+interview+with+Alberto+Melucci+*.-a0128599432. [Accessed 20 May 2016].
Mertig, Angela and Dunlap, Riley (1997). "Global Environmental Concern: An Anomaly for Postmaterialism". *Social Science Quarterly*, 78(1), pp. 24–29.
Meyer, David S., Whittier, Nancy and Robnett, Belinda (eds.) (2002). *Social Movements: Identity, Culture and the State*. Oxford: Oxford University Press.
Miller, Frederic P. , Vandome, Agnes F. and McBrewster, John (eds.) (2009). *Metapolitefsi*. Saarbrücken: VDM.
Mivelaz, Nathalie (2002). "Greece: Greece: Evictions of Roma as part of the Preparation for the 2004 Olympic Games". *World Organisation Against Torture*. Available at: www.omct.org/escr/urgent-interventions/greece/2002/02/d934/ [Accessed 20 May 2016].
Moore, Ryan (2007). "Friends Don't Let Friends Listen to Corporate Rock: Punk as a Field of Cultural Production". *Journal of Contemporary Ethnography*, 36(4), pp. 438–474.
Morris, Aldon D. and Mueller, Carol McClurg (eds.) (1992). *Frontiers in Social Movement Theory*. New Haven, CT: Yale University Press.
Muldoon, Paul (2008). "The Moral Legitimacy of Anger". *European Journal of Social Theory*, 11(3), pp. 299–314.
Muller, Kathryn V. (2009). "Holding Hands With Wampum: Haudenosaunee Council Fires from the Great Law of Peace to Contemporary Relationships with the Canadian State". Unpublished PhD thesis. Queen's University (Canada). Available at: http://search.proquest.com.simsrad.net.ocs.mq.edu.au/pqdtft/docview/287981775/abstract/138028DCC951EC3F5A7/2?accountid=12219 [Accessed 20 May 2016].
Musico, Inga (2002). *Cunt: A Declaration of Independence*, Emeryville: Seal Press.

Nepstad, Sharon Erickson and Smith, Christian (2001). "The Social Structure of Moral Outrage in Recruitment to the U. S. Central America Peace Movement". In Jeff Goodwin, James Jasper and Francesca Polletta (eds.), *Passionate Politics. Emotions and Social Movements*, pp. 158–174. Chicago, IL: University of Chicago Press.

Ness, Immanuel (ed.) (2009). *The International Encyclopedia of Revolution and Protest. 1500 to the Present*. Malden, MA: Blackwell.

Newman, Saul (2011). "Postanarchism and Space: Revolutionary Fantasies and Autonomous Zones". *Planning Theory*, 10(4), pp. 344–365.

Noonan, Rita (1997). "Women Against the State". In Doug McAdam and David A Snow (eds.), *Social Movements: Readings on Their Emergence, Mobilization and Dynamics*, pp. 252–267. Los Angeles: Roxbury.

Nosotros (2013). *Nosotros Social Space*. Available at: http://nosotros.gr/ [Accessed 20 May 2016].

De Oca, Rodolfo Montes (2013). *Prometeos Y Tántalos Aproximaciones Históricas a Figuras Y Anécdotas Del Movimiento Anarquista Griego [Prometeos and Tantalos: Historical Approximations of Significant People and Anecdotes of the Greek Anarchist Movement]*. Barcelona: Por La Libertad Ediciones

Occupied London (2010). "What Do We Honestly Have to Say about Wednesday's Events?" *Occupied London: From the Greek Streets*. Available at: http://blog.occupiedlondon.org/2010/05/07/what-do-we-honestly-have-to-say-about-wednesdays-events/ [Accessed 9 October 2013, inactive as at May 20, 2016].

Occupied London (2011). "Greek Parliament Votes in Education Reform Bill that Abolishes Academic Asylum". *Occupied London: From The Greek Streets*. Available at: http://blog.occupiedlondon.org/2011/08/24/greek-parliament-votes-in-education-reform-bill-abolishing-academic-asylum-free-course-readers/ [Accessed 8 February 2013, inactive as at May 20, 2016].

Occupied London (2012). "Golden Dawn MP Attacked in the City of Volos". *Occupied London: From The Greek Streets*. Available at: blog.occupiedlondon.org/2012/05/26/golden-dawn-mp-attacked-in-the-city-of-volos/ [Accessed 8 February 2013, inactive as at 20 May 2016].

Occupied London (2013). "Fascist Pulls a Gun and Shoots Ten Times in the Air at an Anti-fascist Demo in Dafni, Athens". *Occupied London: From the Greek Streets*. Available at: http://blog.occupiedlondon.org/2013/09/20/fascist-pulls-a-gun-in-an-anti-fascist-demo/ [Accessed 12 November 2013, inactive as at 20 May 2016].

Occupied London (2014). *Occupied London: From the Greek Streets*. Available at: http://blog.occupiedlondon.org/ [Accessed 24 January 2014, inactive as at 20 May 2016].

OECD (2014). "Average Annual Hours Worked per Worker". *OECD.Stat*. Available at https://stats.oecd.org/Index.aspx?DataSetCode=ANHRS [Accessed 20 May 2016].

Offe, Claus (1985). "The New Social Movements: Challenging the Boundaries of Institutional Politics". *Social Research*, 52, pp. 817–868.

Oliver, Pamela (2003). "Mechanisms of Contention", *Mobilization*, 8, pp. 119–122.

Oliver, Pamela and Marwell, Gerard (1992). "Mobilizing Technologies for Collective Action". In Aldon Morris and Carol Mueller (eds.), *Frontiers of Social Movement Theory*, pp. 251–272. New Haven, CT: Yale University Press.

Olson, Mancur (1965). *The Logic of Collective Action: Public Goods and the Theory of Groups*. Cambridge, MA: Harvard University Press.
Opp, Karl-Dieter (2009). *Theories of Political Protest and Social Movements*. London: Routledge.
Organise! (1995). "Greece and the Anarchist Movement". *Organise* 40. Available at: http://flag.blackened.net/af/org/greece.html [Accessed 20 May 2016].
Owen, Paul (2012). "Greek Elections: New Democracy Try to Form Coalition". *Guardian*. Available at: www.theguardian.com/world/greek-election-blog-2012/2012/jun/18/greek-elections-new-democracy-try-to-form-coalition-live [Accessed 20 May 2016].
Pagoulatos, George (2001). "The Enemy Within: Intragovernmental Politics and Organizational Failure In Greek Privatization". *Public Administration*, 79(1), pp. 125–146.
Pakulski, Jan (1991). *Social Movements: The Politics of Moral Protest*. Melbourne: Longman Cheshire.
Pallister-Wilkins, Polly (2009). "Radical Ground: Israeli and Palestinian Activists and Joint Protest Against the Wall". *Social Movement Studies*, 8(4), pp. 393–407.
Papadimitropoulos, Panagiotis (2010). "You Talk About Material Damages, We Speak About Human Life: Perceptions of Violence Among Greek Anarchists". In A.G Schwarz, Tasos Sagris and Void Network (eds.), *We Are an Image from the Future: The Greek Revolt of December 2008*, pp. 57–72. Oakland, CA: AK Press.
Paredes, Julieta (2002). "An Interview with Mujeres Creando". In Dark Star Collective (ed.), *Quiet Rumours: An Anarcha-Feminist Reader*, pp. 111–112. Edinburgh: AK Press.
Passey, Florence (2001). "Socialization, Connection, and the Structure/Agency Gap: A Specification of the Impact of Networks on Participation". *Mobilization*, 6, pp. 173–192.
Paulsen, Krista E (2009). "Ethnography of the Ephemeral: Studying Temporary Scenes Through Individual and Collective Approaches". *Social Identities*, 15(4), pp. 509–524.
Paz, Abel (2007). *Durruti in the Spanish Revolution*. Oakland, CA: AK Press.
Perseus999 (2015). "Anarchists Occupy the Headquarters of the Governing Party SYRIZA (March 8th, 2015)". YouTube. Available at www.youtube.com/watch?v=jfWKqXo-WRE [Accessed 20 May 2016].
Peterson, Abby, Wahlström, Mattias, Wennerhag, Magnus, Christancho, Camilo and Sabucedo, José-Manuel (2012). "May Day Demonstrations in Five European Countries". *Mobilization*, 17(3), pp. 281–300.
Peterson, Abby (2001), *Contemporary Political Protest*. Aldershot: Ashgate.
Pharr, Susan J. and Putnam, Robert D. (eds.) (2000). *Disaffected Democracies: What's Troubling the Trilateral Countries?*. Princeton, NJ: Princeton University Press.
Pichardo, Nelson (1997). "New Social Movements: A Critical Review". *Annual Review of Sociology*, 23, pp. 411–430.
Piven, Frances Fox (2010). "Mobilizing the Jobless". *The Nation*. Available at: www.thenation.com/article/157292/mobilizing-jobless [Accessed 20 May 2016].
Piven, Frances Fox (2012). "Protest Movements and Violence". In Seraphim Seferiades and Hank Johnston (eds.), *Violent Protest, Contentious Politics, and the Neoliberal State*, pp. 19–28. Surrey: Ashgate.

Plant, Sadie (1992). *Most Radical Gesture: The Situationist International in a Postmodern Age*. New York: Routledge.
Platt, Gerald M (2004). "Unifying Social Movement Theories". *Qualitative Sociology*, 27, pp. 107–116.
Pleyers, Geoffrey (2013). "From Local Ethnographies to Global Movement: Experience, Subjectivity, and Power among Four Alter-Globalization Actors". In Juris, J. S. and Khasnabish, A. (eds.), *Insurgency Encounters: Transnational Activism, Ethnography, and the Political*, pp. 108–126. Durham, NC: Duke University Press.
Plows, Alexandra (2008). "Social Movements and Ethnographic Methodologies: An Analysis Using Case Study Examples". *Sociology Compass*, 2(5), pp. 1523–1538.
Polletta, Francesca and Jasper, James M. (2001). "Collective Identity and Social Movements". *Annual Review of Sociology*, 27, pp. 283–305.
Pomonis, Paul (ed.) (2004). *The Early Days of Greek Anarchism: 'The Democratic Club of Patras' and 'Social Radicalism in Greece'*, London: Kate Sharpley Library.
Proudhon, Pierre-Joseph (1970 [1840]). *What is Property?*, Dover: Humbold.
Psimitis, Michalis (2011). "The Protest Cycle of Spring 2010 in Greece". *Social Movement Studies*, 10(2), pp. 191–197.
Razsa, Maple and Kurnick, Andrej (2012). "The Occupy Movement in Zizek's Hometown: Direct Democracy and a Politics of Becoming". *American Ethnologist*, 39(2), pp. 238–258.
Reason, Peter and Bradbury, Hilary (2001). *Handbook of Action Research*, London: SAGE Publications.
Reed-Danahay, D. (1997). "Introduction". In D. Reed-Danahay (ed.), *Auto/ethnography: Rewriting the Self and the Social*, pp. 1–17. London: Berg.
Reiter, Bernd (2009). "A Genealogy of Black Organizing in Brazil". *Revista Nera*, 14, pp. 48–62.
Reuters (2010). "Timeline: Greece's economic crisis". *Reuters*. Available at: www.reuters.com/article/2010/03/03/us-eurozone-greece-economy-timeline-idUSTRE62230T20100303 [Accessed 20 May 2016].
Rich, Adrienne (1986). "Notes Towards A Politics of Location". In Adrienne Rich, *Blood, Bread, and Poetry: Selected Prose 1979–1985*, pp. 210–231. New York: Norton.
Risley, Amy (2011). "Rejoinder". In Jeff Goodwin and James M. Jasper (eds.), *Contention in Context: Political Opportunities and the Emergence of Protest*, pp. 108–213. Stanford, CA: Stanford University Press.
Robben, Antonius C. G. M. (2012). "Fieldwork Identity: Introduction". In Antonius C. G. M. Robben and Jeffrey A. Sluka (eds.), *Ethnographic Fieldwork: An Anthropological Reader*, pp. 85–91. Oxford: John Wiley and Sons.
Robben, Antonius C. G. M. and Sluka, Jeffrey A. (eds.) (2012). *Ethnographic Fieldwork: An Anthropological Reader*. Oxford: John Wiley and Sons.
Roosevelt, Theodore (1901), *First Annual Message to Congress: Theodore Roosevelt*. Messages and Papers of the Presidents, vol. XIV. Available at http://historynewsnetwork.org/article/274 [Accessed 20 May 2016].
Rosenfeld, Jesse (2015). "This Is What Greece's Refugee Crisis Really Looks Like". *The Nation*. Available at www.thenation.com/article/this-is-what-greeces-refugee-crisis-really-looks-like/ [Accessed 20 May 2016]
Roth, Andrew L. (1995). "'Men Wearing Masks': Issues of Description in the Analysis of Ritual". *Sociological Theory*, 13(3), pp. 301–327.

Routledge, Paul (2009). "Toward a Relational Ethics of Struggle. Embodiment, Affinity, and Affect". In Randall Amster, Abraham DeLeon, Luis A. Fernandez, Anthony J. Nocella II and Deric Shannon (eds.), *Contemporary Anarchist Studies: An Introductory Anthology of Anarchy in the Academy*, pp. 82–92. London: Routledge.

Routledge, Paul (2013). "Activist Ethnography and Translocal Solidarity". In Jeffrey Juris and Alex Khasnabish (Eds.), *Insurgency Encounters: Transnational Activism, Ethnography, and the Political*, pp. 250–268. Durham, NC: Duke University Press

Routledge, Paul and Simons, Jon (1995). "Embodying Spirits of Resistance". *Environment and Planning*, 13, pp. 471–498.

Rucht, Dieter (2012). "Political Violence in Germany: Trends and Exploration of Causes". In Seraphim Seferiades and Hank Johnston (eds.), *Violent Protest, Contentious Politics, and the Neoliberal State*, pp. 55–70. Surrey: Ashgate.

Ruins, Ashen (2002). "Against the Corpse Machine: Defining A Post-Leftist Anarchist Critique of Violence". *The Anarchist Library*. Available at: http://theanarchistlibrary.org/library/ashen-ruins-against-the-corpse-machine-defining-a-post-leftist-anarchist-critique-of-violence [Accessed 20 May 2016].

Ruiz-Junco, Natalia (2013). "Feeling Social Movements: Theoretical Contributions to Social Movement Research on Emotions". *Sociology Compass*, 7(1), pp. 45–54.

Rule, James B. (1988). *Theories of Civil Violence*, Berkeley, CA: University of California Press.

Russell, B. (2014). "Beyond Activism/academia: Militant Research and the Radical Climate and Climate Justice Movement(s)". *Area* (Mar [online]): pp. 1–8.

Sagris, Tasos (2010). "The Street Has Its Own History". In A.G Schwarz, Tasos Sagris and Void Network (eds.), *We Are an Image from the Future: The Greek Revolt of December 2008*, pp1–2. Oakland, CA: AK Press.

St John, Graham (2008). "Protestival: Global Days of Action and Carnivalized Politics in the Present". *Social Movement Studies*, 7(2), pp. 167–190.

Sanford, Victoria (2006). "Introduction". In Victoria Sanford and Asale Angel-Ajani (eds.), *Engaged Observer: Anthropology, Advocacy, and Activism*, pp. 1–18. New Brunswick, NJ: Rutgers University Press.

Sanford, Victoria and Angel-Ajani, Asale (eds.) (2006). *Engaged Observer: Anthropology, Advocacy, and Activism*, New Brunswick, NJ: Rutgers University Press.

Saunders, Benjamin, Kitzinger, Jenny and Kitzinger, Celia (2014). "Anonymising Interview Data: Challenges and Compromise in Practice". *Qualitative Research* (September 23, online version): 1–17.

Saunders, Clare (2008). "Double-Edged Swords? Collective Identity and Solidarity in the Environment Movement". *The British Journal of Sociology*, 59(2), pp. 227–253.

Shannon, Deric (Ed.) (2014). *The End of the World as We Know It? Crisis, Resistance, and the Age of Austerity*. Oakland, CA: AK Press.

Scheff, Thomas J (1994). *Bloody Revenge: Emotions, Nationalism, and War*. Boulder, CO: Westview Press.

Scheper-Hughes, Nancy (1995). "The Primacy of the Ethical: Propositions for a Militant Anthropology". *Current Anthropology*, 36(3), pp. 409–440.

Scheper-Hughes, Nancy (2000). "Ire in Ireland". *Ethnography*, 1(1), pp. 117–140.

Scheper-Hughes, Nancy (2001). *Saints, Scholars, and Schizophrenics: Mental Illness in Rural Ireland* [20th Anniversary]. California: University of California Press.
Schrock, Douglas, Holden, Daphne and Reid, Lori (2004). "Creating Emotional Resonance: Interpersonal Emotion Work and Motivational Framing in a Transgender Community". *Social Problems*, 51, pp. 61–81.
Schwartz, Michael (1976). *Radical Protest and Social Structure: The Southern Farmers' Alliance and Cotton Tenancy, 1880–1890.* New York: Free Press.
Schwarz, A.G, Sagris, Tasos and Void Network (eds.) (2010a). *We Are an Image from the Future: The Greek Revolt of December 2008*. Oakland, CA: AK Press.
Schwarz, A.G, Sagris, Tasos and Void Network (2010b). "Chronology: 19th-20th Century". In A. G. Schwarz, Tasos Sagris and Void Network (eds.), *We Are an Image from the Future: The Greek Revolt of December 2008*, pp. 5–7. Oakland, CA: AK Press.
Schwarz, A.G, Sagris, Tasos and Void Network (2010c). "Glossary". In A. G. Schwarz, Tasos Sagris and Void Network (eds.), *We Are an Image from the Future: The Greek Revolt of December 2008*, pp. 368–371. Oakland: AK Press.
Schwarz, A.G, Sagris, Tasos and Void Network (2010d). "Chronology: September 2000–November 2008". In A. G. Schwarz, Tasos Sagris and Void Network (eds.), *We Are an Image from the Future: The Greek Revolt of December 2008*, pp. 27–29. Oakland, CA: AK Press.
Scott, Alan (1990). *Ideology and the New Social Movements*. London: Routledge.
Scott, Alan (1996). "Movements of Modernity. Some Questions of Theory, Method and Interpretation". In John Clark and Marco Diani (eds.), *Alain Touraine*, pp. 77–92. London: Falmer.
Sedghi, Ami (2011). "Greek unemployment: how bad is it for youths?" *The Guardian*. Available at: www.theguardian.com/news/datablog/2011/aug/04/greece-youth-unemployment-rate [Accessed 20 May 2016].
Seel, Benjamin and Plows, Alex (2000). "Coming Live and Direct: Strategies of Earth First!" In Brian Doherty, Matthew Paterson and Benjamin Seel (eds.), *Direct Action in British Environmentalism*, pp. 112–132. London: Routledge.
Seferiades, Seraphim and Johnston, Hank (eds.) (2012a). *Violent Protest, Contentious Politics, and the Neoliberal State*, Surrey: Ashgate.
Seferiades, Seraphim and Johnston, Hank (2012b). "The Dynamics of Violent Protest: Emotions, Repression and Disruptive Deficit". In Seraphim Seferiades and Hank Johnston (eds.), *Violent Protest, Contentious Politics, and the Neoliberal State*, pp. 3–18. Surrey: Ashgate.
Seidman, Steven (1995). "Deconstructing Queer Theory or the Under-Theorization of the Social and the Ethical". In Linda Nicholson and Steven Seidman (eds.), *Social Postmodernism: Beyond Identity Politics*, pp. 116–141.Cambridge: Cambridge University Press.
Serano, Julia (2007). *Whipping Girl: A Transsexual Woman on Sexism and the Scapegoating of Femininity*. Berkeley, CA: Seal Press.
Shantz, Jeff (2010). *Constructive Anarchy: Building Infrastructures of Resistance*. Burlington: Ashgate.
Shaw, Karena (2003). "Whose Knowledge for What Politics?" *Review of International Studies*, 29, pp. 199–221.

Shepherd, Laura J. (2013). "Feminist Security Studies". In Laura J Shepherd (Ed.), *Critical approaches to security: An introduction to theories and methods*. pp. 11–23. London: Taylor and Francis.
Shepherd, Nicole (2002). "Anarcho-Environmentalists. Ascetics of Late Modernity". *Journal of Contemporary Ethnography*, 31(2), pp. 150–172.
Shukaitis, Stevphen, Graeber, David and Biddle, Erika (eds.) (2007). *Constituent Imagination: Militant Investigations. Collective Theorization.* Oakland, CA: AK Press.
Simiti, Marilena (2012). "The Volatility of Urban Riots". In Seraphim Seferiades and Hank Johnston (eds.), *Violent Protest, Contentious Politics, and the Neoliberal State*, pp. 133–145. Surrey: Ashgate.
Singer, Daniel (2000 [1970]). *Prelude to Revolution: France in May 1968*. Cambridge: South End Press.
Sitrin, Marina (2013). "Occupy Trust: The Role of Emotion in the New Movements". *Cultural Anthropology*. Available at: http://culanth.org/fieldsights/76-occupy-trust-the-role-of-emotion-in-the-new-movements [Accessed 20 May 2016].
Slater, David (1998). "Rethinking the Spatialities of Social Movements: Questions of (B)orders, Culture, and Politics in Global Times". In Sonia Alvarez, Evelina Dagnino and Arturo Escobar (Eds.), *Cultures of Politics, Politics of Cultures: Re-visioning Latin American Social Movements*. pp. 380–401, Boulder, CO: Westview Press.
Smallman, Guy and Mara, Kate (2013). *Into the Fire: The Hidden Victims of Austerity in Greece*. Available at: http://intothefire.org [Accessed 20 May 2016].
Smelser, Neil J. (1962). *Theory of Collective Behavior*. New York: Free Press.
Smelser, Neil J. (1964). "Theoretical Issues of Scope and Problems". *Sociological Quarterly*, 5(2), pp. 116–122.
Smith, Helena (2009). "Papandreou unveils radical reforms to salvage Greece's public finances". *Guardian*. Available at: www.theguardian.com/world/2009/dec/14/greece-unveils-reforms-to-public-finances?guni=Article:in%20body%20link [Accessed 20 May 2016].
Smith, Helena (2010). "Greek protesters storm the Acropolis". *Guardian*. Available at: www.theguardian.com/business/2010/may/04/greek-protesters-storm-acropolis?guni=Article:in%20body%20link [Accessed 20 May 2016].
Smith, Helena (2012a). "Antonis Samaras sworn in as Greek prime minister". *Guardian*. Available at: www.theguardian.com/world/2012/jun/20/greek-samaras-coalition-pasok-bailout [Accessed 20 May 2016].
Smith, Helena (2012b). "Golden Dawn MP's live TV assault shocks Greece". *Guardian*. Available at: www.theguardian.com/world/2012/jun/07/golden-dawn-tv-assault-greece [Accessed 20 May 2016].
Smith, Helena (2013a). "Greek Golden Dawn member arrested over murder of leftwing hip-hop artist". *Guardian*. Available at: www.theguardian.com/world/2013/sep/18/greece-murder-golden-dawn/print [Accessed 20 May 2016].
Smith, Helena (2013b). "Greece's birthrate falls as austerity measures hit healthcare". *Guardian*. Available at: www.theguardian.com/world/2013/sep/18/greece-birthrate-austerity-measures-healthcare [Accessed 20 May 2016].
Smith, Helena (2013c). "Greeks protest against Golden Dawn attack on Communists". *Guardian*. Available at: www.theguardian.com/world/2013/sep/13/greeks-protest-golden-dawn-attack-communists/print [Accessed 20 May 2016].

Smith, Helena (2013d). "Greece moves to ban far-right Golden Dawn party". *Guardian*. Available at: www.theguardian.com/world/2013/sep/18/greece-ban-golden-dawn-pavlos-fyssas/print [Accessed 20 May 2016].
Smith, Helena (2013e). "Fears over disappearance of 150 Syrian refugees from Greek village". *Guardian*. Available at: www.theguardian.com/world/2013/dec/24/greeks-protest-refugees-disappear-praggi/print [Accessed 20 May 2016].
Snow, David A (2001). "Collective Identity and Expressive Forms". *Centre for the Study of Democracy Papers*. Available at http://repositories.cdlib.org/csd/01-07 at 7 January 2007. [Accessed 20 May 2016].
Snow, David A (2004). "Framing Processes, Ideology and Discursive Fields". In David A. Snow, Sarah A. Soule and Hanspeter Kriesi (eds.), *The Blackwell Companion to Social Movements*, pp. 380–412. Oxford: Blackwell.
Snow, David A and Benford, Robert (1988). "Ideology, Frame Resonance, and Participant Mobilization". *International Social Movement Research*, 1(1), pp. 197–217.
Snow, David A and Benford, Robert (1992). "Master Frames and Cycles of Protest". In Aldon D. Morris and Carol McClurg Mueller (eds.), *Frontiers in Social Movement Theory*, pp. 133–155. New Haven, CT: Yale University Press.
Snow, David A and McAdam, Doug (2000). "Identity Work Processes in the Context of Social Movements: Clarifying the Identity/Movement Nexus". In Sheldon Stryker, Timothy Joseph Owens and Robert William White (eds.), *Self, Identity, and Social Movements*, pp. 41–67. Minneapolis: University of Minnesota Press.
Snow, David A, Rochford, E Burke Jr, Worden, Steven and Benford, Robert (1986). "Frame alignment Processes, Micro-mobilization, and Movement Participation". *American Sociological Review*, 51, pp. 464–481.
Snow, David A and Trom, Danny (2002). "The Case Study and the Study of Social Movements". In Bert Klandermans and Suzanne Staggenborg (eds.), *Methods of Social movement Research*, pp. 146–172. Minneapolis: University of Minnesota Press.
Snow, David A., Soule, Sarah A. and Kriesi, Hanspeter (eds.) (2004). *The Blackwell Companion to Social Movements*. Oxford: Blackwell.
Soja, Edward W. (1996). *Thirdspace: Journeys to Los Angeles and Other Real-and-Imagined Places*. Oxford: Blackwell.
Sorel, Georges (1999 [1908]). *Reflections on Violence*. Cambridge: Cambridge University Press.
Sotros, James (2004). *The Greek Speaking Anarchist and Revolutionary Movement (1830–1940)- Writings for a History*. Melbourne: No Gods No Masters.
De Sousa, Ronald (1987). *The Rationality of Emotions*. Cambridge, MA: MIT Press.
Spyropoulos, Philippos K. and Fortsakis, Théodore (2009). *Constitutional Law in Greece*. Frederik: Aspen.
Squat!net (2013). "Lelas Karagianni". *Squat!net*. Available at: http://en.squat.net/tag/lelas-karagianni/ [Accessed 20 May 2016].
Squatting in Europe Kollective (ed.) (2013). *Squatting in Europe. Radical Spaces, Urban Struggles*. London: Minor Compositions.
Staggenborg, Suzanne and Lang, Amy (2007). "Culture and Ritual in the Montreal Women's Movement". *Social Movement Studies*, 6(2), pp. 177–194.

Stake, Robert E. (1995). *The Art of Case Study Research*. Thousand Oaks, CA: SAGE Publications.
Staller, Karen M (2013). "Epistemological Boot Camp: The Politics of Science and What Every Qualitative Researcher Needs to Know to Survive in the Academy". *Qualitative Social Work*, 12(4): 395–413.
Stampacchia, Mauro (2009). "Fo, Dario (b.1926)". In Immanuel Ness (ed.), *The International Encyclopedia of Revolution and Protest. 1500 to the Present*, pp. 1204–1205. Malden: Blackwell.
Starhawk (1988). *Truth or Dare: Encounters with Power, Authority and Mystery*. San Francisco, CA: HarperCollins.
Starr, Amory, Fernandez, Luis A. and Scholl, Christian (2011). *Shutting Down the Streets: Political Violence and Social Control in the Global Era*. New York: NYU Press.
Starr, Amory, Fernandez, Luis, Amster, Randall, Wood, Lesley J. and Caro, Manuel J (2008). "The Impacts of State Surveillance on Political Assembly and Association". *Qualitative Sociology*, 31, pp. 251–270.
Stein, Arlene (2001). "Revenge of the Shamed: The Christian Right's Emotional Culture War". In Jeff Goodwin, James Jasper and Francesca Polletta (eds.), *Passionate Politics. Emotions and Social Movements*, pp. 115–131. Chicago, IL: University of Chicago Press.
Stein, Arlene (2010). "Sex, Truths, and Audiotape: Anonymity and the Ethics of Exposure in Public Ethnography". *Journal of Contemporary Ethnography*, 39(5), pp. 554–568.
Stets, Jan E and Turner, Jonathan H. (eds.) (2007). *Handbook of the Sociology of Emotions*. New York: Springer.
Steven (2007). "Bresci, Gaetano, 1869–1901". libcom.org. Available at: http://libcom.org/history/bresci-gaetano-1869-1901 [Accessed 20 May 2016].
Stroobants, Jean-Pierre and Perrier, Guillaume (2011). "Plans for a wall on Greece's border with Turkey embarrass Brussels". *Guardian*. Available at: www.guardian.co.uk/world/2011/jan/11/greece-turkey-wall-immigration-stroobants [Accessed 20 May 2016].
Stryker, Sheldon, Owens, Timothy Joseph and White, Robert William (eds.) (2000). *Self, Identity, and Social Movements*. Minneapolis: University of Minnesota Press.
SubMedia (2012). "The Greek Anarchists". *Dissident Voice*. Available at: http://dissidentvoice.org/2012/07/the-greek-anarchists/ [Accessed 20 May 2016].
SubMediaTV (2012). "This is Athens • Esto es Atenas • C'est Athènes". *SubMedia*. Available at: www.submedia.tv/stimulator/2012/07/09/this-is-athens/ [Accessed 20 May 2016].
Sullivan, Sian (2004). "*'We Are Heartbroken and Furious!' Violence and the (anti-) globalisation movement(s)*", Working Paper, Centre for the Study of Globalisation and Regionalisation No 133/04. Coventry: University of Warwick.
Swim, Janet K., Mallet, Robyn and Stagnor, Charles (2004). "Understanding Subtle Sexism: Detection and Use of Sexist Language". *Sex Roles*, 51(3/4), pp. 117–128.
Tamtakos, Yiannis (2003). Αναμνήσεις Μιας Ζωής στο Επαναστατικό Κίνημα [Memories of a Life in the Revolutionary Movement], Thessaloniki: Κύκλοι Αντιεξουσίας.
Tarrow, Sidney (1992). "Mentalities, Political Cultures, and Collective Action Frames: Constructing Meaning through Action". In Aldon D. Morris and Carol

McClurg Mueller (eds.), *Frontiers in Social Movement Theory*, pp. 174–202. New Haven, CT: Yale University Press.

Tarrow, Sidney (1994). *Power in Movement: Social Movements and Contentious Politics*. Cambridge University Press.

Tarrow, Sidney (2000). "Mad Cows and Social Activists: Contentious politics in the Trilateral Democracies". In Susan J. Pharr and Robert D Putnam (eds.), *Disaffected Democracies: What's Troubling the Trilateral Countries*, pp. 270–290. Princeton, NJ: Princeton University Press.

Tarrow, Sidney (2008). "Charles Tilly and the Practice of Contentious Politics". *Social Movement Studies*, 7(3), pp. 225–246.

Taylor, Verta (2003). "Plus ça change, plus c'est la même chose". *Mobilization*, 8, pp. 122–126.

Taylor, Verta and Van Dyke, Nella (2004). "'Get up, Stand up': Tactical Repertoires of Social Movements". In David A. Snow, Sarah A. Soule and Hanspeter Kriesi (eds.), *The Blackwell Companion to Social Movements*, pp. 262–293. Oxford: Blackwell.

Taylor, Verta and Rupp, Leila J. (1991). "Researching the Women's Movement: We Make Our Own History, But Not Just As We Please". In Mary M. Fonow and Judith Cook (eds.), *Beyond Methodology: Feminist Scholarship as Lived Research*, pp. 119–132. Bloomington, IN: Indiana University Press.

Taylor, Verta and Rupp, Leila J. (2002). "Loving Internationalism: The Emotion Culture Of Transnational Women's Organizations". *Mobilization*, 7(2), pp. 141–158.

Taylor, Verta and Whittier, Nancy (1992). "Collective Identity in Social Movement Communities: Lesbian Feminist Mobilization". In Aldon D. Morris and Carol McClurg Mueller (eds.), *Frontiers in Social Movement Theory*, pp. 104–129. New Haven, CT: Yale University Press.

Taylor, Verta and Whittier, Nancy (1995). "Analytical Approaches to Social Movement Culture: The Culture of the Women's Movement". In Hank Johnston and Bert Klandermans (eds.), *Social Movements and Culture*, pp. 163–187. Minneapolis: University of Minnesota Press.

The Children of the Gallery (2011). "The Rebellious Passage of a Proletarian Minority Through a Brief Period of Time". In Antonis Vradis and Dimitris Dalakoglou (eds.), *Revolt and Crisis in Greece: Between a Present Yet to Pass and a Future Still to Come*, pp. 115–131. Edinburgh: AK Press.

The Children of the Gallery (2013). Τα Παιδιά της Γαλαρίας [The Children of the Gallery]. Available at: www.tapaidiatisgalarias.org/ [Accessed 20 May 2016].

The Curious George Brigade (2012). *Anarchy in the Age of Dinosaurs*, Strangers in a Tangled Wilderness / Combustion Books.

The Economist (2007). "School for scandal". *The Economist*. Available at: www.economist.com/node/8972460 [Accessed 20 May 2016].

The Economist (2012). "Illegal Immigration: The Crossing Point". *The Economist*. Available at: www.economist.com/node/21549012 [Accessed 20 May 2016].

The Invisible Committee (2009) *The Coming Insurrection* [online]. Available at http://libcom.org/files/thecominsur_booklet%5B1%5D.pdf [Accessed 20 May 2016].

The Potentiality of Storming Heaven (2009). Documentary. Available from: http://voidmirror.blogspot.com.au/2009/08/potentiality-of-storming-heaven-film.html [Accessed 20 May 2016].

Thomopoulos, Elaine (2011). *The History of Greece*. Santa Barbara, CA: ABC-CLIO.

Thompson, A. K. (2010). *Black Bloc, White Riot: Anti-globalization and the Genealogy of Dissent*. Edinburgh: AK Press.
Thompson, Kenneth (ed.) (1997). *Media and Cultural Regulation*. London: SAGE Publications.
Tilly, Charles (1978). *From Mobilization to Revolution*. Reading: Addison-Wesley.
Tilly, Charles (1986). *The Contentious French*. Cambridge, MA: Harvard University Press.
Tilly, Charles (1988). "Social Movements, Old and New". In Louis Kriesberg (ed.), *Research in Social Movements, Conflicts and Change*, pp. 1–18. Greenwich: JAI Press.
Tilly, Charles (1999). "Wise Quacks". *Sociological Forum*, 14(1), pp. 55–61.
Tilly, Charles (2002). "Mechanisms in Political Processes". *Annual Review of Sociology*, 3, pp. 449–474.
Tilly, Charles (2003). *The Politics of Collective Violence*. Cambridge: Cambridge University Press.
Tilly, Charles (2004). "Wise Quacks". In Jeff Goodwin and James M. Jasper (eds.), *Rethinking Social Movements: Structure, Meaning, and Emotion*. Lanham, MD: Rowman and Littlefield.
Το Βημα [The Vima] (2013). "Editorial: The Droplets of the Hellenic Police". *Το Βημα*. Available at: www.tovima.gr/en/article/?aid=531617 [Accessed 20 May 2016].
Tolstoy, Leo (2005). "The Slavery of Our Times". In Robert Graham (ed.), *Anarchism. A Documentary History of Libertarian Ideas*, vol. I: *From Anarchy to Anarchism (300CE to1939)*, pp. 157–160. Montreal: Black Rose Books.
Touraine, Alain (1971). *The May Movement: Revolt and Reform: May 1968 – The Student Rebellion and Workers' Strikes – The Birth of a Social Movement*. New York: Random House.
Touraine, Alain (1985). "An Introduction to the Study of Social Movements". *Social Research*, 52, pp. 749–787.
Touraine, Alain (2000). *Can We Live Together?: Equality and Difference*. Stanford, CA: Stanford University Press.
Touraine, Alain, Hegedus, Zsuzska, Dubet, Francois and Michael Wieviorka (1983). *Anti-Nuclear Protest: The Opposition to Nuclear Energy in France*. Cambridge: Cambridge University Press.
TPTG (2011). "Burdened With Debt: 'Debt Crisis' And Class Struggles In Greece". In Antonios Vradis and Dimitris Dalakoglou (eds.), *Revolt and Crisis in Greece: Between a Present Yet to Pass and a Future Still to Come*, pp. 245–278. Edinburgh: AK Press.
Traynor, Ian (2010). "EU debt crisis: Greece granted €110bn aid to avert meltdown". *Guardian*. Available at: www.theguardian.com/world/2010/may/02/eu-debt-crisis-greece-aid-meltdown [Accessed 20 May 2016].
Trocchi, Alex (2011). "For the Insurrection to Succeed, We Must First Destroy Ourselves". In Antonis Vradis and Dimitris Dalakoglou (eds.), *Revolt and Crisis in Greece: Between a Present Yet to Pass and a Future Still to Come*, pp. 298–328. Edinburgh: AK Press.
Trott, Ben (2011). "Just Do It? A Review of the Coming Insurrection". *Social Movement Studies*, 10(1), pp. 113–118.
Tsiliopoulos, Efthymios (2008). "Thessaloniki's Bloody May of 1936". *Athens News*. Available at: www.athensnews.gr/old_issue/13286/17773 [Accessed 20 May 2016].

Turner, Jonathan H. and Stets, Jan E. (2005). *The Sociology of Emotions*, New York: Cambridge University Press.
Turner, Ralph H. (1988). "Collective Behavior Without Guile: Chicago in the Late 1940s". *Sociological Perspectives*, 31(3), pp. 315–324.
Turner, Ralph H. and Killian, Lewis M. (1957). *Collective Behavior*. Englewood Cliffs, NJ: Prentice Hall.
Uncreative (2011). "Speras, Constantinos, 1893–1943". *Libcom.org*. Available at: http://libcom.org/library/constantinos-speras [Accessed 20 May 2016].
Valocchi, Stephen (2013). "Activism as a Career, Calling, and Way of Life". *Journal of Contemporary Ethnography*, 42(2), pp. 169–200. Void Network (2013). *Void Network*. Available at: http://voidnetwork.blogspot.com.au/ [Accessed 20 May 2016].
Van Maanen, John (1988). *Tales of the Field: On Writing Ethnography*, 2nd edn. Chicago, IL: University of Chicago Press.
Void Network (2013). Void Network. Available from: http://voidnetwork.blogspot.com.au/ [accessed 20 May 2016].
Vortex (2010). "The Occupation of the National TV". In A.G Schwarz, Tasos Sagris and Void Network (eds.), *We Are an Image from the Future: The Greek Revolt of December 2008*, pp. 173–176. Oakland, CA: AK Press.
Vradis, Antonios and Dalakoglou, Dimitris. (2009). "Anarchism, Greece". In Immanuel Ness (ed.), *The International Encyclopedia of Revolution and Protest. 1500 to the Present*, 126–127. Malden, MA: Blackwell.
Vradis, Antonios and Dalakoglou, Dimitris. (eds.) (2011). *Revolt and Crisis in Greece: Between a Present Yet to Pass and a Future Still to Come*. Edinburgh: AK Press.
Wacquant, Loïc J. D. (1992). "Toward a Social Praxeology: The Structure and Logic of Bourdieu's Sociology". In Pierre Bourdieu and Loïc J. D. Wacquant (eds.), *An Invitation to Reflexive Sociology*, pp. 1–59. Chicago, IL: University of Chicago Press.
Warner, Michael (1993). *Fear of a Queer Planet: Queer Politics and Social Theory*, Minneapolis, MI: University of Minnesota Press.
Waters, Sarah (2008). "Situating Movements Historically: May 1968, Alain Touraine, and New Social Movement Theory". *Mobilization*, 13(1), pp. 63–82.
Weber, Max (1947). *The Theory of Social and Economic Organisation*. New York: Free Press.
Weber, Max (1978 [1922]). *Economy and Society: An Outline of Interpretative Sociology*, Berkeley, CA: University of California Press.
Weber, Max (2011a [1949]). *Methodology of Social Sciences*, ed. and trans. Edward Shils and Henry A. Finch. New Jersey: Transaction.
Weber, Max (2011b [1949]). "'Objectivity' in Social Science and Social Policy". In Max Weber *Methodology of Social Sciences*, pp. 49–112. New Jersey: Transaction.
Wettergren, Asa (2005). "Mobilization and the Moral Shock: Adbusters Media Foundation". In Helena Flam and Debra King (eds.), *Emotions and Social Movements*, pp. 99–118. New York: Routledge.
White, Julie, Drew, Sarah and Hay, Trevor (2009). "Ethnography Versus Case Study Positioning Research and Researchers". *Qualitative Research Journal*, 9(1), pp. 18–27.

White, Robert William and Fraser, Michael (2000). "Personal and Collective identities and Long-Term Social Movement Activism: Republican Sinn Féin". In Sheldon Stryker, Timothy Joseph Owens and Robert William White (eds.), *Self, Identity, and Social Movements*. pp. 324–346. Minneapolis: University of Minnesota Press.

Whittier, Nancy (1995). *Feminist Generations: The Persistence of the Radical Women's Movement*, Philadelphia: Temple University Press.

Whittier, Nancy (2001). "Emotional Strategies: The Collective Reconstruction and Display of Oppositional Emotions in the Movement against Child Sexual Abuse". In Jeff Goodwin, James Jasper and Francesca Polletta (eds.), *Passionate Politics*, pp. 233–250. Chicago, IL: University of Chicago Press.

Whittier, Nancy (2002). "Meaning and Structure in Social Movements". In David S. Meyer, Nancy Whittier and Belinda Robnett (eds.), *Social Movements: Identity, Culture and the State*, pp. 289–309. Oxford: Oxford University Press.

Wieck, David (1979). "The Negativity of Anarchism". In Howard Ehrlich, Carol Ehrlich, David De Leon and Glenda Morris (eds.), *Reinventing Anarchy: What Are Anarchists Thinking These Days?*, pp. 138–155. London: Routledge.

Willful Disobedience (2003). "Giuseppe Ciancabilla: A Biographical Note". *Willful Disobedience*, 4(3–4). Available at: www.reocities.com/kk_abacus/vb/wdv4n3-4.html#ciancabilla [Accessed 20 May 2016].

Williams, Clive (2014). "Black Rose Shapes as Blooming Problem for Brisbane G20". *The Canberra Times*. Available at: www.canberratimes.com.au/comment/black-rose-shapes-as-blooming-problem-for-brisbane-g20-20140119-312hw.html [Accessed 21 January 2015].

Willis, Jerry (2008). *Qualitative Research Methods for Education and Instructional Technology*. Charlotte, NC: Information Age.

Wilson, Kathi (2005). "Ecofeminism and First Nations People in Canada: Linking Culture, Gender and Nature". *Gender, Place and Culture*, 12(3), pp. 333–355.

Wood, Elisabeth Jean (2001). "The Emotional Benefits of Insurgency in El Salvador". In Jeff Goodwin, James Jasper and Francesca Polletta (eds.), *Passionate Politics. Emotions and Social Movements*, pp 267–281. Chicago, IL: University of Chicago Press.

Woodcock, George (2004 [1964]). *Anarchism: A History of Libertarian Ideas and Movements*. Ontario: Broadview.

Woodcock, Jamie (2014). "The Workers' Inquiry from Trotskyism to Operaismo: A Political Methodology for Investigating the Workplace". *Ephemera: Theory of Politics in Organization*, 14(3): 493–513.

Wright, Steve (2002). *Storming Heaven: Class Composition and Struggle in Italian Autonomist Marxism*. London: Pluto Press.

Yang, Guobin (2000). "Achieving Emotions in Collective Action". *The Sociological Quarterly*, 41(4) pp. 593–614.

Yanoulopoulos, Yanis (2009). "Greek Nationalism". In Immanuel Ness (ed.), *The International Encyclopedia of Revolution and Protest. 1500 to the Present*, pp. 1451–1456. Malden: Blackwell.

Youtube (2012). *Ο Ηλίας Παναγιώταρος στο BBC 17.10.2012 [Ilias Panagiotaros on BBC]*, Available at: www.youtube.com/watch?v=IyLgAwuD1SUandfeature=youtube_gdata_player [Accessed 20 May 2016].

Yin, Robert (1998). "The Abridged Version of Case Study Research. Design and Method". In Leonard Bickman and Debra J. Rog (eds.), *Handbook of Applied Social Research Methods*, pp. 229–260. Thousand Oaks, CA: SAGE Publications.

Young, Michael (2002). "Confessional Protest: The Religious Birth of U.S National Social Movements in the 1830s". *American Sociological Review*, 67, pp. 660–688.

Zald, Mayer N. and Ash, Roberta (1966). "Social Movement Organizations: Growth Decay, and Change". *Social Forces*, 44, pp. 327–340.

Zald, Mayer N.. and McCarthy, John David (eds.) (1987). *Social Movements in an Organizational Society: Collected Essays*, New Brunswick, NJ: Transaction.

Zemlinskaya, Yulia (2010). "Social Movements Through the Gender Lens". *Sociology Compass*, 4(8), pp. 628–641.

Zournazi, Mary (2002). *New Philosophies for Change*. London: Pluto Press.

Zwerman, Gilda and Steinhoff, Patricia (2012). "The Remains of the Movement: The Role of Legal Support Networks in Leaving Violence while Sustaining Movement Identity". *Mobilization*, 17(1), pp. 67–84.

INDEX

AK *see* Anti-Authoritarian Current
anarchist and anti-authoritarian
   milieu 2–3, 11–17, 109, 123–4
   movement
      in Athens 2, 3, 5, 11, 91–3, 127
      concept 15–16
      history 68–79, 82, 85–101
      identity 106, 117, 129–40
      politics 12–13, 17, 81, 100
      praxis 2, 13, 38, 46, 53, 61, 79, 81, 96–7, 104, 117, 127, 138, 154
      space 15–17, 52, 64, 81, 91, 93, 142
      symbolism 69, 129
anarcho-syndicalism 12, 14, 19, 75–7, 81
Anti-Authoritarian Current 13, 96–7, 117, 119, 156
austerity 1, 6–8, 104, 150–1

banners 18, 69, 87–8, 119–20, 130
Black Bloc tactics 14, 19, 78, 89, 95–6, 115–16, 130–2, 138, 156

Children of the Gallery, The 91
The Coalition of the Radical Left 1, 8–9, 150
collective behaviours 20–3
collective identity 2, 34–5, 39–40, 85, 129–40
   emotions 35–8, 139–47, 142, 144–6
The Communist Party of Greece 1, 10, 18, 76, 88
Conspiracy of Fire 99, 125

Democratic Club of Patras 70–1, 79
direct action 12, 17, 41, 54–6, 66, 72, 74, 78, 81, 85, 92, 95, 97–8, 104–6, 118–19, 130, 132, 142, 151

ethnohistory 66–7, 102–3
European Central Bank 1, 7
European Commission 1, 7
European Union 6, 96
Eurozone 6, 105
Exarcheia 15, 45, 48, 89, 97, 119

fascism 9–11, 104, 153, 155
fascists 10, 18, 58, 86, 89, 98, 106, 139, 147, 155

gender 109–14
global financial crisis (2008–09) 1, 6
globalisation of movement 94, 132
Golden Dawn 1, 9–11, 99, 106, 156
graffiti 84, 99
Greek Communist Party *see* The Communist Party of Greece
Grigoropoulos, Alexandros 89, 100–1, 103

homophobia 109–11, 155

industrial action 121–4
Indymedia 96–7, 99, 120
insurrectionist anarchists 14, 65, 69, 73, 79, 81, 85, 104–5, 118–19, 123, 154, 157
International Monetary Fund 1, 7, 95, 105

Jura Federation 70–1

KKE *see* The Communist Party of Greece

media 97, 99, 101, 119–20
Melucci, Alberto 2–3, 30, 33–8, 40–3, 148, 154

militant ethnography 46, 50–64, 153
  benefits 54–5
  ethics 57–9
  physical violence 59–63
  practicalities 53–4, 56–7
militants 2, 125–6
Molotov cocktails 89–90, 104, 116, 121, 130, 142

ND *see* New Democracy
neo-liberalism 5, 50, 93–4, 100, 148, 150, 153
New Democracy 1, 8, 91, 94, 104, 150
new social movement theory 30–3
  criticism 40–2
non-violence 132–3, 136, 143
Nosotros Free Social Space 97

pacifism *see* non-violence
Panhellenic Socialist Movement 1, 6, 8, 150
PASOK *see* Panhellenic Socialist Movement
performative violence 129–32, 134, 148
  symbolism 134–6, 143, 151
political process theory 25–6
  criticism 26–8
  culture and emotions 29–31, 36
political violence 134–7, 143, 145
  arson 137

property damage 134–5
protests 8, 18, 119, 121–2, 129–30, 138–9, 142–3, 147–8, 151

resource mobilisation theory 23, 36
riot-porn 80–1, 105–6

sampling 48–9
sexism 111–17
sexuality 109–10
social movement theory 15, 18
  actors 27
solidarity campaigns 97–8
squats 15, 28, 47–9, 54–5, 90–2, 108–11, 115
SYRIZA *see* The Coalition of the Radical Left

tear gas 48, 53–4, 60, 128, 134, 142, 146
trust 52–4, 59, 132, 140–2, 147–8, 153–4, 156

unemployment 1, 7, 150

Void Network 91

We Are an Image 12–13, 48–9, 77

EU authorised representative for GPSR:
Easy Access System Europe, Mustamäe tee 50,
10621 Tallinn, Estonia
gpsr.requests@easproject.com

www.ingramcontent.com/pod-product-compliance
Lightning Source LLC
Chambersburg PA
CBHW030121240426
43673CB00041B/1356